QUIRKY, YES

HOPELESS, NO

QUIRKY, YES
HOPELESS, NO

PRACTICAL TIPS TO HELP YOUR
CHILD WITH ASPERGER'S SYNDROME
BE MORE SOCIALLY ACCEPTED

Cynthia La Brie Norall, Ph.D.
FOUNDER OF THE FRIENDS' CLUB

with Beth Wagner Brust

ST. MARTIN'S GRIFFIN ☙ NEW YORK

This book is a reference work for readers to use in conjunction with the advice and care of their health-care providers. The ideas, procedures, and suggestions contained in this book are not intended as a substitute for consulting with your physician. The opinions expressed in this book represent the personal views of the authors and not of the publisher. Readers are solely responsible for their own health-care decisions. Neither the publisher nor the authors accept any responsibility for adverse effects individuals may claim to experience, either directly or indirectly, from the information contained in this book.

Friends' Club is a trademark registered by Cynthia Norall.

Social Story is a trademarked term by Carol Gray.

DSM-IV-TR diagnostic criteria for Asperger's reprinted with permission from the *Diagnostic and Statistical Manual of Mental Disorders, Text Revision, Fourth Edition,* copyright © 2000 by the American Psychiatric Association.

www.stmartins.com

Book design by Mspace/Maura Fadden Rosenthal

Library of Congress Cataloging-in-Publication Data

Norall, Cynthia La Brie.
    Quirky, yes—hopeless, no : practical tips to help your child with Asperger's syndrome be more socially accepted / Cynthia La Brie Norall, with Beth Wagner Brust.—1st ed.
        p. cm.
    ISBN-13: 978-0-312-55849-9
    ISBN-10: 0-312-55849-X
    Includes index.
    1. Asperger's syndrome in children—Popular works.   2. Asperger's syndrome in children—Social aspects.   1. Title.

    RJ506.A9 N67 2009
    618.92'858832—dc22

                                                    2009010696

10   9   8   7   6   5   4   3   2

To my family: David, Lauren Ashley, and John Lloyd—
You have supported my writing, but more than that,
you have been personally involved in the work
that I do, for which I am truly grateful.

And to my Heroes:
Conner, Evan, Matthew, Ben, Alec,
Nathan, Gavin, Christopher, Adrian, Riley,
Anthony, and so many others who have
added to my understanding of celebrating Aspie differences
and who made me realize that if we believe, they will achieve.
—Cynthia La Brie Norall

For my son, Ben, a wonderful out-of-the-box thinker,
who brought me into the Asperger's world.

And for Jay and Diane Wagner,
who showed such interest and support
in this project every step of the way—thank you.
—BETH WAGNER BRUST

CONTENTS

PART THREE] RESOURCES

NOTE TO THE READER

This book is intended to be a handy, practical resource to help you zero in on specific concerns regarding Asperger's syndrome. Eighty-five topics that challenge Asperger's kids are listed alphabetically from A to Z to make it as easy as possible to find the help you and your child need as fast as possible. Depending on your individual needs, you may choose to either read this book from beginning to end or skip around to the sections you need, in any order.

Quirky, Yes—Hopeless, No is very reader-friendly and conversational. No clinic speak. No obscure words. The few clinical terms that needed to be used are explained clearly. A glossary at the back of this book provides full definitions.

Although I am a trained professional and this book offers insights gained from real interactions with real clients and kids in our Friends' Club, I urge you to always consult a physician regarding diagnosis and treatment for your child.

ACKNOWLEDGMENTS

I am extremely grateful to the following people:

• All of the children and teens who have attended Friends' Club over the years, whose unique perspectives never cease to amaze me

• Employees of C.A.S.E., Inc., past and present, for the wonderful work they do at Friends' Club and in social coaching to make a positive difference in the lives of children and teens with Asperger's syndrome

• Robin La Brie Jackson, Evan Wooton, and many others for all their early efforts, time, and hard work helping me develop this book; I would also like to acknowledge my parents, Lloyd and Phyllis La Brie, for believing in my work and enjoying the stories as I told them. This book is especially written for the two of you to be proud of!

• My mentors, Tony Attwood, Ph.D., Michelle Garcia Winner, Carol Gray, Ron Leaf, Ph.D., and B. J. Freeman, Ph.D., for inspiring and influencing my professional path

• The noble band of critiquers who graciously agreed to read and comment on the manuscript, in particular Dr. Joshua Feder, Dr. Sarita Eastman, Michelle Garcia Winner, Lisa Lundhagen, Suzan Wilson, Lynne Cordes, and Cathy Fritz

• Beth Brust for her gracious offer and hard work in transforming my earlier efforts into a wonderful, user-friendly guide for parents and professionals

• Angela Rinaldi, agent extraordinaire, and Alyse Diamond, a dream editor, both of whom expressed interest in this book at the San Diego State University Writers' Conference right from the start

• And finally, to the parents with whom I've worked at C.A.S.E., Inc., and all of the schoolteachers and special education professionals who have heard my presentations on Asperger's syndrome and shared their own insights—thank you, one and all

INTRODUCTION
HOW FRIENDS' CLUB BEGAN

Friendship improves happiness, and abates misery,
by doubling our joys and dividing our grief.

—Joseph Addison,
POET (1672–1719)

In February 2000, Friends' Club was born. It was to be a place just for kids with Asperger's syndrome, where they could learn behaviors to help them succeed in social settings. They could learn how to be appropriate in a very nonthreatening, nonstressful environment. And, most important of all, they could come here to feel less alone.

Remember, these are the kids who have rarely, if ever, been invited to a birthday party.

These are the kids who sit alone at lunchtime.

These are the kids who get teased and picked on because they are such easy targets. They don't detect the sarcasm or teasing tones in someone's voice. They don't see the smirks and elbowing of other kids toying with them. And they are so eager to connect with anyone that they are a bully's dream.

From the start, our goal was to give them a comfortable place where mistakes could be made as we showed them how to decode the subtle social signals that the rest of us notice and understand intuitively. We wanted to improve how they approached and communicated with people. Most of all, we wanted to help them make new friends and keep them.

We would work with these kids on social awareness, something that does not come naturally to Asperger's folks. We would teach them simple yet important skills—greeting others, asking questions, listening without interrupting, looking someone in the eye and smiling, taking turns when talking or playing a game, paying compliments, etc.

The good news is that these kids can become more socially aware and these skills *can* be taught. With practice, your child *can* learn to communicate better and be more accepted by their peers. With specific guidance and coaching, they can learn people skills.

Friends' Club began with only three groups and a total of fifteen Asperger's kids. There were two groups of boys aged six to ten years and one group of girls aged ten to eleven years. I enlisted the help of an instructional assistant with whom I had worked at a school where I consulted. As coleaders, we met with each group for one hour, one after the other.

At the end of those first sessions, I was exhausted. Things hadn't gone as planned. But with Asperger's kids, things rarely go as planned because these children are such original thinkers. A major part of Friends' Club, right from the start, has been to be flexible, to expect the unexpected, and to model appropriate behavior by breaking each social skill into very small steps. We then practice, practice, practice through games, role-playing, activities, and conversation.

Asperger's children and teens are often made fun of, taken advantage of, or humiliated because they are so unsuspecting. They misinterpret facial expressions, if they look at someone's face at all. They find it difficult to predict what will happen next. And they cannot determine the true intentions of others or their desires.

What I wanted from the beginning, the whole premise of Friends' Club, was to provide a safe place where Asperger's kids are understood by adult leaders who can teach them how to make and keep friends. "Safe" means without the stress of usual social situations. Research has proven that stressful events turn off an Aspie's memory, making it impossible for them to really hear or learn if they're under duress.

The unique aspect of the Friends' Club is that it is for Asperger's kids only. No neurotypical children are involved. This is contrary to conventional wisdom, but it works.

Without neurotypical kids present, Asperger's kids can relax and be themselves. We've discovered that our club members thrive when they are with others like them and are not around neurotypical kids who are more skilled at social interaction, which makes an Aspie feel like a failure. They get enough of that in the real world—at school, at home, and out in public.

For these kids, Friends' Club becomes a weekly safe haven—a sanctuary where they can feel the kinship of others who think outside the box and who have suffered the same slights and put-downs.

I meet with all of the children and teens who have Asperger's or ASD (autism spectrum disorders), to determine their placement in the right group. My cognitive behavioral program is for kids with average or above-average intelligence, good verbal skills, and a desire to learn about being friends and keeping friends. It is not for kids with classic autism, but for high-functioning Asperger's children and teens.

Our formula, if you want to call it that, is to provide a balance of empathy, support, mediation, education, boundaries, practice, and time to "be with one's own species."

Within each group meeting, leaders respond to situations as they arise while still following a basic structured lesson to introduce various themes and to work on particular social skills. We use books, games, and multimedia to teach these lessons while also taking advantage of unexpected teachable moments.

Much of our success comes from our adult leaders having learned—and they are still learning—to see what the Asperger's kids see and to try to think the way they think in order to help them.

One really has to enter their world because it's so different from the way the rest of us perceive things. Often I feel like a dual translator, decoding two languages: I interpret the neurotypical world to the Aspies, and in reverse, I decode the Asperger's kids' unique point of view and behavior to parents, teachers, school professionals, and others. For both sides to understand each other, their very different perspectives have to be made clear and allowed to coexist.

So many Asperger's children get in trouble unintentionally because people misunderstand why they act as they do or say what they say. Much of the time, it's a matter of sensory overload and they simply can't cope. Smells, sounds, and sights can suddenly upset them. They yell. They refuse to cooperate. They run away. To most adults, that looks like disruptive, uncooperative, disrespectful, or argumentative behavior.

At the Friends' Club, we take into account that Asperger's kids feel bombarded by a world that, too often, is too loud, too bright, and too distracting for them to pay attention to what we neurotypicals deem to be important. They are not trying to misbehave or be defiant. Theirs is a neurological condition that results in a social disability. And they don't yet have the skills to explain themselves.

We know that typical discipline will not work. This is not a battle of strong wills, it is not a psychological issue. We focus on helping them cope so that they can function.

So many parents have told me, "If my son would just try it, then he could do it." We take the opposite approach. We say, "If he could, he would." We know that these kids want to cooperate but they can't help their hypersensitivities to sensory stimulation or their inability to see from someone else's perspective, because they are locked in their own point of view.

At Friends' Club, we've learned to read the kids' sensory systems and to recognize when they need a quick break. We've learned to be flexible and to customize each group experience to make the most of the hour a week that they're with us. This leads to a session where they can learn.

Another thing we have to take into account is how Asperger's kids process information. They are concrete, finite, and specific thinkers. They look for patterns and have to consciously think about what they are seeing before it makes sense to them.

As neurotypicals, we notice things unconsciously all the time and, without realizing it, we do what's called *social thinking*, a term coined by Michelle Garcia Winner, a speech language pathologist and specialist in social cognition. We'll notice other people as we walk down the street and make guesses about them. We interact with people in subtle ways, sometimes saying things we don't mean, but also saying things we do mean.

Asperger's people don't understand the abstract. For them to handle an abstraction, they need to associate it with a pattern or have something shown to them so they can see what the person means. This makes it hard for them to process the vague, often invisible nuances of social interactions. And if emotions are expressed, then it really can confuse them.

So at Friends' Club, we've learned to keep our session on a logical, rational plane. We show the behaviors through pictures or video or by modeling them ourselves, so our Friends can grasp the notion. We break down the social behavior—greetings, compliments, responding to others, compromise—into small pieces and then practice each one until it becomes a fluid, whole skill again.

To date, Friends' Club has mushroomed into 21 groups, each meeting for one hour a week, with more than 125 Asperger's kids and teens of all ages involved at any given time. Based in Carlsbad, California, we now have satellite offices in Napa, California; Vancouver, Canada; and Oahu, Hawaii.

At parents' and kids' requests, we have also launched Saturday camps, summer day camps, Playground Patch (which takes Friends' Club to the playground), social coaching, and other special activities.

The experiment of allowing just Asperger's kids to be together has succeeded. Many of our Friends' Club members have made new friends for the first time, not just in their group, but in their community and at school.

Many parents have said that their children have become more relaxed and happier at school, which is welcome news since that is what we were trying to achieve all along. Our quest is, and always will be, to improve our Friends' ability to make and keep friends, one child and teen at a time.

ABOUT THE EXPERTS CITED

Tony Attwood, Ph.D., is an internationally recognized author, speaker, and practicing clinical psychologist specializing in Asperger's syndrome who is based in Queensland, Australia. His books include *The Complete Guide to Asperger's Syndrome* and *Asperger's Syndrome: A Guide for Parents and Professionals*.

Simon Baron-Cohen, Ph.D., is a University of Cambridge professor of psychology who coined the term *mindblindness*. His books include *The Essential Difference: Male and Female Brains and the Truth About Autism* and *Mindblindness: An Essay on Autism and Theory of Mind*.

Eric Courchesne, Ph.D., is a professor of neuroscience at University of California, San Diego (UCSD), and director of the Center for Autism Research at Children's Hospital in San Diego. Courchesne has conducted many long-term studies on autistic children and has published extensively.

Barbara Doyle, M.S., is a special education professional with more than thirty years of experience in developmental disability services who is based in Springfield, Illinois. Her books include *Autism Spectrum Disorders from A to Z: Assessment . . . Diagnosis & More*.

Michael Fitzgerald, Ph.D., is the first professor of child and adolescent psychiatry in Ireland, with a special interest in Asperger's syndrome. His books include *The Genesis of Artistic Creativity: Asperger's Syndrome and the Arts* and *Genius Genes: How Asperger Talents Changed the World*.

B. J. Freeman, Ph.D., is Professor Emerita of Medical Psychology at University of California, Los Angeles (UCLA) School of Medicine. An international authority in the diagnosis and treatment of children and adults with autism, she has published more than one hundred articles in scientific journals and books in the area of autism.

Temple Grandin, Ph.D., is an associate professor of animal sciences at Colorado State University, a business consultant, and a well-known speaker. Her books include *Thinking in Pictures: And Other Reports From My Life with Autism* and *The Way I See It: A Personal Look at Autism and Asperger's.*

Carol Gray is director of the Gray Center for Social Learning and Understanding in Grand Rapids, Michigan. Gray is the originator of Social Stories and Comic Strip Conversations, which were based on her work with students with autism and Asperger's syndrome. Her books include *The New Social Story Book* and *Gray's Guide to Bullying* (the latter includes her *Bully Workbook*).

Ami Klin, Ph.D., is director of the Autism Program and Harris Associate Professor of Child Psychology and Psychiatry at Yale Child Study Center, Yale University School of Medicine in New Haven, Connecticut. His work includes the textbook *Asperger Syndrome.*

Richard Lavoie, M.A., M.Ed., is an author, speaker, and consultant on learning disabilities. His work is based on thirty years of heading residential homes for children with special needs in Cape Cod, Massachusetts. His books include *The Motivation Breakthrough: 6 Secrets to Turning On the Tuned-out Child* and *It's So Much Work to Be Your Friend*, as well as the acclaimed video, *Last One Picked . . . First One Picked On.*

Ron Leaf, Ph.D., is codirector of the Autism Partnership and executive director of the Behavior Therapy and Learning Center. He worked closely with Ivar Lovaas at UCLA, where Leaf received his degrees. His books include *A Work in Progress: Behavior Management Strategies and a Curriculum for Intensive Behavioral Treatment for Autism.*

Vilayanur S. Ramachandran, M.D., Ph.D., is director of the Center for Brain Cognition at UCSD and adjunct professor at the Salk

Institute. His books include *Phantoms in the Brain: Probing the Mysteries of the Human Mind* and *A Brief Tour of Human Consciousness.*

Michelle Garcia Winner, SLP-MA, CCC, is director of the Center for Social Thinking in San Jose, California, and a practicing speech language pathologist and specialist in social cognition. Winner coined the term *social thinking.* Her books include *Thinking about YOU, Thinking about ME* and *Inside Out: What Makes a Person with Social Cognition Deficits Tick?*

PART ONE

ASPERGER'S SYNDROME AND
YOUR CHILD

WHAT ARE THE SIGNS OF ASPERGER'S SYNDROME?

The range and degree of characteristics associated with Asperger's syndrome vary considerably, but the most typical are these:

- **Generally unaware about people, social situations, time, place.** Aspies live very much in the present, in the immediate moment, or many light-years from now, but have no clue what's happening next. They can only see from their point of view and need help in becoming aware of others' thoughts and feelings. They tend to be quite awkward around people and lack social skills.

- **Rigid, prefer routine, very literal-minded, and are such purveyors of truth that they are too blunt and inadvertently insult others.** Fortunately, they can be taught how to be less direct.

- **Have difficulty making eye contact.** Some say it's too confusing, even painful, to look someone in the eyes; others say it's distracting and they can't remember what they want to say.

- **Have special interests, which for some become obsessions, and they will talk about these topics continuously,** whether anyone else is interested or not.

- **Act inappropriately,** yet have no idea that they are being inappropriate. It is difficult for them to read body language.

- **Out-of-the-box thinking lets them see the world very differently than we do** and leads to some odd conclusions and odd behavior by conventional standards. It's best to ask them why they are doing something before you get angry. It's easier to be understanding if you know their reasoning.

- **Highly sensitive to touch, sound, light, taste, and other stimuli** to the degree that a tag in a shirt bothers them, sunlight is too bright, and they prefer to stay indoors much more than be out-doors, where their sensory system is bombarded.

- **Need help staying on track and being organized** and can become easily overwhelmed by too many directions, too many details, timed tests, and deadlines.

- **Lack self-awareness skills and may have bouts of anger and frustration** beyond their control. They can learn to cope through repetition and reinforcement.

FREQUENTLY ASKED QUESTIONS ABOUT ASPERGER'S SYNDROME

Ever since founding the Friends' Club in 2000, and performing thousands of assessments for children of all ages, I have heard certain questions over and over from parents just learning that their child or teen has been diagnosed with Asperger's syndrome. As they begin to wonder what it means for their child and for the whole family, these are the questions I hear most often.

1. IS THERE A CURE? WILL MY CHILD OUTGROW IT?

No, there is no cure and they won't grow out of it, but Asperger's kids can learn to cope in the real world with help and guidance. And the good news is that most Asperger's kids really don't care if they're like everyone else. They like their uniqueness and creativity.

Because this is a neurological condition, and not a psychological issue, conventional Freudian or play therapies will not work. There is no interpreting dreams or getting in touch with their feelings, because Asperger's kids are *not* naturally connected to their feelings. They live more in their minds and imaginations.

To help them cope with daily life and people, cognitive behavior therapy is extremely helpful in raising Aspies' awareness. Kids practice social skills and they learn to associate more successfully with others. Psychotherapy can be effective as long as it's carried out in an engaging manner with a balanced interactive approach. It won't help if the Aspie is allowed to talk on and on about his special interest. But if the session has a mutual, reciprocal interaction, through play or talking, then such therapy can lead to social problem solving and improvement.

2. WHY CAN'T I DISCIPLINE THIS CHILD THE WAY THAT I DO MY OTHERS?

First of all, the emotional carrot that many parents can use with their other children won't work with their Asperger's child. Trying to drum up caring, trying to make them feel ashamed, or trying to get them to please you won't work. Such tactics don't mean anything to an Asperger's child of any age. They don't care about meeting parents' expectations or anyone else's, just their own. **The best approach is a totally rational one.**

Keep emotion out of your message as much as possible.

Focus on the facts and logical reasons why they should or shouldn't do something and present your case as calmly and clearly as possible. If you make it sound like a rule, all the better, because they are natural-born rule followers. And by following rules, they can please you.

Second, to only tell an Asperger's child what he is doing wrong doesn't work. They are not abstract thinkers, so they can't intuit the next step. **You need to tell them exactly what they should be doing, and even show them, if possible.** Modeling the desired behavior is extremely helpful to them. And being natural-born rule followers, they will usually comply once they understand, as long as their sensitivities to sounds or smells or light don't get in the way.

Another stumbling block can be that the **Asperger's child needs to do things his own way.** This makes them seem like they're acting out or misbehaving when really they are just stuck on the idea of doing something a certain way. This is where discipline is less important than being more flexible as a parent. You can't spoil Aspies by letting them do it their way, as might happen with your other children. Giving in to an Asperger's child does not usually lead to manipulative behavior on her part.

Instead **the best strategy is to pick your battles,** giving in to the smaller deviations from what they're supposed to do, and then making them comply with the truly important requests. Since give-and-take does not come naturally to them, you will have to explain and keep reminding them of how you gave in on the last issue, so now it's their turn to give in and do it your way.

Their opposition can be their way of keeping things predictable— they want to know what comes next. So if you use their desire to do something a certain way to gently force them to be more reciprocal, you both win.

3. CAN MY CHILD CONTROL HIS DISRUPTIVE BEHAVIOR OR NOT?

Again, Asperger's children are not like your neurotypical children, who intentionally push parental buttons to get what they want. A tantrum by an Aspie is more often caused by an overload of sensory stimuli or an inability to loosen up about his own ideas. It is nothing like a spoiled child's tantrum, which is manipulative and should be ignored to discourage such behavior.

An Asperger's child's tantrum needs understanding and patience, a lessening of sensory overload, and a return to calm. While you may enjoy being around people, it is one of the most exhausting and overly stimulating activities for these children.

The main thing for parents to remember is that these children are struggling to make sense of the world around them. And **if they could do something, they would, but they often can't**—at least, not right away. Things that we don't think twice about are a challenge for Aspies—greeting people, making small talk, planning the next thing to do, being on time, getting organized, navigating anywhere. These are all struggles for them and they get exhausted.

So **understanding and communication are the best tools to tackle disruptive behavior**. Ask them why they are upset. If they don't know, suggest some possible reasons to help them figure it out. And give them the time and quiet space they need to calm down.

When it comes to obsessive behavior, something that has worked for us at the Friends' Club is to show the child a box and tell him that you are putting that topic in the box. Then close the lid and say, "It's closed. You can't talk about it anymore." This kind of concrete action helps curb the compulsion.

4. WHY DO THEY DO SUCH QUIRKY THINGS?

Asperger's children do not see the world the same way the rest of us do, so they are not bound by convention. They do unconventional things because they are unconventional people. They are not even aware of how different they can be, and the good news is that it doesn't bother them to be different.

Some of our greatest geniuses are thought to have had Asperger's— Albert Einstein, Sir Isaac Newton, Thomas Jefferson, Hans Christian Andersen, Mozart, Vincent van Gogh. These different thinkers didn't let conventional thinking box them in, and they produced ground-breaking theories and creative works that are revered to this day.

When Asperger's kids have the various tics and sporadic movements— hand waving, flapping, twitching—that some children on the autism spectrum have in order to be more aware of their bodies or to release stress, they seem really quirky. We've found that placing a bean bag object on their shoulders or neck will calm some of them, and reduce the random body movements. Anything weighted compresses joints, triggering a series of signals to the brain that makes them feel better.

5. WHY DON'T THEY UNDERSTAND WHAT I WANT THEM TO DO?

First, ask yourself if you're being emotional, because that can make any-one with Asperger's shut down and stop hearing your message. Recent neurological research suggests that people with Asperger's have a neu-ronal process that automatically shuts down their memory if they are socially or emotionally overwhelmed. They cannot hear or understand whatever you have to say, nor can they communicate their own thoughts or feelings. The best thing to do is to deal with them logically and with-out emotion.

Also, remember that **if you are proposing something abstract, then often your child won't be able to grasp what you want her to do**. As concrete thinkers, Aspies respond better to visual images. Write out what you want them to do or, better still, show them what you want them to do.

6. WHY CAN'T I GET MY CHILD OUT OF THE HOUSE?

It's true that Asperger's kids are most comfortable at home. There they experience fewer sensations, fewer surprises, and less social discomfort. They put so much effort into just holding it together when they're out of the house and interacting with people that they need a retreat where they are comfortable and they can decompress. The best thing that you can do as their parents is to allow them this time alone and a quiet space at home, for a certain amount of time each day. Please accept that they prefer—and need—this sanctuary from the real world. Being alone does not mean they are lonely. And in solitude, they do better at problem solving and calming themselves.

Also, since Asperger's kids do not usually have the best gross motor skills, they are not drawn to physical outdoor activities. They need a nudge to play sports or to go walking or biking. It is good for them to get fresh air and to exercise, if you are able to talk them into it.

7. WILL MY SON OR DAUGHTER EVER DATE OR GET MARRIED?

Asperger's kids are definitely late bloomers. Emotionally and socially, they are often a couple of years behind their peers while intellectually they are on par or way ahead.

Because social situations are a struggle for them and the basics of building friendships elude them, Aspies are usually slower to make the kinds of connections that lead to dating and long-term relationships. But yes, they can have relationships that turn into dating, and yes, they may marry.

Once they make friends, Asperger's kids and teens are loyal, truthful, and reliable. The grass is never greener. As adults, they are hard workers and can be solid, steady partners who earn a decent income. It will probably be the other person who makes the first move toward a friendship or romance because, by nature, people with Asperger's do not take the initiative. They will react, but they rarely reach out to people or take the first step themselves.

Parents of female teens with Asperger's should be aware that their daughters may be **in danger of being taken advantage of by unscrupulous males, because these girls can't read between the lines**. Dating language is particularly full of innuendo, murky meanings, and smooth talking. You will want to keep tabs on your Aspie daughter, and help put things in perspective as well as ward off possibly misleading situations.

8. ARE THEY GOING TO BE ABLE TO BE INDEPENDENT ENOUGH ONE DAY TO GO TO COLLEGE OR TO GET A JOB AND MOVE OUT OF THE HOUSE?

The short answer is "Yes, possibly." Many Asperger's teens are capable of learning enough life skills to be able to move out and live on their own . . . eventually. With going to college or working at a job, there are so many variables that it is impossible to predict exactly when they will be ready. It all depends on the individual.

Often, they need to stay at home longer than your other children because they need extra time to mature and pick up organizational and other skills to make sure they can plan their days, feed themselves, do their laundry, and show up to classes or work on time. Going to a junior college the first two years and living at home is often best for some teens. This would ease the transition to higher education and give them time to take on more personal responsibility.

A set routine always helps. Asperger's kids prefer a predictable pattern in their lives because it gives them something to count on, something regular and unchanging to expect. The good news is that they will adhere to routine, which pleases employers and professors. Still, their safety is the main concern. They should not be expected to live on their own until it's certain that they can do so safely.

9. WILL THEY EVER TAKE THE INITIATIVE AND REACH OUT TO OTHERS?

No, probably not. Part of having Asperger's is being unable to take the initiative because they don't see things the same way as others do. They will need your help to coax them to call potential friends, or even existing ones, to ask them over. Or you may need to call the child's parent yourself and set up a playdate for your Asperger's child.

Talking on the phone is also very difficult for Asperger's kids because they cannot see the other person and there are slight delays in the transmission of voices. Even more debilitating is that they are very poor at making small talk to begin with. Add that to all the confusing details involved in making plans to get together with someone, and it just seems too hard to them to take that first step.

It's best to at least have your child practice dialing the number and start the invitation (with you on hand to feed some lines for them to say). Then you can ask to speak to the other parent to solidify the details.

10. WHY DON'T THEY TRY HARDER WHEN THEY ARE CHALLENGED?

Asperger's kids are prone to perfectionism. They are afraid to be wrong, so they won't do something if they think they may make a mistake. At Friends' Club, we try to help them understand that guessing is just that—a guess, which doesn't have to be right. Asperger's kids won't make a guess if they're not sure it's the right answer.

This perfectionist bent keeps them from predicting events or actions in stories. When their struggles comprehending abstract and referential ideas are added to their quest to be right all the time, predicting becomes even harder.

Ironically, their problem is not that they don't notice details. It's the opposite—they notice too much detail. This can also confuse them and prevent them from figuring things out, so they don't try.

GETTING THROUGH TO YOUR ASPERGER'S CHILD OR TEEN

As hard as it can be to understand someone with Asperger's, it's often even harder to be understood *by* someone with Asperger's. Taking a conventional approach rarely works because they are unconventional thinkers. They get tripped up by their social blindness and their inability to see another person's point of view. Asperger's kids have a hard time understanding what is upsetting you, why you want them to do something, or how they should behave.

Here are some tips that I'd like to share from my years of working with Asperger's children and teens, both at the Friends' Club and elsewhere. In order for you to help them make sense of their world, first you have to reach them. And to do that, you should know the following:

1. IF YOU SEE ODD BEHAVIOR, DON'T ASSUME THE WORST—INSTEAD, ASK THEM, "WHY?"

The younger they are, the harder it is to figure out what your Asperger's children are doing and why. That's because they don't always know themselves and often have fewer verbal skills. But know that they do have their own logic. What appears to the rest of us to be odd or quirky or makes no sense does, in fact, make perfect and logical sense to them, coming from their unique perspective.

So it's best to ask calmly, "Why?" or "How come you're doing that?" rather than criticizing or punishing them without asking. Once they've explained what they're up to, then you can understand their logic and let them know why that's inappropriate or impolite or is better done in a less obvious way.

2. YOU WILL NOT BE ABLE TO DISCIPLINE ASPERGER'S CHILDREN THE WAY YOU DISCIPLINE OTHER CHILDREN.

Although some Aspies are very sensitive to being punished, a time-out might be a reward! They love spending time alone in their room, so to be sent there probably will not teach them a lesson or leave much of an impression.

Also, to punish them for being rude by telling them not to do something only leaves them wondering, "What's not being rude?" They honestly don't know. **Asperger's kids need to be told, in a calm voice, exactly what they need to do, not what they shouldn't be doing.**

They need clear instructions, step-by-step, to achieve the desired behavior. Once spelled out so they know what is expected, they will usually comply because you've now made it a rule and they are rule followers.

3. KEEP YOUR EMOTIONS IN CHECK OR THE ASPERGER'S CHILD WILL SHUT DOWN.

The best way to deliver any information to a person with Asperger's is in a calm, logical, and very direct manner. If there is any anger or any outburst, the Asperger's brain is wired to shut down. Aspies are very sensitive and can't handle the emotional overload and stress, so nothing is heard or remembered until things calm down.

The good news is that you can get through to someone with Asperger's, as long as you speak as unemotionally as possible. Make your message very clear, very logical, and very calm. Writing it down also works very well. Written words give them a concrete message to see.

4. IF YOU WANT THEM TO LEARN A NEW SKILL, REDUCE THE SOCIAL STRESS OF THEIR ENVIRONMENT AS MUCH AS POSSIBLE.

Research done in 2001 by Eric Courchesne, Ph.D., of the University of California, San Diego, revealed that social stress triggers a memory neuronal system to shut off in an Asperger's brain. This creates memory loss because they are unable to retain information if highly stressed. So if your child is having a tough time in a new social situation, it's not the time to expect him to learn how to handle it. They will need your understanding and guidance, and perhaps need to escape to a calm room until they can regain their footing.

5. BREAK EVERYTHING DOWN INTO SMALL STEPS.

Asperger's kids have trouble processing information. Things that seem simple to us, like tying a shoe or making conversation, are baffling to them. They need to have everything broken down into very small, clear parts to follow.

This is especially true for anything social. Interactions with people need explaining, step-by-step, for the Asperger's child to be able to understand what to do and to be able to practice the behavior. Whether it's as simple as greeting someone and shaking hands, or something more complicated like attending a holiday event, Asperger's kids will need coaching. They need to be reminded over and over again of what the desirable behavior will be. They are not being uncooperative or discourteous intentionally. They are just clueless, and need your help to figure out what is expected of them.

6. THEY WILL NEED YOUR HELP TO EXPRESS THEMSELVES POLITELY.

Since Asperger's kids are purveyors of truth, they can be very blunt and even outright rude and hurtful without realizing it. Part of their disability is a lack of understanding of other people's feelings. They have to be taught a semblance of empathy since it does not come naturally to them.

They also need explanations about why the truth hurts. They don't understand why they can't say what seems so obvious to them. They are not aware of social standards, which deem it best not to say certain truths in order to spare the other person's feelings. They will need to practice such restraint over and over again. You will need to be their constant reality check.

7. TURNING THEIR OBSESSIONS INTO CONCRETE CONCEPTS HELPS MAKE THEM MORE MANAGEABLE.

Being black-and-white thinkers, Asperger's kids tend to see patterns and form pictures in their minds to help them process what they see around them. It gives them something to hang on to, but unfortunately for them, life doesn't always have a nice, tidy order about it. Consequently, Asperger's kids can tend to become obsessed with things that give them a sense of order like trains, schedules, maps, dinosaurs, outer space, a certain video or computer game, etc.

If your child's obsessions interfere with what he needs to be doing, you could hold up a small box and say, "I'm putting that subject in this box and locking it up. No more talking about it." And make sure he watches as you open the box and pretend to put something in it, then close it.

If he tries to talk about it again, say, "No, that's locked up. End of discussion." Aspies cannot argue with the box because it is a concrete object. Your child sees the closed lid, which ends that option.

8. APPRECIATE THEIR STRENGTHS, CREATIVITY, AND UNIQUE VIEWPOINTS AS MUCH AS POSSIBLE WHILE ALSO WORKING ON REDUCING THEIR DEFICITS.

While Asperger's kids face daily struggles to navigate the complex, rough seas of the social world, they usually have certain areas where they excel. These assets should be cultivated to encourage them and to boost their sense of self-worth.

Just as Thomas Edison's mother let him loose in the family's basement to do chemistry experiments after recognizing his love of science, it's best to find out your child's passions and strengths and play to those. It keeps up their excitement and imagination, while you still work on coaching them in the other areas where they struggle.

See also Depression, Embarrassment,
Parental Sainthood and Your Need for Support,
Strengths and How to Cultivate Them, *and* Telling
Your Child That He or She Has Asperger's
Syndrome

DIAGNOSIS

Some of our Friends were diagnosed with Asperger's before they became school-age, while many of them were in third or sixth or even eighth grade before their condition was identified.

Interestingly, as many as 60 percent of children diagnosed with Asperger's have also been diagnosed with attention-deficit/hyperactivity disorder (either the hyperactive-impulsive or the inattentive type). Both ADHD and Asperger's include the frontal lobe deficits, which make our Friends unable to gauge time or to be organized.

Six main descriptors of Asperger's syndrome were proposed by Christopher Gillberg, a Swedish physician who studied AS extensively. They were incorporated in the *Diagnostic and Statistical Manual of Mental Disorders*, fourth edition, text revision (DSM-IV-TR) in 1994. All or a majority of these may be present to diagnose Asperger's:

- Social impairments

- Narrow interests

- Repetitive routines

- Speech and language problems

- Nonverbal communication problems

- Motor clumsiness

Since Asperger's truly is a social disability, it becomes more obvious once more social interaction is expected of children as they go through elementary school and interact with more people outside of the home and away from their family.

Like the whole spectrum of autism, Asperger's is something of a hidden disability. Also commonly referred to as pervasive developmental disorder (PDD), autism has blurry lines that make it hard to pinpoint exactly what type of disorder it is, but the kids are usually quirky, exhibit what is considered to be "odd" behavior, and struggle in conventional learning or social situations. Ask your child's primary care physician to do a thorough physical exam, especially a hearing test, to rule out other issues.

Once your child has been diagnosed with Asperger's, here are the first steps that I recommend to launch them on the right path. If your child is still of preschool age, then **keep encouraging and modeling the best social behavior**. For example, if your child doesn't respond to your good-night hug, then pull his arms up around your neck and show him. Or if your daughter slides off your lap when you're reading to her, keep reading while she plays nearby, and then try again to have her sit in your lap next time. It's also good to join her in play so she's not always alone.

Experts agree that early intervention is very important for significant progress. The sooner your child can get help developmentally, the better. **Ask your local school for any prekindergarten special services that your child may need**—speech, adaptive physical education, and occupational therapy may all be available for early intervention. Or look into private services, which your insurance may pay for or you may have to pay for yourself.

If your child is already in elementary school and recently diagnosed, **make an appointment with the special education department to discuss services or accommodations** that would be available to help your child. If you show that you're willing to meet them halfway and are actively supporting the school's efforts, then they may be more cooperative. No one can just "fix" your child—it's a group effort to help an Asperger's child succeed in school.

During the Individualized Education Program (IEP) meeting with school officials, consider checking the "autism" box if that is an option. Then your child is eligible for resource help as well as homework modification and test accommodations in the classroom. Having a diagnosis of Asperger's or autism is a benefit over having your child's condition unidentified and grouped into the general pervasive developmental disorder (PDD) category. An ADHD diagnosis may warrant a 504 accommodation, which allows extra time on timed tests and exams, but ADHD does not qualify for an IEP.

To label or not to label?

Many parents struggle with this question. While files remain confidential, as does the label, some parents find it hard to accept that their child is being branded a certain thing. Other parents welcome the specific identification of their child's condition so that it takes the guesswork out of what he has and how to help him. A diagnosis helps professionals know which treatments to use for maximum effectiveness.

Most parents already have an inkling that their child has issues, especially by the time he or she reaches school age. But as one of our Friends' parents said, nothing prepared him for the actual diagnosis.

Upon hearing an autism spectrum disorder diagnosis, the grieving process begins. Parents may mourn the loss of their expectations and dreams for their child. Typical emotions reflect the grief cycle: shock, disbelief, denial, anger, confusion, guilt, anxiety, physical illness, loss of sleep, withdrawal, and despair. The grief is for the death of the idealized child, and can be chronic, continuing over the child's lifetime as the discrepancy grows between who the child is now and who the child could have been.

The acceptance of the diagnosis is a gradual process. Unlike with the finality of a child's death, the grief process for an autistic or Asperger's child may be reopened at each transition, such as a change of schools or a transitional period in development.

Having a child with a chronic disability often causes parental stress, so it's important to learn how to cope. Hearing the initial diagnosis can activate defense mechanisms like numbness, allowing the mind to shut down until the parent can accept this new reality. One of our Friends' dad said that when he learned about his son's autism, he felt a massive heartache that moved to his muscles and head. It seemed impossible to start the car and drive away from the specialist's office.

For many parents, it's only when a second opinion has been delivered that the grieving process can start. And that is followed by the fear that the child will stay the same and never improve or develop.

In time, parents learn that with appropriate treatment (the sooner, the better) and support services, their autistic child will be able to maximize their potential. There is hope for advances on all fronts, as long as help is sought and implemented.

Parents should know that guilt often surfaces as the family searches for reasons for the autism. One parent may blame the other. The mother may wonder if it was something she did during her pregnancy that led to this development. There is an inherent need to assign blame or to claim it was someone's fault in the mistaken belief that it was something that we have control over.

After all, it is a blow to one's self confidence and self esteem to hear the news that one's child has a lifelong disability. Sometimes the blame is projected outward—at the doctor making the diagnosis or the teachers who did not tell the parents of their suspicions.

Parental anger is common and expressed in different ways, depending on the individual's personality. It may be outward, showing how hurt the parent is, or held inside with unnatural quietness and resentment. Having an autistic child may make you resent your friends who have neurotypical children. Or one parent may become angry with the other if that spouse was more insistent about having children in the first place.

It is quite common for parents to be resentful of their autistic child because the condition means so many changes for the family. They may also feel scrutinized by others as they try to cope with having a special needs child.

This kind of misplacement of anger is part of the grieving process. The best step is to put all blaming aside, or better still to banish it completely so that you are able to become a team working together to help your child, rather than remaining adversaries at odds with each other. If blaming continues despite your best efforts, then seeking help through therapy and/or a support group is a wise next step so that you will be able to move on.

PARENTAL SAINTHOOD AND
YOUR NEED FOR SUPPORT

How many of you have been criticized for being overly protective of your Asperger's child? Or the reverse, condemned for not watching him closely enough?

It hurts when other people think that they know better than you do what your child is like and how to handle him. It hurts to be accused outright, or subtly hinted at, that you're either not doing your job as a parent well enough to control your child or that you're doing too much for your child, which is keeping him from being more independent.

Most days, it feels like you're caught between a rock and a hard place, doesn't it? And it stinks more than you'd care to admit, I'll bet.

How frustrating it must be to think that you have figured out your Asperger's child only to have an odd new behavior surface, or a sudden outburst occur over something that you had no idea would bother him. As we've learned to say at the Friends' Club, "Expect the unexpected."

But no one said that the unexpected is easy.

Well, I want to tell you that while none of you may have been bucking for sainthood, it comes with the territory.

No one plans on becoming the parent of a special needs child, but how you approach this challenge, and the ways you choose to help your child, vary with every parent I meet.

After years of parent-child interviews for the Friends' Club and thousands of outside evaluations for individual families and schools, I can assure you that I think you're all champions. The daily struggles that all of you go through to guide your Asperger's child through life and school as safely, happily, and successfully as possible can be mind-boggling.

The injustice is that as admirable as your efforts are, you receive little praise or external repayment. Not even from your own child, because Asperger's kids aren't the kind to give you a hug or to climb into your lap as a cuddly reward for all you've done.

I'm so impressed with those families who have sacrificed much for their Asperger's child, both financially and in time or effort— staying home for closer monitoring, extra tutoring, various therapies, numerous doctor visits, evaluations, etc. I'm also in awe of those parents who learn as much as they can about Asperger's syndrome to help their son or daughter navigate through life, knowing there is no cure, striving to maximize their potential, encouraging eventual independence.

Hearing their child diagnosed as having Asperger's syndrome is a relief for some parents, who finally know why their quirky child behaves the way he or she does. It also qualifies their child for extra help and services at school if the whole team agrees during an Individualized Education Program (IEP) meeting, and the parents decide to check the "autism" box.

For others, such news is not welcome and there is parental resistance and denial.

Either way, the child will be the same and will still have Asperger's.

In my experience, those parents who accept the diagnosis and begin to get help for their child fare better than those who refuse to believe it. You can keep hoping your child will snap out of it, or grow out of it, but it won't happen.

Again, Asperger's is not a disease and there is no cure at this time. It is a neurological condition. Getting help for your child—the earlier the better—can modify the impact through behavioral training and practice.

Let me make one thing clear—when I speak of sainthood, please don't think that I'm advocating or encouraging martyrdom to achieve it. Parents should not become martyrs to their child's special needs. It doesn't help you and it doesn't help your child.

That's where support comes in.

Support is available in all forms and sizes. Emotional support from family, friends, other parents, and experts. Academic support from teachers, school psychologists, and staff. Financial support from insurance companies and outside foundations and grants.

The key is to get the support that you need at any given time so that you can continue to do the best for yourself and your Asperger's child. If a crisis erupts because you've had too many rough nights with your

Aspie child or too much bad news from the school and you're at your wit's end, *get some help*. You don't have to do this alone.

You are never alone.

Not with support groups, professionals, and organizations to help you. (See Part Three: Resources.)

Remember the airplane emergency rule. When a plane is in crisis and there's a sudden drop in cabin pressure, the breathing masks drop down. Who goes first? You do, as the parent. You are supposed to cover your own mouth first and start breathing before covering your child's mouth.

Why? Because if you're suffocating and can't function, then your child is also going to suffer and won't be able to function.

As the caregiver for your Asperger's child, as the chief architect and administrator of your child's day-to-day living and future, if you become overwhelmed or exhausted or overly discouraged, then you will become nonfunctional. It's a disservice to your child to do too much for him, and not enough for yourself to keep you afloat.

So please remember that you are not alone, no matter how isolated or helpless or hopeless you may feel. *You are not alone!* Trust me on this.

So many families are going through exactly what you're going through—well, maybe not *exactly*, because, after all, we're talking about Asperger's kids. No two are alike. But so many of the trials and tribulations—or "challenges" for a more positive spin—that I hear about and consult families about are along the same lines.

And I can tell you right now, you're not the only parent of an Asperger's child who has ever felt frustrated or confused or helpless or defeated. And fortunately, there are good days when you feel surprised and excited for your child, encouraged by a positive development.

To those people who criticize or tell you "You're doing it all wrong," feel free to speak up. Whether you say "My child has Asperger's syndrome and needs extra help" or "My child needs this consideration even if your child does not," either one addresses the issue and may even educate the person a bit. You'll feel better for saying something, so go ahead.

Again, for moral support, turn to friends and other parents whose children have Asperger's. For more information, turn to books and local or national Asperger's and autism organizations. For more school support, talk with the special education department at your child's school. If they are not responsive, go to the district office. And always follow up a phone call with a written letter or e-mail.

Whatever you do, identify the kind of support you need and seek it out. Your child will benefit. Your family will benefit . . . and so will you.

PART TWO

85 LESSONS FOR DECODING ASPERGER'S CHILDREN

See also Anxiety, Change and "Change-ups," Curiosity About People, Perfectionism and Unrealistic Expectations, *and* Perspectives and Point of View

ACCEPTANCE

Usually, I have an opportunity to meet each of our new Friends' Club members before the first meeting. But once there was a teenage girl whom I met for the first time on the night of her group's first meeting. When I greeted her at the door with my usual, "Hi! I'm Dr. Norall, but my friends call me Cynthia," she answered, "Well, Cynthia, it's about time you put this together for my species."

Often, that is how Asperger's kids feel—like another species. That's why parents have been so grateful for Friends' Club, because they tell us that this is the first time their sons or daughters have been with a group of kids who are like them.

When typical kids come together, they tend to smile, goof around, ask questions, and generally get to know one another without really thinking about it.

Asperger's kids tend not to smile, which makes them seem rather serious. They think their own thoughts, and are not at all curious about other people—ideas and things, yes, but not people. This makes it difficult for them to connect with and be accepted by their peers.

Ironically, by the very nature of the Aspie mind, it's hard for the Asperger's child to accept other kids because acceptance is a two-way street. That, in and of itself, is a hard concept for Asperger's kids to understand because reciprocity does not occur to them.

While Asperger's children need to be taught that they have to accept other people, flaws and all, if they want to connect with others and make friends, they also have to realize that they are not perfect themselves. To be accepted, others will have to overlook the Asperger's child's flaws. This can be a startling notion to them.

So at Friends' Club, what we work on is flexibility training. Our

Asperger's Friends cultivate a certain order of things to keep from feeling anxious about the unknown. They avoid change. We try to help our clients to loosen up in small ways at first and then build up to bigger things.

For example, just learning to play with an object in a new way that is different from how they normally play is a good place to start. We take a toy plane and put it on a train track.

Would you accept that? Sure. But our Friends would have a hard time with this at first. They will not want to do it because it's "wrong" in their view of the world. Planes don't belong on tracks.

What we are doing is teaching them that it's okay to do it differently and that their world won't fall apart if a plane goes on a train track. The typical order can change and, if they are more flexible, things will still be all right.

Once they learn to accept these kinds of small changes, then we might write their schedule differently. We teach them what we call "change-ups," when the unexpected happens. We talk about how all of us have to learn to adjust and accept what wasn't planned or something that's done out of order.

One of the biggest and most unpredictable things in any Asperger child's life is people. To interact with people requires much flexibility and acceptance.

One surprisingly effective teaching tool to help our Friends practice being more accepting around people is to have them read scripts of conversations or social situations while being videotaped. They like reading the scripts, they enjoy watching themselves in a "movie," and they learn by hearing and seeing themselves address a social episode. By facing the camera and reading the words written on butcher paper taped to a wall behind the camera and out of the viewers' eyeshot, children practice saying what will eventually become more natural for them to say without prompting.

See also First Friendships, Remembering Names, *and* Talking with Peers

ACQUAINTANCE VERSUS FRIEND

There are many degrees of friendship. It depends on how much you share with the other person—not just time spent together, but also mutual outlook, experiences, humor, and helpfulness. Do you see each other often and get beyond the superficial level? Is there a connection beyond living in the same neighborhood or going to the same school?

Remembering someone's name is expected with friends, but not necessarily with a casual acquaintance. Distinguishing between friends and acquaintances is very difficult for our Asperger's kids. Of course, it doesn't help that they have such a hard time remembering names, too.

When new children are going to join one of our Friends' Club groups, I try to meet with the child one-on-one. I find out more about him and determine which group would be the best fit. During this interview, I ask him what a friend is. The most common answers are "Someone who is nice to you" and "Someone who plays with you." Notice that there is no mention or understanding that a friend is someone who shares a similar interest or with whom they have something in common.

When I ask the younger ones how many friends they have, they'll say a number like nineteen or twenty-four—the same number of kids in their class. They think that everyone is their friend, and don't understand that other students are just acquaintances until something more develops between them.

In fact, when I told a teen whom I was meeting that I have different friends for different activities, his face turned red and he blustered, "You normal people are so confusing—I told you that I just wanted a friend."

At Friends' Club, we teach our groups that saying "hi" and talking about general things makes someone more of an acquaintance. And while talking on the phone with someone is a friend activity, it takes more than that to become better friends. You have to share an experience together, like going to the movies or having a meal or playing at each other's house to begin a friendship. And then you both have to want to see each other again to be considered friends.

With our groups, we'll start by making the topic more concrete by writing on a board: "What is a friend?" and "What is an acquaintance?"

Then we ask the group to offer some answers and to discuss the similarities and differences. One girl said that she had some friends at school, but she didn't know their names. Another asked if friendship was determined by how long you knew someone.

We pointed out that just because you've known your mail carrier your whole life and you might talk a little, like "How are you?" and "Nice day," that unless you invited her over for dinner or did something together, she would be considered an acquaintance.

We also teach them that even if you call to initiate a friendship with someone, you won't really know if the other person wants to be friends until he also calls you as well. Reciprocity is a tough concept for our kids, but it's an important signal as to whether the desire to spend time together is mutual so that a friendship can grow.

With our younger Friends, we emphasize that a true friend shares a connection with you. As C. S. Lewis said, "Friendship is born at that moment when one person says to another: 'What! You, too? Thought I was the only one.'"

With our older Friends, we must teach them to show an interest in others. As Dale Carnegie once said, "You can make more friends in two months by becoming interested in other people than you can in two years by trying to get other people interested in you."

Since our Asperger's kids tend to start any conversation by talking about *their* special interests or what they've been doing, we work on teaching them that they have to *act* interested in others by asking people questions.

We use the activity What's *Up*? to practice this social skill. First, we start with one Friend telling about what he did recently. Then each Friend in the group asks a question about his statement. We pass out links, small metal or plastic hoops that can be chained together. Each time someone asks an appropriate question (appropriateness is often a

challenge for our Asperger's Friends), they get a link. It's a tangible reminder that listening has its own rewards. We want them to understand
that the more they stay on topic, the better the conversation will go.

Another game we'll play in a group is called What Am I Thinking?
We encourage our Friends to make guesses about what someone else in
the group is thinking about just by noticing where the person is looking. One of the boys who enjoyed this game said, "My eyes are like
arrows. Just look at where my eyes are pointing." Most Asperger's kids
don't look at other people's eyes, which is why they miss most of the
nonverbal message being relayed. This game helps them cue into the
other person's eyes, and also risk being wrong by guessing (another
thing they don't like—being wrong).

For our teen Friends, we let them know that the Internet can be
a way to connect with other teens, especially with those who have
Asperger's. The Web site Wrong Planet (at www.wrongplanet.net) is
dedicated to just this audience and purpose.

But we also warn our kids of the possibility that the contacts that
they make online may not be who they say they are. We've discovered
that especially our teen girls need to be careful. They don't perceive
questions as being as personal as others would. And they may give out
more information than they should about themselves.

One girl in a Friends group announced that she'd made a friend on
the Internet. She said that she hadn't given out any personal information. But by probing further, we found out that the online "friend" was
really a thirty-plus-year-old male who had asked for her panty size and
whether she wore a thong!

Worse still, she had given him her address. We had to explain to
our Friend that those were, indeed, very personal questions and totally
inappropriate, and we also notified the sheriff's department.

See also Anxiety, Calming Down and Focusing, Fear, *and* Sensory Sensitivities

ADMITTING WHEN YOU'RE SCARED

With their high sensitivity to sound, light, smell, taste, and textures, Asperger's kids are more prone to being afraid of ordinary things. What we might not even notice or can easily ignore is scary to them.

For example, a simple visit to the beach resulted in one of our young Friends covering himself up with a beach towel from head to toe. His mother thought that he was afraid of the waves or just didn't like the gritty sand. But he was really trying to hide from all the sensory stimuli that were overwhelming him.

He felt bombarded and afraid of sunlight that was too bright, waves that were too loud, sand that was too hot, and people who were making too much noise, yet he was too young to say so. He was eager to go home almost as soon as his family arrived.

Other times, an Aspie child hides his fear, especially as he gets older, but it doesn't go away. The experience is just buried until a later date, maybe a month or months later, when your child tells you about how very afraid he was even though there was no hint of anything being wrong at the time.

Since our Friends have a hard time understanding and expressing their emotions, it's hard for them to pinpoint what's bothering them and to put it into words. Your best course is to ask them directly what's bothering them, and acknowledge the fear. But don't dwell on it, because that can make the fear stronger.

A simple statement is helpful, like "Sometimes things are scary and that's okay," which puts the fear into perspective. Then make a suggestion of how to alleviate the fear. Writing down both the fear and the solution is even better, creating a visual for them to see and refer to.

For an immediate strategy, using calming techniques like steady breathing can help. Focusing on breathing buys some time for the body to stop reacting and provides more oxygen, which has a calming influence.

At Friends' Club, we also encourage our kids to think of something else to make them feel better. Diversions work. With our younger children, we'll make a "Happy Book." This is a scrapbook of photos and cutouts of things that make the child feel happy. We encourage them to look at the Happy Book when they are afraid, so their minds turn to more soothing, pleasant thoughts.

Fears are exaggerated with Asperger's children, and there can be many—fear of change, of the new and unknown, of sensory overload, of being wrong, etc. Facing their fears is actually the best way to overcome them. We work on that in our groups, but as with anything else we address, it's broken down into very, very small steps and we move at our Friends' pace.

See also Leaving the House, Physical Inactivity, *and* Sensory Sensitivities

ALONE TIME

After a busy day at school or work, many people seek out other people for relaxation and recreation. They like to hang out together to visit or play something, often sharing what went on that day, perhaps discussing whatever is bothering them to find a fresh perspective from someone else's viewpoint.

Not an Asperger's child or teen. What they want most is alone time.

At school, they are forced to socialize all day long in class. And recess is no respite. If anything, recess time is often more stressful than being in the classroom. It's noisy. It's chaotic. And everyone expects students to run around and play together, while what an Asperger's kid really wants is to be left alone.

Unfortunately, going off on their own looks like they're being antisocial and unfriendly. But seeking out alone time is self-protection, and must be allowed. It's an Aspie's way of regrouping and restoring himself before having to navigate another round of social dynamics. Plus, the ruckus of recess is sensory overload for these kids, and they just can't cope with the noise, confusion, and unruliness.

At home, the stimulation doesn't stop if there are siblings needing attention or appointments to go to or homework to be done. Once an Asperger's kid gets home from school, he would rather retreat to his bedroom and close the door to gain some peace and quiet than to talk about his day. Please let him go for a while. Give him that quiet time.

You should know that these kids are not being rude. They're not intentionally shutting you out. They just need time to decompress and restore their inner calm.

The best thing that you can do is to let them have their solitude, even if it's only for five or ten minutes. Being alone will help unfray their nerves and keep them from becoming too agitated. The less anxious they are, the better they will be able to do their homework or to join the family for an outing.

And at school, when they wander off to a quiet corner of the playground or classroom, Asperger's kids need to be allowed to remove themselves from overstimulation to find peace in being alone. Again, they're not trying to be rude. They're just trying to get through another demanding day of sensory overload.

However, at home and at school, it's important to balance how long they're on their own and how much time they spend with people. It's especially crucial that Asperger's kids are not alone too much at school or they will become more likely targets for bullies.

The other risk is that the longer they're alone, the more comfortable these kids become *not* socializing and the less they practice their social skills (and they *do* need practice!). It's important that they stay engaged and interacting with other people for at least part of the day, and that they are not allowed to withdraw more and more.

Time limits for video games up to an hour are recommended. Setting a timer so it dings or buzzes helps make the end of their playtime more tangible. Then it's time for some other activity. This will help them learn to achieve more balance, by stopping one thing and moving on to another.

Our Aspie Friends need to be wooed into our world and lured out of theirs on a regular basis if they are to become more comfortable in social settings and make friends.

See also Acceptance, Anxiety, Asking for Help,
Calming Down and Focusing, Compromise,
Letting Go and Refocusing, Losing Gracefully,
Meltdowns, Perspectives and Point of View,
Sportsmanship, Staying Calm, Waiting, *and*
Writing Things Down

ANGER AND FRUSTRATION

With their lack of flexibility and their need for control and structure, Asperger's kids and teens endure endless frustration.

Life and social interactions are loose and unpredictable.

Surprises and the unexpected happen all the time.

People often break rules, or at least bend them.

When playing a game, for example, the humor and fun arise from all of the surprises. Only by loosening up can everyone have a good time. Yet whenever an activity or situation seems out of control, Aspie children and teens can become highly anxious, frustrated, and even angry.

With our Friends, we've found how important it is to discuss this "feeling out of control" and for our kids to practice ways to calm themselves. Since Aspie kids are verbal and very vocal, it's important for them to learn how to express their feelings, something that is *not* easy for them to do. Otherwise, their suppressed emotions may erupt into sudden outbursts of anger, blindsiding them and others.

We've found that by playing games like SPLAT!, feelings of frustration quickly surface and need to be discussed. This game has Play-Doh "bugs" as game pieces, which make their way around the board. The unexpected is when your bug is tagged and goes "splat," forcing you out of the game.

Even older children are lured into expressing their emotions by playing SPLAT! because everything happens so fast and can seem so unfair. That's what's so great—our goal is *not* to have a smoothly running game, but a frustrating one! Our Friends learn more when someone accidentally knocks over their piece or doesn't do something exactly as he's supposed to, which creates objections and strife.

Finding ways for these kids to express their feelings of frustration helps them get over the anger or anxiety of a conflict.

During one session, a newer member was having fun playing SPLAT! Yet he felt frustrated as well that players were going around the rules. We were able to point out that while it was important for him to express his annoyance, it was just as important for him to learn that it was okay if the rules were being bent, given that he and the others were indeed having fun. **The key is to have frustration spoken out loud**, not bottled up where it can accumulate and become true anger.

Asperger's kids' rigidity makes it hard for them to relax and enjoy the game. Yet if they're ruled by the rules, it also prevents them from having fun and being fun, which puts off potential friends.

The bottom line is that learning how to be flexible is paramount to their success with other people and in life. And being flexible will keep their frustrations to a minimum and their anger under control.

One thing we've noticed with children on the spectrum is that they can become "stuck" in an emotion. While we always want to acknowledge what they're feeling, we also want to limit its duration.

Clinical psychologists have found that we must help these children connect their emotional state to their intellect before they can understand what they're feeling. By reaching an intellectual connection, the children are able to learn to "feel" and to express themselves more.

One way of helping an Asperger's child get unstuck emotionally is to use **visual cues**, like an hourglass or any visual timer, to show exactly how long they are allowed to feel that way and that they then must move on.

Or try associating the feeling to an object, like a file on a computer. I've done this successfully with many of our Friends. I'll say, "Okay, now it's time to close that file and take it off your desktop." The child envisions what that means in computer terms and accepts its removal.

We've also found that if we simply say, "Okay, put that feeling in a drawer," that works, too. By making the feeling seem concrete, the Aspie child sees it as something that can be tucked away.

When frustrations go unexpressed, they tend to build and suddenly turn to anger, even to the surprise of the Asperger's child. Several techniques help defuse such anger and manage it.

First and probably most effective is for the child to **simply walk away** from whomever or whatever is making him so frustrated. This will give the Aspie's emotional brain, the amygdala, a chance to cool down and give the rational brain, the neocortex, a chance to kick in and help make sense of the situation. Removing oneself from the frustration is good. Talking about it with an understanding adult is even better.

The old standby technique of **counting to ten** also works for much the same reason—anger erupts first from the emotional brain, so counting to ten gives the rational brain the chance to catch up to what's going on. Then it can send calming thoughts, which will counter the feelings of anger in the upset child.

Our leaders often write a countdown on the white board: 5-4-3-2-1, and wipe away one numeral at a time. First the 5, then the 4, and so on. This shifts the focus to time and the kids see it going away. Writing things down like this works very well with our born-to-be-visual Friends.

If you do **measured breathing** with your child, slowly and steadily, deep inhales and exhales a few times, this models how to overcome anger. You are showing her instead of just telling her to do it.

And of course, the simple act of **redirecting** your child's attention away from what's bothering him and toward something else is quite effective and easy to do. This does not mean offering something new or using bribery. It's just pointing out something he may not have noticed, or pointing to something he may have an interest in, which will take his mind (and emotions) off the source of his frustration or anger.

If you know an upcoming situation or activity may trigger frustration or anger in your child, it is also effective to draw a sequence of pictures to show and prepare her for what to expect. Or to even simply write down a list of the things that may be there.

For example, one of our social coaches knew that a boy she was working with was very anxious about going to an after-school recreation center. So she wrote him a note:

> *Foosball might be available.*
> *Basketball might be available.*
> *Board games might be available.*

She folded the note and handed it to the boy, who put it in his pocket. Later, he used it like a touchstone, pulling it out and looking at it from time to time. Knowing the possibilities meant minimizing the surprises. This was very reassuring to the boy and reduced his stress considerably.

See also Bluntness and Unintentional Insults, Letting Go and Refocusing, Obsessions and Obsessive Behavior, *and* Self-regulation or "Stimming"

ANNOYING BEHAVIOR

To be human means to be annoying to someone at some point in our lives.

We're all annoying when we talk too loudly, fidget when we're bored, grab things that don't belong to us, or say things that aren't necessarily true. While most of us can cut others some slack and ignore such behavior, an Asperger's child notices and often can't stop noticing.

His focus becomes glued to the one thing the other person does that annoys him. He begins to resent that person and become overly upset, even though the other person is just being himself.

One of the first things we do at Friends' Club is to teach our kids how to let people know that their behavior is annoying without offending them or making them mad. Tact is not easy for an Asperger's child because bluntness comes much too easily.

So we model the right way to approach the annoying person. We practice the right words to say to ask them to stop or to tone down what they're doing. For example, "Please stop kicking my seat," is better than "Why are you whacking my chair? Stop it!"

What's particularly surprising to our Aspie kids is to find out that they, too, are annoying to others. Given their one-way mentality, they don't realize that things that they say and do can be just as annoying to their classmates or family members as what the other person is doing that annoys them.

By making our Friends aware of this possibility, it helps them to realize that they, too, need to alter their behavior to get along, just as they expect the other person to do. While some involuntary behavior, like arm flapping or pacing, might not be controllable, our Friends can become self-aware enough to not ask the same question over and over or to stop talking about the same topic when others seem disinterested. Self-awareness can curb their annoying behavior.

But how do you help curb an Asperger's child's annoyance with another person? We've found one way is to try to find some common ground between your child and the other person. If the Aspie realizes that the other child has similar interests or experience, then she will see him in a more kindly way and be able to refocus.

For instance, one of our fourth-grade Friends was upset with another student in his class because the boy was exaggerating and twisting a fact to get a laugh. Being a purveyor of truth, our Asperger's Friend was irate that this boy would lie to the other kids. He worried that the others would believe his false fact.

This annoyance kept getting stronger and stronger. What worked to stop this irritation was when our Friend's mother found out that the other boy liked James Bond movies, just like our Friend did. Once our Friend learned that they had something in common, it made the exaggerator more acceptable. A bridge was formed to allow them to talk and get along, even if on a superficial level.

See also Admitting When You're Scared,
Calming Down and Focusing, Change and
"Change-ups," Fear, Further Information About
Bullying, Meltdowns, *and* Sensory Sensitivities

ANXIETY

Life throws us all a lot of curveballs and unexpected situations, but for Asperger's kids, most of the real world is a total surprise to them and easily stirs up anxiety.

That is why our Friends prefer familiar places and familiar faces. This keeps them from feeling so off balance, so unsettled and anxious all the time.

Take a party, for instance. We neurotypicals may cover up our discomfort in a new social situation with a twitter of nervous laughter or an overly loud greeting, or perhaps we'll hover around the food too much.

Asperger's kids have more unconventional reactions to such social stress and anxiety. Some will retreat to a corner of the room. Some hide outside. Some start talking in baby talk or flapping their arms.

Even something as routine as school can throw our Friends off if, for instance, their teacher is absent and there's a substitute. Or they may get anxious if there is a sudden change in projects or assignments.

How can we help these kids adjust to stressful situations without their resorting to baby talk or hiding or flapping their arms?

At the Friends' Club, we work on several stress-reducing techniques almost weekly, with noticeable results. The first and easiest is deep breathing. We've found that if we can teach our Friends to stop for just a moment and breathe deeply several times in a row, this deliberate action helps calm them down. If they can count to five as they inhale and five as they exhale each breath, all the better. That can distract them from the trigger event, and shift their attention to something calmer.

We've also encouraged them to advocate for themselves. When our Friends are feeling overly anxious in the classroom, we've told them to go up to the teacher and ask for permission to have some quiet time, either in the classroom, in another room, or in the library, until their distress passes.

At home, during a social event, it helps tremendously if you allow your child to leave whenever the noise, crowd, or confusion become too much for him. Retreating to his room, or going outside if that's quieter, is not being rude. For our Friends, it's a matter of stress relief and survival in the real world.

Of course, if your child's anxiety is severe and nothing seems to reduce it, you should consult a doctor. Stronger measures may be necessary, such as cognitive behavior therapy or medication.

See also Bluntness and Unintentional Insults, Perfectionism and Unrealistic Expectations, Rudeness, *and* Writing Things Down

APOLOGIZING

The matter-of-fact mind of the Asperger's child and adult—and the certainty that they're right—makes it hard for them to accept that they've done or said something wrong.

Making a mistake makes them see themselves as less than perfect. And perfectionism is one of the things that many Asperger's children strive for, in their own way. Saying "sorry" for the mistake is inconceivable, especially if the mistake was unintentional (which most of our Friends' social faux pas are!).

With their strong sense of right and wrong, our Friends can be quick to point out that someone is wrong or "stupid" or "an idiot." But it's difficult to make Aspies understand why they need to apologize for calling someone a name or for being outright rude, because they didn't mean to be rude. They were just speaking the truth as they saw it, and the other person should want to hear the truth . . . even if it hurts their feelings. So since any hurt feelings were unintended, our Friends don't believe that they have to apologize for unintentional behavior.

Again, when it comes to Asperger's behavior, typical compassion and social norms do not come naturally. While our Friends want others as well as themselves to follow the rules of politeness at all times—and Aspies even answer correctly on language tests about saying "sorry" for a mistake—from their point of view, one should only have to apologize if there was an intentional hurt. And even then, they usually think "sorry" is only necessary for a physical hurt.

So, if one of our Friends bumps into someone accidentally, she sees no reason to say sorry. It was an accident. It wasn't meant to happen. Why should she say "sorry"? She does not realize that it's rude not to apologize. She doesn't see the disrespect or disregard for the other person's well-being. She doesn't see that it looks like she doesn't care and, maybe, that it appears as if she did it on purpose.

Again, Aspie children are not mean-spirited or trying to be rude. Their complete lack of social sensitivity makes them unaware that they've hurt someone, especially when it comes to feelings. Lacking natural empathy, the Asperger's child doesn't realize how unkind his words sound. Plus, he doesn't hear his own tone of voice or read the other person's reaction.

Small slights and offenses can become major offenses if the Aspie doesn't apologize, or the other person is not aware of this inability to recognize the feelings of others and the seeming insensitivity of our Friends.

Good news—there is hope. Our Friends can be taught to say "I'm sorry." Ideally, we can catch the rudeness right at the moment it happens. We'll say, "Oh, that was one of those times when you need to apologize" or "You need to apologize for that because . . ." It's important to state the logic behind it, to give them a sound reason why an apology is needed.

They understand physical hurt more easily because that is more obvious. It's harder to make our Friends understand the concept of hurting someone's feelings because this is totally foreign to them. Emotional hurt is invisible, and besides, our Friends can't put themselves in the other person's shoes.

So in our Friends' Club sessions, we practice using different tones of voice so that they can learn to hear the difference between a rude voice and a friendly voice.

We also incorporate it into games and other activities, so if incidents of rudeness arise, then we are "in the moment" and can work with the child to help him understand what he said or did, why it was rude, and why he needs to apologize.

Classically Asperger's folks struggle with apologies more than high-functioning autism types. While the latter often don't talk as well, they have a better sense of when to say "sorry" and they can apologize more easily than the true Asperger's person.

It also helps to make Asperger's children aware that not everyone has read what they've read, not everyone knows what they know. Aspies must be told that people are smart in many ways and in many areas, and just because someone doesn't know what the Aspie knows, that doesn't mean that the person should be dismissed and called "stupid" or an "idiot."

Eventually, if all goes well, the Asperger's child realizes how unfair and rude he or she has been. Once that realization sinks in, he may cringe to think of it. It can take a while, but such a realization should happen, just not right away.

Then practicing an apology comes next, so that your child is more prepared to make amends the next time he sees the person he's insulted. If your child argues a lot about why he should not have to apologize, then it's best to just write down the apology and ask your child to read it aloud to the other person so that the apology is made.

See also Grooming and Personal Hygiene *and* Sensory Sensitivities

APPEARANCE

Not only do Asperger's kids tend to be gender blind, they are usually fashion blind as well. They rarely notice or care what they are wearing as long as it doesn't poke, itch, or irritate them in some way.

Many have acute sensitivities to tags in their clothes, tightness around their waistbands or cuffs, and rough seams that rub their skin. Consequently, comfort becomes the driving factor—not being fashionable or fitting in.

Many of our Friends have favorite outfits, which they prefer to wear all the time. While working at the Swiss patent office, Albert Einstein would wear green slippers with flowers on them. While teaching at Princeton University, he wore sweatshirts instead of suits and ties. His hair was long and wild, not at all in keeping with the clean-cut, 1950s crew cut, but he didn't care. Typical of people with Asperger's syndrome, Einstein couldn't care less about his appearance or being conventional. He only cared about being comfortable.

Clean clothes? Complementary colors? Current fashions?

Most of our Friends have no idea why any of those are important to the rest of us, or why they should have to think about such things to conform. Being presentable, and even being well-groomed, just doesn't register with them.

While it's not critical that wearing our Friends follow the latest trends in fashion, it does help them to be more accepted by their peers if they are wearing clothes that at least blend in.

But even more important than wearing current styles is having clean hair, no body odor, and no scruffy facial hair, yet it is often hard to make our Friends understand this. As usual, even though they want friends, they don't see why they have to work at it. We work on making them see why in the Friends' Club.

First, we address cleanliness. As one of our teen boys said, "I wish I was living in the cowboy time. Then I wouldn't have to bathe more than once a month." It seems that the force of the shower water, the scraping of razors (or buzzing of electric shavers), and the possibility of getting shampoo in their eyes make becoming clean not very appealing to our Friends, young and old. It's the process that they object to, with their sensory sensitivities, not the result.

Consequently, it's up to parents to encourage them to bathe and groom. And it's up to parents to keep an eye out for spots and stains on their clothes. You'll need to train your child to examine shirts, pants, or skirts before putting them on.

Next, as you've undoubtedly noticed, some odd combinations of colors and clothing come up if Aspies are left to dress themselves. With comfort being the prime concern, coordination isn't even considered. Again, with some coaching, they can be made aware of clashing colors and fashion faux pas (stripes with checks or long pants that are too short). They can learn how to dress more appropriately, but it takes guidance from parents as well as checking their clothing and overall appearance before they head out into public.

A simple remedy is to buy shirts, shorts, pants, and socks in complementary colors so that any combination of colors and styles is interchangeable.

Now if our Friends are clinging to certain clothes because of sensory issues, but those clothes will set them up to be teased or are inappropriate, then we've discovered that a gradual, step-by-step approach can work for introducing new clothes while slowly weaning them from their favorites.

For example, one of our fourteen-year-old boys preferred the soft feel of leggings to regular pants. But leggings were totally inappropriate and out of step with his peers, setting him up for ridicule. Along with a social coach, I talked with the boy's mother and came up with a solution.

By finding jeans and popular, baggy parachute pants that would fit over the leggings, the boy could continue to wear leggings for the soft feeling he liked while getting used to the feel of other clothing. Eventually, he gave up the leggings under his pants. He did wear long underwear in the winter, but the parachute pants with their soft insides and nylon outer side worked during the other seasons.

Another boy needed to wear a collared shirt for an upcoming wedding that his family would be attending. Noticing that our Friend was most relaxed while playing video games, our social coach recommended having the young man wear a collared shirt while he played those games. Eventually, the calm that he felt while playing video games encompassed wearing the collared shirt, which helped the sensory issue to disappear.

Sometimes, it is very useful to ask for help from a behavioral therapist or social coach when tricky issues come up and creative solutions are needed. With this nonconformist Asperger's group, an unconventional and inspired approach is usually required.

See also Perfectionism and Unrealistic Expectations, Time Blindness, *and* Writing Things Down

ASKING FOR HELP

Often children with Asperger's do not know where they are supposed to go, do not know where they actually are, and do not know that they might even be lost! A sense of time, direction, and place is not their forte. Like those with attention-deficit/hyperactivity disorder (ADHD) and Tourette's syndrome, Asperger's kids have frontal lobe deficits, which sabotage their sense of time and place, and make them unable to get organized on their own.

Unfortunately, they very rarely know to ask for help. It's not a pride issue. It might be a bit of a perfectionism issue, because to ask for help seems like you're not perfect. But most of the time, it truly and simply just doesn't occur to them.

With little sense of direction, time, or place, Asperger's kids can be chronically late to school to the point of being suspended for failing to get to class on time. What is fundamentally missing is their sense of knowing that they need help in order to ask for it.

Some Asperger's children, especially teens, think that they can figure it out themselves rather than have to ask for help. This kind of approach can appear to be stubbornness, but it's really just overconfidence and believing that they are always right, and therefore couldn't possibly be wrong.

For example, one of our Friends was almost suspended from school once. Why? Because instead of going inside the classroom before the bell rang for first period, he waited *outside* the class until he saw the teacher start talking. It never occurred to him that he was supposed to be in his seat when class started and that he would be marked late if he wasn't. Unfortunately, it didn't occur to the teacher to ask him why he was so consistently late either. "Why?" is a very important question to ask Aspie kids because their reasoning is so different from what we expect.

Richard Lavoie, a recognized learning disabilities expert, was a consultant for a high school student also on the verge of suspension for chronic tardiness to all of his classes. When Lavoie talked with the boy, he discovered that the student's homeroom was on the first floor of a four-story building. While his other classes were scattered on the fourth, third, and second floors, this boy would go back to the homeroom each time before his next class, because that was his only point of reference for navigating the campus.

The boy had no idea why he was always late and he couldn't understand how everyone else was on time. Yet it never occurred to him to ask someone for help to find a better way of getting to class. While school officials had declared him to be an unmotivated student due to his chronic lateness, Lavoie was able to clear up the mystery and help the boy find more efficient routes to all of his classes.

We encourage our Friends' Club parents not to wait for their child to ask them for help. If he's going somewhere, ask him if he knows where he's supposed to go and, if on foot, what direction he will go to get there. Better still, go with him! Even teens need help the first time, but subtlety is advised since other teens may be watching.

At least the first time or two, it's best to go with your child to make sure he's on the right path, heading the right way, and knows which landmarks to look for to figure out where he is.

You'll also want to make sure that he knows how to cross streets safely, by looking drivers in the eyes before he steps off the curb. With cell phones and other distractions these days for drivers, our Friends are even more at risk because they'll follow the signal light when it turns green or says "walk" and may not watch the cars and drivers to make sure that they stop when they're supposed to.

Never drop your Asperger's child off to find her own way somewhere, because she may get lost. Be sure to accompany her to where the group is meeting, and make it clear where she should wait for you to pick her up after the event or activity is over.

We recommend to parents that you carry a small whiteboard or tablet with you. That way you can write down what is expected of your child, which can alleviate a lot of anxiety. One of our five-year-old Friends was having a difficult time accepting that it was time to leave my office after our session, but he didn't know how to ask for help in making the transition.

Seeing that he was stuck and knowing he was an advanced reader, I pulled out a whiteboard and wrote, "It's time to go. The best thing to do is to say 'Good-bye, Cynthia.'" He got up, said, "Good-bye," and left with his parents, without a single complaint!

Writing down what the child needs to do or directions for where she needs to go makes it more concrete. The message is in black and white, which is easier for her to absorb.

As for school, we encourage parents to take our younger Friends to the campus *before* the first day of school to orient them when there is less noise and confusion. If classes have been assigned, then you can go find your child's new classroom. It also helps to practice navigating the school yard from that starting point.

If your child is starting middle school or high school, ask the counseling office to give you your child's schedule the week before school starts, if possible. That way, you can accompany your child around campus to orient her.

If she is switching periods, be sure to go to each class and then find the most direct route to the next classroom so that your child develops a sense of where to go. By doing it a few days ahead of the first day, she'll have a chance to sleep on it and get used to the idea of the changes.

If you have pictures that you can show your child of a new place or new activity, that is helpful, too. For a new field trip, for example, pictures provide a visual social story of where the group will be going and what your child can expect to see there.

An online resource that some of our Friends' parents have found useful is Autism Shopper (at www.autismshopper.com) for a wide variety of aids that will help your children.

See also Conversation, Depression, Eye Contact, Perfectionism and Unrealistic Expectations, Remembering Names, Sensory Sensitivities, *and* Thinking in Pictures and Patterns

AWARENESS

To varying degrees, most of us are aware of our surroundings. Of what day and time it is. Of where we're going and when we'll get there. Of who is with us and how they feel and how we feel about them.

We're aware of what's appropriate to say or do in front of others and what isn't. Aware of what others are thinking without them telling us and of how we are perceived by them. Simply put, we take our awareness for granted.

And the more conscious we are of our strengths, the more we can make the most of them, along with the knowledge of our weaker points that we can work on to improve. Any kind of personal growth and change is dependent on the first basic step of self-awareness. How can we become better at something if we don't know what needs improving?

Asperger's folks lack awareness on many fronts, especially in the people department. They don't read people's faces (they don't even look people in the eyes). They don't catch the underlying meaning of what people are saying, the "hidden" messages. And they miss so much of the body language, which tips off the rest of us as to how people really feel about things.

The one awareness our Friends seem to register is that they are different from other kids. Usually it's when they are around six years old and at school all day, but sometimes it is when they are "tweens" in fifth or sixth grade, and for a few, it can even be as late as high school.

Maybe they notice that other kids in their classes can write a whole page while they're still on their second sentence. Or when the teacher says, "Draw any picture you want," and our Friends just sit there with no idea what to draw or how to start while all the other kids are diving right in and making pictures easily. If the teacher had said, "Draw a person" or "Draw an animal," our kids would have had a starting point. But if it's as abstract as "draw anything," they are lost.

Being slower with pencil or pen, or simply not knowing what to do, or not having the answer because the assignment is too vague and they're unable to predict what's expected—all of these make them very aware of their differences from the other kids.

And while most of the time Asperger's kids are smart and know it, and are happy playing by themselves and don't really seem to care if they're like anyone else, there are times when their natural perfectionism and their deep-seated need to not be wrong fuels their frustration at being different.

Often their perfectionism is what goads them into caring once they realize that they are different. In the tween years, or preadolescence, when some start to not want to appear as different from others as they often are, it can actually help boost their awareness.

For example, I was in a meeting for one of our fourteen-year-old Friends at his high school when the boy started looking out the window. He kept fidgeting and seemed eager for the meeting to end.

Later, outside, his father told me that it wasn't the meeting that made his son antsy. It was the desire that no one see him in that special meeting because he didn't want his friends to think that he was different.

This is actually a great thing, a true milestone, to have one of our Friends become aware of himself in relation to his peers. This opens up the boy to learn how to make some changes, which will make him better able to interact with his peers. This awareness motivates our kids to learn from group activities at the Friends' Club, to truly make progress in becoming more socially skilled, and motivates them to make connections with others.

Since awareness comes at different stages and ages, we make sure all of our groups participate in consciousness-building activities. Our aim is to open our kids' eyes, minds, and hearts to recognize the world beyond their tightly focused point of view.

There are three steps that you can take to help your Asperger's child achieve heightened awareness:

STEP ONE

Help them become more aware of who they are with and where they are. This is called "the setting" or social referencing.

Our Asperger's Friends are so bright, yet also so unaware of those around them. For example, two of our younger boys got together outside of the Friends' Club. While playing in the living room, one boy suddenly got up and left the room without an "excuse me" or "good-bye" or "I'm going to play upstairs." He just left.

The remaining boy, true to Aspie form, kept playing with his toys, totally unaware that the other boy had left. Only when an adult pointed out that the first boy had left the room and said, "Maybe you should find him," did the boy notice and say, "Oh, yeah." Only then did he go look for the missing boy.

Neurotypical kids are aware of another child's presence by an early age, at less than a year old. Asperger's kids are so immersed in their world and their point of view, they do not notice who or what is around them even at much older ages.

If they leave a room or gathering, they honestly don't even think of saying "good-bye." They just leave. It simply does not occur to them to say something and they have no idea how rude such behavior seems to others.

At every group session, we practice "hello" and "good-bye." As simple as that seems, it's a huge step if our Friends can become more automatic in these basic greetings and then seem less rude or uncaring.

With our younger kids, we play Name-Name-Goose (our version of Duck-Duck-Goose), where the group sits in a circle. One child taps each person's head as he walks around and says their name until he says "Goose." Learning others' names is a challenge for Asperger's children, but it's an important first step in becoming aware of others.

We also write the group members' names on the whiteboard, so everyone can see them. And we teach our Friends that if they have trouble figuring out a member's name they should ask for help or look for a clue.

And if one of our kids is just talking blankly to the group and not addressing anyone in particular, not using a name, we often say, "We're not sure who you're talking to right now." This makes them look at the person or use the person's name.

I believe that being aware of the setting—who you are with and what's going on around you—is key to developing general social awareness. And setting awareness must be in place before the next step is possible.

STEP TWO

Help your Asperger's child become aware of "the audience," as I call it, or as speech language pathologist Michelle Garcia Winner says, "social thinking."

When typical kids see someone, they will think about that person—what she may be thinking, what previous experiences they've had with her, what her belief system is (religious, political, or any of the -isms, like vegetarianism, feminism, etc.), so as not to say something that will offend the person.

We think about that other person who will become our audience as we interact. We talk differently to different people. We think, or try to, before we speak to avoid saying something unpleasant by accident and hurting someone's feelings.

However, Asperger's kids don't think of their audience. They are *not* aware and tend not to think about what they're going to say to a particular person or group of people. They tend to blurt things out.

Case in point: I was observing one of our teen Friends at his charter high school where group presentations are the norm. As others in his group were speaking, he was quiet. Then, when it was his turn to talk, he said, "I was so surprised to hear my voice on the video. It was so deep. When did my voice get so deep?"

While this kind of self-reflection is typical of a teen, what is not typical is to tell an entire class! It's a frequent occurrence for Aspies to say things publicly that should be said privately.

So much of social thinking also involves ambiguous language with implied meanings. If a teacher says, "Everyone should be on page three," that really means, "Go to page three," but Aspies don't get that. This is why we teach them that if someone says, "I've seen *Star Wars* five times," that really means that this person loves *Star Wars*. We don't have to ask because we can *assume* that they like a movie if they've seen it that many times.

As for activities, we love the ones that delve into likes and dislikes. Games like Apples to Apples and Whoonu are natural and fun ways to teach thinking about others and what they like. Both games have cards about a wide variety of objects and activities. The goal is to guess what someone else who is the "judge" or "whoonu" would like. Whoonu players receive points and Apples players collect cards when their guess is the one chosen. We play that the winner becomes the next judge. If he has already been a judge, then he can choose the next one so everyone has a turn.

Once an awareness of setting and audience are heightened, then it's more likely for the next step to take hold.

STEP THREE

Help them develop an awareness of themselves. By nature, Asperger's kids are unaware of the thoughts and feelings of others, and also their own feelings. That does not mean that they can't become more perceptive, but it takes exposure, experience, and practice in talking with others. As in most things, gains are made in very small increments, but improvement can be seen.

Rather than specific lessons for self-awareness, it's more that all the lessons we teach at the Friends' Club, how we teach them and how comfortable the kids feel about learning, help them to progress and gradually become more self-aware.

One of our group leaders and social coaches has Asperger's. He started out as a young client of mine and is now a young man. I have watched him grow in his own awareness of himself, especially since he started making occasional presentations to parents to describe what growing up with Asperger's was like and how he handles things now. It seems that in the telling and thinking about it, his self-awareness has increased.

So our Friends' consciousness of others and themselves can improve, but like other skills that they learn, it will be bit by bit, ever so gradual. The reward is that they can be better at socializing and making friends and not feel so different and so disconnected.

One of our teen boys told me recently, "Cynthia, Asperger's is like having a big brain with no internal map." These kids are smart, but their lack of perception makes them feel lost. They often have no idea where they are supposed to be and what they're supposed to do next. Awareness is the map they need to get along in life and with people.

In addition to the social realm, Asperger's folks can be surprisingly unaware of their physical condition.

As supersensitive as so many of our Asperger's kids are to all kinds of sensory stimuli—noise, light, touch, smell, taste—and as bombarded as they often feel by the world around them, our Friends can be very unaware of how their body feels and whether they're in pain.

When it comes to big injuries, high pain thresholds are common among Asperger's kids. I've seen a boy fall and have blood dripping down his leg, yet not feel it at all. One of our eight-year-old Friends split his chin open in a scooter accident, but never flinched while lying on a table in the emergency room for two hours or when the doctor put in nine stitches.

I know a young girl who threw herself onto the living room floor, chest first, to get the maximum impact possible in order to "feel" the sensation. She's also had great difficulty becoming toilet trained because she is not aware of the sensation of being wet.

There is danger in not recognizing one's body and its current condition. These kids can be hurt in a big way, bleeding and in need of stitches, and they may not be aware of it.

As a parent, this must seem ironic, given all the tiny irritants that your child has pointed out and been bothered by: shirt tags, scratchy pants, a sock seam, or a particular comb or brush.

As contradictory as it seems given their hypersensitivities, the lack of physical awareness is a real issue that benefits from *your* awareness. It's up to the adult caring for the child to recognize this tendency to not feel pain. What children need to be taught is how to register the sensory input.

According to occupational therapists with whom I've worked, such awareness requires intervention. Occupational therapists who are trained in sensory integration can help these children and teens learn to register sensations, but it is difficult and will not happen overnight.

While we do not do anything specific at the Friends' Club to increase our kids' physical awareness—because the range and degrees are too vast and require special training and techniques—we do refer our members to specialists who can help them the most. If it becomes a problem during group time, we turn it into a social-thinking lesson. For example, we say that friends won't like it if you keep bumping into them.

See also First Friendships, Meltdowns,
Sensory Sensitivies, Social Stories,
and Writing Things Down

BIRTHDAY PARTIES

Something I learned very early on in working with Asperger's children, even before founding the Friends' Club, is that these kids do not get invited to birthday parties. Unless the whole class is invited to a birthday party, our Friends are usually left out. And even if the entire class is invited, I've seen Aspie kids still be left out.

As young as three years old, children notice the Asperger's child's lack of social skills and just don't include them. Some of our Friends who are eleven years old have never been invited to a birthday party.

Ami Klin, Ph.D., an autism/Asperger's expert and head of Yale's Child Study Center, has quoted one of his patients as saying that he liked the first day of school the most "because no one knows yet." No one knows about the boy's Asperger's and he gets one day to be treated like everybody else.

It seems sad in its own way. Fortunately for our Friends, they are quite happy playing by themselves and enjoy being alone with their thoughts most of the time. Also, they don't like loud noises and chaos, which are part and parcel of children's birthday parties. So your child probably won't notice or care about not being invited, which is good news, really.

What we've found is that when one of our Friends is finally asked to a birthday party, it can be difficult because of so much sensory overload. With a group of squirrelly children running around, playing an assortment of games, yelling and calling to one another, demanding that presents be opened, and begging for cake to be served, it can be an overwhelming sensory experience for any Asperger's child.

That's why we recommend that one parent stay at any party attended by their Asperger's child, and maybe even when their child is a teenager. It depends on your child's challenges. There needs to be someone keeping an eye on your child's stress thermostat, seeing how well he's handling the confusion and cavorting that occurs at any birthday party. If his senses get overloaded, there could easily be a meltdown.

One of our Friends went to a birthday party for someone in his preschool class. Midway through, the parents slung a piñata over a tree branch. Kids lined up to take turns whacking at it, trying to break the piñata open so candy would pour out. That's when a huge problem arose for the boy.

While he'd been just fine and happy throughout the whole party, he suddenly ran over to his mother, crying and yelling that he wanted to go home immediately. His mother was completely baffled by this sudden hysteria.

Being a preschooler, the boy couldn't explain what was so upsetting, but his mother finally figured out that it was the piñata spinning around, as people hit it, that bothered him so much.

Wisely, she had him face another way and they took a short walk, until that portion of the party was over. This is the kind of thing that can suddenly crop up when our Friends are in new social situations, experiencing new things. As we say at the Friends' Club, "Expect the unexpected." It's also the reason that parents need to stay nearby, and can't just drop off their Asperger's children expecting everything to be fine. You'll need to be around to monitor their stress level.

What helps the most for our Friends is to prepare them for what might happen at the birthday party. Give them more details than just saying it's a birthday party, which is vague and means nothing to them if they've never been to one before. If they know better what to expect and what may happen, they will feel less unsettled.

For example, if the party has a carnival theme, then you should explain what a carnival is and the possible games and activities that might go with it. Better still, when you RSVP, ask the host parents what they have planned, and then share those details with your child. If there will be a clown, prepare your child. Even neurotypical kids are scared of clowns, but they especially bother Asperger's kids.

Still better, and if possible, find some pictures in magazines or books or catalogs that would give your child a concrete image of what she might see or do at the party. I know it sounds like a lot of work, but I've found that once our Friends have a first success at a birthday party, then they are more willing and able to enjoy other parties.

Something else that has helped is when I've written down a Social Story to be read before the party by children and sometimes by recently diagnosed teens who need this kind of help. By tucking it into their pocket to take with them, they can pull it out and read it if they start to feel stressed. The story might say something like this:

> When there are a lot of kids, it is noisy and busy. That's okay. I will try to be with the other kids at the party. I will try to listen to the adult's directions so that I can play fairly and everyone can have fun. If I get tired or the party is too busy, I will ask for a break in a quiet spot. That's okay, because I can go back to the party when I am ready. When we are done, then we will go to our home.

Also, finding any children's books or stories about birthday parties is very helpful. Again, this is a black-and-white, tangible medium to help our Asperger's Friends understand what birthday parties will be like, and that they will need to be flexible in the new, unfamiliar environment of a party at someone else's home. The more ways you can coach your child to cope, the better.

What you also should be aware of is that there are small things at birthday parties that can trigger sudden fear in our Friends. Some are afraid of candles because, to them, all fire seems dangerous.

Others may be afraid of balloons because they are like ticking time bombs, prone to pop at any second and make a loud noise, which will hurt their ears and scare them.

Some may feel at a loss when it's time to sing the "Happy Birthday" song. They usually can't remember the words, since they only hear the song every now and then. They probably won't know or remember the birthday child's name either.

To help them with the song, encourage them to do the "cha-cha-cha" part between the "happy birthday to you" lines. This is good for humor and it's a phrase they can manage.

To help with the fear of balloons popping, show them a pattern, since they understand and see life in patterns. Show them that a balloon filled up and tied off is not going to keep growing because no more air is going into it. It's only if it gets really, really big and fills with more air that it will pop.

Of course, if something sharp hits it, the balloon will pop unexpectedly, but that is out of your control. You can warn your child that while popping may happen, most people want to see the pretty balloons during the whole party, so few want to pop them.

Now there is difficulty in the reverse situation—if you throw a birthday party for your child, who will come?

Socially successful kids are the ones everyone wants to have over to their parties. But will they come to your child's party, if your child wants to ask them?

First, ask your child whom he wants to invite and why. Usually there are quieter or "fringe" kids who will be glad to come to the party and will appreciate the invitation the most. If your child insists on inviting the most popular kids, call ahead and ask their parents about their availability. This gives them an opportunity to say no without rejecting your written invitation or their child saying no to your child directly.

Believe it or not, as long as you make the event so cool it's irresistible, most kids will say yes and will want to come. So think up something fun and original to pique their interest.

Whether it's a train ride to a nearby destination with something to explore at the other end, or Chuck E. Cheese's with its video games and stage show (warning—it is loud), rock climbing, or a new-release movie, there are plenty of possibilities, and the busier the kids the better.

The bonus to a movie: No talking is allowed, making it easier for your Asperger's child by minimizing the amount of socializing. One drawback is that, depending on their sensory challenges, some kids may find a movie too loud. That's why some of our parents bring headsets to muffle the volume for their child.

The key is to make your child's birthday party event too tempting for other kids to turn down. Also be careful how many you invite, so your child is not overwhelmed by her own party. Asking a half-dozen kids or so is plenty. After calling ahead to see who's available and interested, you can send written invitations as reminders.

For our teen Friends, one of our mothers came up with a perfect idea for her son's new group of friends from middle school. About eight of them had all discovered one another while lunching outside the media center, and they loved talking about computer and video games.

As this boy's thirteenth birthday was approaching in June, his mother asked him to get the boys' names and phone numbers so she could call their parents about setting up a date to celebrate his birthday. (True to form, it had taken her son until April to learn the boys' first names and he had no idea what their last names were.)

Since computers and video games were the main glue bonding this group together, the mom reserved an afternoon at the local computer game store called Cyberstore, which hosted birthday parties for all ages. She asked parents to drop off their kids, and then she supervised them for the two hours they were playing an assortment of games with and against one another.

Afterward, she and another parent ferried the group to a pizza place, where the conversation zinged because they had so much to talk about after playing those games. And for the rest of the summer, her son had a group of friends to call whenever he wanted to get together with someone, because they all felt closer after their shared experience.

See also Apologizing, Conversation, Empathy, Manners, Rudeness, *and* "White Lies" and Sparing Others' Feelings

BLUNTNESS AND UNINTENTIONAL INSULTS

Because Asperger's children and adults see the world in black and white, they do not "make nice" to soften anything and can be very blunt when they speak. They are far more concerned about telling the truth than sparing anyone's feelings. Why? Because feelings really don't register with them, only ideas and facts.

Precision is more important than diplomacy. Often, they have no idea how harsh or even hurtful their words sound to others. It's just the truth—their truth—and they see nothing wrong with that.

The irony is that Aspies themselves are often the targets of other kids' cruel remarks and jokes made at their expense. But the difference is that the bully intends to hurt the unaware Asperger's child while the Aspie has no intention of hurting anyone. It is just through the Aspies' own fierce adherence to the truth that they end up sounding just as mean as the bully.

What can be done about this?

As always, self-awareness is the starting point.

At the Friends' Club, we work on teaching our boys and girls to stop before they blurt out exactly what they're thinking. We coach them to take a few seconds to choose their words more carefully, and not say whatever immediately comes to mind. That little pause can help them find better words that won't offend or insult the other person.

As neurotypicals, we have an overseer in our mind to edit what we really want to say so that we can be more diplomatic. It's based in the frontal lobe, where a "stop and think" mechanism develops when we're eight years old or so.

Asperger's kids and adults have no such gatekeeper because their frontal lobe doesn't develop the same way. So they need to practice what they should say, and monitor what they should not say.

They also need to be more aware of *how* they say things, since tone/speed/style is 38 percent of the whole message in everything we say, while body language is 55 percent, and the actual words themselves are only 7 percent of the message.

Of course, Asperger's folks aren't the only ones to say the wrong thing or to be too honest or too critical. We're all guilty of that from time to time, especially if we're tired, frustrated, or stressed. However, we also usually catch ourselves doing it and notice the other person's reaction. Once we realize that we've offended someone, we apologize for our hurtful remarks.

Those are two things that Asperger's folks struggle with. First, they don't notice the other person's reactions because they have trouble reading other people's emotions.

And second, they see no need to apologize if it was an unintentional hurt (which most of them are). Aspies only think that they should apologize if they have done something on purpose, and even then that's hard for them to do because they would be admitting that they made a mistake.

One of our longtime Friends once confessed to his mother when he was fifteen, "I have a knack for saying the absolute worst thing at the worst possible time."

Since so many of our Friends have this same knack, we work with all of our kids to try to instill a type of gatekeeper. Through conversations during game playing and other activities, we catch our kids at the moment that they blurt out a too-truthful statement that hurts another child's feelings, and address it right away. We ask them to think about how else they could say something so that it is not hurtful, and we ask them to apologize.

Another strategy that we've used at Friends' Club with kids about ten years old and up is to compare their unintentional insult to a pebble thrown into a pond. With a whiteboard and a felt pen, I'll draw the "ripple" effect triggered by what they said or did. This visual helps them see all the layers of hurt caused by their words or actions, making it more tangible and understandable.

If you are present when your child is overly blunt and saying something offensive, please stop him at that moment. In a calm and unemotional voice, let him know that what he said was unacceptable and hurt someone's feelings.

Then ask him to apologize, even if he protests. You could say something like, "That was too harsh. Please apologize now and we will talk about it some more later."

And finally, still keeping any emotion out of the interaction, pull him aside right then or find a time later to explain in greater depth why saying "sorry" was necessary. Sometimes it takes a few tries—and time—before it sinks in, but keep trying.

See also Anxiety, Fear, Further Information
About Bullying, Listening to Others, Literal
Language, Meltdowns, Peer Pressure and
Avoiding Dares, Sarcasm, Talking with Peers,
and Teasing

BULLYING AND BULLIES

Anyone with Asperger's is a bully magnet. Their inability to read others' intentions and their lack of awareness make them very easy targets.

This problem is so prevalent among our Friends that it is one of the main trigger events for parents to seek out the Friends' Club. There is a more in-depth section addressing bullies and bullying in Part Three: Resources.

Here is an overview of our approach to teaching Asperger's kids and teens how to recognize bullying in all its forms, since they do not correctly perceive others' motivations, and how to stop it.

First, we discuss and identify the three types of bullying:

1. **Physical bullying:** This includes hitting, tripping, throwing things at you, taking things away from you, sexual harassment, etc.

2. **Verbal bullying:** This is teasing, taunting, name-calling, insulting, making fun of, writing nasty comments or spreading rumors, making threats, etc.

3. **Insincere, "taking advantage of you" bullying:** Usually the hardest for our Friends to detect because the bully is smiling and seems so friendly, which confuses Asperger's kids. When bullies smile and laugh as they're doing the mean thing, this tricks Aspies because they don't see the bully's hidden intentions.

Next, we discuss how to handle being bullied and that different situations need different strategies. The main points that you must teach your child boil down to this:

- It is *not* a good idea to fight back.

- It *is* a good idea to tell a trusted adult (parent, teacher, librarian, counselor) to alert him or her to what is going on at school or in the neighborhood.

- It is *not* good to ignore the verbal bully because it tends to escalate the bad behavior in search of a reaction.

- It *is* good to look the bully in the eye and say something brief, so it won't attract more teasing, and then walk away. Something like "This is boring" or "That's mean" or even "If you say so." And then walk away. That way, the bully has gotten a reaction and the target will be allowed to walk away more easily than if he or she says nothing.

For verbal bullying, it's the child's reactions to the bullying words that affect the situation, not the words themselves. Research shows that to say nothing causes repeated bullying attempts, so it's best to confront it quickly and unemotionally, then leave.

Finally, we role-play the various strategies to help our Friends feel more confident in how they would handle bullying situations. We especially delve into friendly and mean teasing, and how to tell the two apart, since that type of teasing tricks our Friends the most.

Because most bullies are savvy enough to make their move when no one else is watching, we encourage our Friends to get help from an adult. Be sure to ask any aides assigned to your child at school to stay with your child during recess and then take their break *after* recess is over.

We also go over how to say "no" to someone daring them to do something bad, because the other person is taking advantage of them and that's bullying. We teach our Friends that they must walk away and not fall for the dare just to please the other person or to feel accepted.

An important point for parents and teachers to know is that if a bullying incident is not resolved, Asperger's kids do not shake it off like other kids. They tend to relive the experience over and over. This makes it seem like many episodes rather than just one.

According to Tony Attwood, an internationally known autism and

Asperger's expert, it's best for Asperger's kids to talk about any bullying episode so that it can be examined and put into perspective for the child, to allow her to move on and not relive the incident.

The irony is that a bully is often a fringe person, someone who feels left out, just like an Asperger's child. Unfortunately, this type of bully is more aggressive than an Aspie and is in search of a victim to make himself feel superior to someone else. But not all bullies feel badly about themselves. Some have plenty of friends but may be emotionally troubled. They use intimidation and even violence to get attention, status, or whatever they're seeking.

As the parent of an Asperger's child, you need to know that your child will not make up bullying incidents in order to get your attention. If he is bothered by an episode at school or closer to home, do not dismiss it. It should be taken seriously and addressed, because our Friends do not go out of their way to report unkind things said or done to them. (There are times when they may perceive someone to be a bully or an enemy and it's really a case of needing to find a common ground, but those instances are rare.)

Whether bullying is coming from a sibling at home or a student at school, it is never a good idea to leave the Aspie child alone with the bully to "work it out." That only gives the bully another chance to mistreat the Asperger's child, who already feels like a victim.

It's very important for adults, whether parents or teachers or school administrators, to meet *separately* with the Asperger's child and listen to what he says happened. If the bully is present, our Friends usually become flustered and are unable to explain exactly what went on. This allows the more people-savvy, manipulative bully to further incriminate the Asperger's child and make it seem like the Aspie's fault.

Also, do not believe school administrators who say that they do not have bullies and that they are able to maintain and enforce a zero-tolerance zone, because it just isn't possible. The digs, slights, taunts, physical pokes, trip-ups, and stolen lunch money are widespread and usually undetected. A no-tolerance zone is simply not enforceable or possible.

So if your child reports a case of bullying once, believe it. Otherwise, if it's dismissed, he may come back with the same complaint, not because the bullying was repeated, but because the child's mind keeps repeating the incident until it's put into perspective for him. So the sooner it's talked over and dealt with, the better for your child.

Some great books about bullying to help your child understand what it is and what to do are:

Enemy Pie by Derek Munson, illustrated by Tara Calahan King
King of the Playground by Phyllis Reynolds Naylor, illustrated by Nola Langner Malone
The Meanest Thing to Say (part of the Little Bill series) by Bill Cosby
The Recess Queen by Alexis O'Neill, illustrated by Laura Huliska-Beith
Stand Tall, Molly Lou Melon by Patty Lovell, illustrated by David Catrow

As Aristotle once wrote, "The antidote for fifty enemies is one friend." Research has shown that if just one person steps in and tells the bully to stop, then the majority of the time, the bullying will stop. Doing nothing to stop bullying signals that it's okay. Doing something to help the child being bullied breaks the spell and usually breaks up the incident.

That's why having just one friend can make such a difference for our Asperger's kids.

Many of our Friends love computers and the Internet, but this is a new frontier for bullying—cyberbullying. Technology offers new ways of spreading vicious rumors, posting humiliating photos, or sending threatening messages.

What's particularly insidious about cyberbullying is its cloak of anonymity, huge audience, and lack of censorship. In nanoseconds, kids can send text messages, e-mails, and instant messages, or post photos. It can be difficult to determine where it's coming from.

Many children have been bullied into giving up their passwords, which are then changed while the bullies lock them out of their own account. Then the bully is free to send messages posing as the victim.

You'll want to monitor your child's time on the computer anyway, given how truly naïve our Friends are and how vulnerable they are to anyone looking to take advantage of someone. Cybertrollers on the prowl can easily fool our Asperger's Friends.

Monitor your child's screen name(s) and Web sites for appropriateness, and you'll also want to have them show you Web sites like MySpace, Facebook, and YouTube, if they have been going there, so you can see what's being shown and said. Tell them never to share their passwords except with you.

There is monitoring and filtering software available. You can find free downloads at K9 Web Protection (www.K9webprotection.com) and Safe Families (www.safefamilies.org) The nonprofit organization Web site WiredSafety (at www.wiredsafety.org) offers further tips on Internet safety and how to deal with cyberbullies, as does Cyber-bullying (at www.cyberbullying.org) and Bullying.org (at www.bully ing.org).

If your child is being cyberbullied, save and print out the evidence and then decide where to get help, whether from a teacher, school administrator, or, if it's a serious threat, the police. States and school districts are beginning to take steps to halt such behavior on the grounds that it affects children's abilities to learn.

See also Alone Time, Anxiety, Letting Go and Refocusing, Meltdowns, Self-regulation or "Stimming," Sensory Sensitivities, *and* Staying Calm

CALMING DOWN AND FOCUSING

Often, it's hard for Asperger's kids to settle down. There can be too much sensory overload—too much sound, light, visual distraction, and too many people—and they get overly excited. With that overload comes anxiety as well. At the Friends' Club, we've developed several approaches for helping our kids calm down.

Some relax if they're holding on to something, which we call a "fidget." As long as the object doesn't distract them or others in the group, then this is fine with us.

What is ideal is for each child to find a method for bringing himself under control as quickly and consistently as possible.

Here are some calming techniques to try with your child:

- **"Breathe and Count"** is a standard method that involves counting each breath before we deeply inhale and slowly let it out. After five or six rounds, usually everyone is calmer.

- **Relaxing your muscles** helps calm the body and mind, so we use this, concentrating on loosening the shoulders and moving down to the feet or vice versa.

- **"The Humming Drill"** has been quite effective. This is when everyone in the group makes the noise "shhhhh—hmmmmm," doing five in a row. This is especially good to do with the younger kids.

- **"The Hum-Along"** also works when the song being hummed has the tempo of a heartbeat (sixty beats per minute). You can also use a metronome to keep time.

- **Silent Snitch or Silent Chicken** is a game that we made up that works well to calm the whole group. We pass around either a bean bag snitch from the Harry Potter movies or a rubber chicken and we don't allow voices. We pretend to put everyone's voice "in a box" (leader lifts the lid of a real box and closes it) so no one can speak, and the silence and simple activity soothe the group.

- **A timer set for five or ten minutes** gives our Friends a set amount of time to get themselves under control. When it dings, they need to be settled or ready to listen. It's amazing how well this works!

- **Basic yoga moves** have been surprisingly well received by our kids and help them feel calmer. Pictures of the positions are shown and the leader demonstrates each pose before the group tries it. Yoga seems to make these kids more aware of their bodies and improves their focus.

If someone in the group is becoming revved up because they are frustrated or annoyed with someone else, we talk to both individuals. By asking them both about things they like to do, we see if there are some common interests that they share in books, toys, video games, movies, or music. Once they discover that they have something in common, the irritation often goes away because a bridge has been built.

Sometimes, we intentionally speed things up to rev up the kids so that they learn how to slow down and calm themselves while we're with them. Self-regulation is often a challenge for this group, especially the younger ones, so the more practice they have, the better they get at it and the more they (and we) find out what works and what doesn't.

See also Compliance, Letting Go and
Refocusing, Meltdowns, Moving On to New
Things, Sensory Sensitivities, Staying Calm *and*
Writing Things Down

CHANGE AND "CHANGE-UPS"

As much as we try to plan ahead, life does not always cooperate and follow that plan. This can be *very* hard for anyone on the autism spectrum.

Asperger's folks find security and comfort in routine and schedules. They truly live in the moment, so they are upset by surprises and change. Our Friends do not cope well with the unexpected. And we neurotypicals don't realize how even the smallest changes will catch our Friends off guard and upset them.

At Friends' Club, we call such unpredictable events "change-ups." To help our kids be more flexible and able to accept changes, we've adopted the motto "Change-ups happen." We teach them that no one has control over everything. Everyone must cope with change in their lives.

Since change is a fundamental part of life, *all* of us must learn to live with it. An essential life skill is to be able to accept sudden and not-so-sudden changes with as much flexibility and as little disappointment or upset as possible.

For each session at the Friends' Club, we write a schedule to orient the kids and let them know what to expect during the hour. We also write the word "change-up" when there is going to be a change of plans, so they also get used to that concept. Then we proceed to model how to cope with change and let that be part of the lesson.

For instance, one night I was unable to lead a group because of a sudden family emergency, which required me to go to the hospital. My absence caught one of the boys in particular off guard. When it came to following the rules for a game that the group was playing, he said, "It isn't the rule when Cynthia is here."

When I was the leader, we had played the game a certain way. Now he was arguing to do it the same way. The substitute leader handled it by writing next to the activity on the schedule board: "Change-up: Rules might change when Cynthia is not here."

Seeing it on the board, in black and white, appeased the boy and he didn't argue any further. He went along with the new rules. What this made me and the other leaders realize is that we needed to incorporate more surprises and change-ups into our schedule, precisely so that our kids would keep learning and practicing how to adjust and cope with the unexpected.

Whether your child is at home or at school, it always helps to write down what it is you expect them to do. And when there is a change, then write down, "change-up," and what the new plan is going to be. Asperger's kids really respond to seeing whatever you're trying to tell them in written words. It makes it clearer for them. They see it as a rule, and then they will usually follow those instructions.

Another thing to remember is that any change of activity, planned or unplanned, requires patience on your part. These kids do not react quickly because it requires more motor planning than they can muster.

If you say, "Okay, stop playing, get your shoes on, grab your coat, and we're going out to dinner," that is *way* too much direction way too fast. They can't process that much information that quickly. You probably lost them at "stop playing," if they even heard that.

It's best to ask them to change, or transition, to another activity by breaking your request into one step at a time. And please *wait* after each step to allow them to absorb the message, realize what they need to do, and then get up to do it.

They're not trying to misbehave and they don't want to make you angry by not responding immediately. Their inability to process the information and act on it slows their reaction time and requires extra patience from you.

What works is if you ask for one thing at a time: "Please close that book" and then wait. They will usually comply. You may need to say it again, but wait until the book is closed before saying, "Now go to the bathroom to brush your teeth, please."

If you wish to get your child more used to changes in general, then plan different ways to do your typical routines, but make the changes in small steps. It's better if you give a warning that there will be a little difference in their routine, and write it down for them to read.

The unfortunate thing is that often, when our Friends argue against change, or refuse to comply, it's seen as a control issue or a matter of task avoidance. This isn't true. It's really back to their sensory sensitivity issues and their comfort with the predictable.

For example, when we changed the layout of furniture in the meeting room, one of our Friends could not adjust to the "new" room. This caught us off guard because, to us, it was the same room, just less cluttered. To him, however, it was too different and unacceptable.

So we set a stool just outside the doorway, and let the boy sit there while we started our session. After a few minutes, we had him move the stool inside the room but still outside our circle where the group was meeting. Soon, on his own, he got off the stool and joined us on the carpet. After that, all was normal again.

It was his anxiety over the "new" look to the room and his inability to accept it that needed addressing. His hesitancy wasn't from trying to avoid a task or from a control issue, as many people might think. It stemmed from his sensory issues, and needed to be addressed calmly, in small steps, at his own pace, to become workable for him.

See also Acceptance, Conversation, Cooperation, Initiative, Letting Go and Refocusing, Listening to Others, Moving On to New Things, Teamwork, Waiting, *and* Writing Things Down

COMPLIANCE

So many parents and teachers ask me, *"Why* is it so hard for Asperger's kids to comply? Why do they have to be so difficult, so uncooperative?"

Please understand that it is not a typical behavior issue.

Such rigidity comes from having Asperger's, which is a neurological condition, not a psychological issue. It's about wiring, not playing games.

Being slaves to facts and the truth, Asperger's folks use their own logic and reasoning to make sense of the world around them. Once they've figured something out, then that's that. They adhere to their own ideas, which make sense to them. Since they are smart enough to be right often, this reinforces their stance and they see no reason to comply.

If it's any consolation, they are not trying to be difficult. They don't mean to be "acting up." They just have very rigid thinking and stick to it until a logical, unemotional reason is presented to them so that they can change.

As you know by now, demanding compliance is not the answer. Emotional arguments, yelling, or disciplinary tactics do not make them cooperative. That only makes these kids stress out, shut down, and hear nothing you say.

First, it's important to be as clear as possible about what it is that you expect your child to do, not what you don't want him to do.

Just because you say what you *don't* want him to do ("Don't run!") that doesn't mean that he knows what you *do* want him to do ("Walk"). Our Friends are literal thinkers, not inferential thinkers. They can't figure out what you mean for them to do. While neurotypical kids can figure out that if you ask them to do something, then that means XYZ is expected, Aspie kids can't make that leap in prediction.

Next, what we've learned at the Friends' Club is to strive for "compliance as an interaction." That means not making it a demand. Instead, we use an experience in the moment as the lesson so it is less abstract.

In each session, we work on many things, but underlying everything is the fact that the kids must comply with certain things in order to be with the other kids. We call this "social responsibility."

Where to start? The key is to first get an Aspie motivated to do something. That is where logic comes in.

If you explain the "why" of doing something (which you can never assume that they know), then it usually clicks. If you can link it to a context, to something that they know already, then that's all the better.

For example, a teen Friend was refusing to do schoolwork and exercises in class, which he considered busywork. But this teen also wants to go to art college and become an animator. Once we linked his classwork to his dream by saying, "You have to do this work to get into college," then he understood why it is necessary and complied.

Sadly, when Aspies become angry at a change in plans or refuse to do something, adults tend to want to punish them. What's best is to tell these kids which behavior you want and expect, and to focus on them understanding, not focus on their refusal.

The process for gaining compliance has five steps, applicable to young children as well as to the older ones:

1. **You must get them to be physically with you**—not running around or standing apart, but seated in a chair or on the floor in a particular spot. Offering a pillow or small mat gives your child a visual reminder of where you want him to sit on the floor. Asperger's kids must be physically present, respecting boundaries, to make the lesson possible.

   The first time one boy came to my office, he kept pacing and saying that he didn't know why he was there. This is typical anxious behavior, but I couldn't talk to him unless he stood still. So I simply said, "You don't have to look at me but you have to stand in one place before we can talk." He complied and I explained.

2. **Check to see if they have quiet hands.** This means that they're not grabbing objects and acting impulsively. So often these kids

touch a lamp, put their hands on a window, pick things up off my desk the first time they come into my office. It's a way for them to get used to a new environment, and the touching goes way down after they get used to a new place, but they need to learn the boundary of "ask before you touch." This rule needs to be established and in place before you begin. It's part of learning self-control, which is hard for these guys but not impossible. It's part of learning social responsibility.

3. **You need to initiate.** So many of our Friends just don't know how to start a conversation or how to make the first move. For example, I often say, "Do you have any questions for me?" While most kids would think of something, often Aspie kids say, "No."

    For a group, I prefer to offer them visual cues written down on a whiteboard or notepad rather than verbal cues, so they don't become dependent on an adult prompting them to speak. Many parents tell their child, "Say 'hi,'" but I know that when the parent isn't there to prompt him, the boy won't initiate a greeting. Of course, initiation is important in conversation, so the more we can train our Friends to speak first, to greet others, to take the first step, the better their connection will be to people.

4. **Check to see if your child is *reciprocating* in a conversation and realizes that she should not go on and on about an idea or experience.** Our Friends know some amazing things, but they often have no clue how to make a conversation interactive—how to make it a dialogue, not just a monologue.

    There was one girl who was fascinated with volcanoes. She was telling me about Pele, the Hawaiian goddess of fire and volcanoes, and other facts. I busied myself, to signal that I wasn't interested anymore, but she just went on and on. Finally, I slipped out of my chair intentionally and slowly sank out of sight, so that I was *sitting under my desk on the floor*, yet she continued on as if nothing were wrong and my presence was unnecessary (shades of Sir Isaac Newton delivering a college lecture to an empty room). If you can't realize that the person with whom you're talking is now sitting under a desk out of view and you're still talking, it doesn't matter how bright you are, you won't learn social responsibility.

5. **The last step is called "out of chair."** This means that we ask the child *to do something* and *come back* to wherever he was sitting. This is hard for them because once they leave a spot, they often get wrapped up in the next thing. For instance, when you send your Asperger's child to go get his shoes and you don't see him again, you will end up finding him in another room doing something completely different.

   While they *seem* noncompliant, it's really just their brain. It moves on, following its own sequence, forgetting to come back. We can teach them to come back, with practice, because they can learn to understand expectations.

What doesn't work as a motivator is delayed gratification. Why? Because Asperger's folks have no sense of time so they hate to wait. They want it now or never mind.

What does work is to jump on the teachable moment. Even if we have to interrupt something else we are trying to teach, it's important to jump on a related episode with these kids while they are in a safe environment with people who understand an Asperger's child's unique perspective.

Aspies are unconventional thinkers who require an unconventional approach in order to give us their cooperation. Their brains are wired differently and so they tend to react differently than how you may expect.

But if you can dig deeper and ask them why they object to your request, and if you can *stay calm* as they explain their point of view behind their refusal, then you'll know how to address their concerns as well as make your own plan make sense to them.

See also Bluntness and Unintentional Insults,
Courtesy, Curiosity About People, Greetings,
Manners, Responding to Others, Social Stories,
and "White Lies" and Sparing Others' Feelings

COMPLIMENTS

While most of us need to hear compliments from time to time to boost our spirits and to feel better about ourselves, Asperger's kids and adults do not. They have no need to hear that you've noticed something positive about them or that you think well of them. In fact, they often don't respond to a compliment and seem to ignore it or not hear it.

Why? Because they already know it. If they consider it to be a fact, then it's not new information. It's obvious, so why state the obvious?

Asperger's kids also have no curiosity about other people, so it never occurs to them to reach out and make the positive kind of connection that a compliment makes. Besides, compliments are not factual, but more opinions and feelings. Where's the merit in that?

In an Aspie's mind, people should know when they've done well or look good or said something worthwhile. Why should you compliment them for what they already know?

This inability to give or receive compliments creates an enormous gulf between the Asperger's person and neurotypicals. There's such a basic need in most of us to hear something positive about ourselves or our actions that when a loved one or friend never speaks kindly of us, well, this is very off-putting and even hurtful.

Yet it's not intentional. Failing to pay compliments is never on purpose to hurt the other person. That's the irony—the Asperger's person has no idea that he has done anything wrong, or in this case, that his lack of doing something is wrong.

Paying a compliment just never enters their heads. The concept is foreign to them, and they are at a loss as to what the other person wants to hear. It literally does not compute in their differently wired brain.

At Friends' Club, we have approached this issue by offering our kids step-by-step ways to pay compliments and to receive compliments. As always, it doesn't help any Aspie to tell them what they should *not* be doing. Then they're still in the dark. What they need is someone to tell them *exactly* what they should do, so they have a specific phrase or action to guide them. Yes, it's hand-holding, but it works!

We've also discovered that it's easier to teach them to compliment someone's appearance with a simple phrase ("Nice haircut" or "Nice shoes") than it is to teach them to say something about how well someone did something. Again, this is because an Asperger's person assumes that you know you've done well, so why should they have to tell you? To state the obvious is a waste of time and just plain foreign to them.

While our Friends can learn to use certain pat phrases, this can backfire. For instance, one boy walked up to me and said, "Nice skirt, Cynthia." This would have been fine except that I wasn't wearing a skirt! His mother had taught him to say this compliment, but being typical Asperger's, the boy didn't pay attention to the relevant detail of noticing whether I was wearing a skirt or not.

So with our groups, we've discovered that it's best to practice compliments in an interactive way. We take advantage of the learning moment while playing games or creating something. We will stop the activity and ask the boys or girls to give their Friends a compliment on how they played the game, etc.

The more they practice this, the more comfortable and willing they seem to be in paying compliments to others. Of course, their literalness may need toning down. One boy, sounding like a dentist, said, "You have nice white teeth." We practiced the more natural phrase, "You have a nice smile."

In one group, the leader told the kids that she had just had her hair cut. She said, "This is something that you could compliment someone for, if they've changed their appearance." That's when one of the boys blurted out, "But what if I think you don't look good?" This is when she took the opportunity to combine the lesson on compliments with a new lesson on "little white lies" and encouraged some social thinking, toning down their truthfulness to spare someone else's feelings.

What you may have noticed with your Asperger's son or daughter is that when you pay them a compliment, it doesn't really seem to register. They don't say "thank you," and sometimes don't seem to hear you at all. This kind of nonreaction is very strange to the rest of us, who are so used to noticing and appreciating a kind word or a positive observation. It's also offensive to not be acknowledged, and leaves the person giving the compliment feeling baffled and ignored.

We've found out that sometimes Asperger's folks don't believe the compliment. It doesn't fit into their perception of what they did or who they are, so they don't believe it and don't respond. But in most cases, they truly just don't hear the compliment. It falls on deaf ears.

Also, to some Aspies, a compliment needs no acknowledgment because if the person saying it believes it, then why react? An answer isn't necessary. A compliment was stated. End of story.

We try to teach them to acknowledge any kind remark because it is good manners. Social rules dictate saying, "Thank you," after a compliment is given to you. Fortunately, our Aspie Friends are rule followers, so they can learn this standard response rather easily.

Carol Gray and Tony Attwood, well-known experts in the Asperger's field, have written a booklet on compliments. See their Web sites for more information, at www.thegraycenter.org and www.tonyattwood.com. They've broken down the very complicated dynamic of giving compliments, basing it on how well you know the person to whom you'd pay a compliment. The main point is that if you don't pay any compliments, it seems like you don't care about that person. Yet if you pay compliments to someone you don't know very well, it seems pushy. They explain the levels of friendship and even offer a formula of how many compliments to pay and when.

Here's a Social Story on compliments that we've written that may be useful for your Asperger's child, to help him understand the role of such comments:

> Compliments are comments that you make to another person. These are usually comments about how a person looks or how someone completed a task. Compliments are not new information, but they show you've noticed something good about them. Our friends and family like to hear compliments. It makes them feel good. I will try to give a compliment to someone when I see them.

See also Acceptance, Awareness, Bluntness and
Unintentional Insults, Compliance, Cooperation,
Letting Go and Refocusing, Perspectives and
Point of View, Sportsmanship, *and* Teamwork

COMPROMISE

Inflexibility goes with the territory of an Asperger's mind.

Our Friends see the world their way and their way only. This natural inability to see things from anyone else's perspective creates a mental rigidity that makes it very difficult for them to understand and accept compromise. Their need for control also gets in the way.

Yet, in order to have friendships and healthy relationships, there must be give-and-take. While we know that we must stay open to others' suggestions and proposals and *bend* enough to make things work, how do you teach an Asperger's child how to be more flexible?

How do you get them to let go of their ideas enough to make room for someone else's?

How do you teach them to compromise?

We practice give-and-take as much as possible at Friends' Club, without the kids knowing it—in conversation, in game playing, and in other activities. This helps Asperger's kids loosen up and learn that if they bend, they won't break. We help them learn to lessen the "my" way to accept an "our" way.

Their need for control is not a power issue. It's just that if you were an Asperger's person, you'd see how alarmingly unpredictable life is. And even worse, how extremely unpredictable people are, so much so that the only way you can feel safe is if you control the situation. The more you get to do things your way, the more you'll know exactly what to expect and the less anxious you'll feel.

Everyday life and people make Asperger's folks very anxious. Change is ever present. Uncertainty is rampant. The unexpected is lurking around every corner. So control is the answer. The more you do things your way, which makes you feel in control, the safer you'll feel.

New situations are when Asperger's people are more likely to want things done their way and when they'll be more entrenched in doing things the same way. It's hard for them to give up their position because they're giving up safety. Again, not because of a lust for power, but because doing it some other way is an unknown. And unknowns are distressing.

In almost every group session, we teach our Friends to let go of wanting total control. We change the rules sometimes while playing a favorite game. Or we'll use a conflict between two kids over a desirable object as a teachable moment to come up with a compromise.

For instance, when one Friend wants the same game piece as another, we stop and say, "Let's work this out." What makes compromise so hard is that one of them is not going to get what she wants. So we encourage both kids to decide who gets their way this time, and then the other person gets what she wants next time.

We'll even write it down (which always helps our Friends). We'll write, "Next week, Jonathan gets the red game piece," as if it's a contract. Sometimes we'll help by taking the game piece in one of our hands, and then having them choose the left or the right hand. Rock, paper, scissors has also worked. But the strategy they like best is to choose a number between one and ten, because numbers have a solid feel and appeal to these folks. Once they're redirected, our Friends usually go along with the compromise.

The main thing is that we do all we can to help them become more flexible and more open to other people's suggestions. We impress upon them that they will win friends and get along better with others if they accept other people's ideas, or at least don't reject them outright.

The bluntness factor of many Asperger's folks can sound like a rude shutdown of someone else's idea. In truth, our Friends don't hear how they really sound. They don't realize that their tone is so negative and dismissive.

We try to make them aware of how an immediate rejection of someone else's ideas is not the way to go. We work on more positive responses, which respect others' feelings and make friendships possible.

Building projects together is another way we continually get our kids to practice compromising, since their natural preference is to work alone.

Whether we give them Legos, K'NEX, or other building materials, we ask our Friends to work as a team, which nudges all of them into sharing, listening to one another, and learning to accept different ideas so that, ultimately, they learn to compromise.

As with other social skills, practice does make possible.

See also Awareness, Compliments, Curiosity
About People, Emotions, Eye Contact,
Greetings, Listening to Others, Literal
Language, Manners, Remembering Names,
Responding to Others, Rudeness, Slang and
Idioms, *and* Talking with Peers

CONVERSATION

Conversation is the cornerstone of all friendships.

Talking to others helps us find out more about them so that we can connect. There is both an art and skill to conversing with people. It is through the give-and-take of questions and answers that we learn about one another.

Unfortunately, such give-and-take is difficult for kids with Asperger's syndrome. Conversation just does not come naturally to them at all, for a number of reasons. The good news is that they can be taught. It won't improve overnight, but improvement is possible.

In the Friends' Club, we've introduced Carol Gray's Conversation Equation as a handy reminder for them: Conversation=Compliment+Comment+Questions. We write this on the board for all to see.

We emphasize that it's not just what you say, but *how* you say it that can be so important. Tone of voice conveys more than our Friends realize. Many are surprised to learn that they have a flat or abrupt delivery. They're also surprised to find out that they sound harsh, or even mean, when they speak in such a serious manner.

So we teach them how to identify and repeat different tones of voice. It's hard for them to hear the difference between a loud voice and screaming. One of our boys said that he uses the same voice for talking to everyone about everything. This led us to discuss how tone of voice reveals clues about other people and about us. We also teach them how to say things in a pleasant voice.

It also doesn't help that our Friends take language so literally. They miss the subtleties of double entendres, sarcasm, and humorous asides. Dubbed "little professors" by Hans Asperger himself in his 1944 paper because of their ablity to talk in great detail about their favorite subjects, Asperger's kids need help listening to others and loosening up their conversational style.

Almost every one of our sessions covers conversation in some way, since it's very hard to make and keep a friend without it. To help our teens and younger kids learn to converse better, we've broken this social skill down into smaller parts to make it clearer for them, and some times we write these out on poster paper for them to see:

- Open with a topic, such as movies or video games

- Stay in the same topic area

- Ask questions to get more information, such as "How did you like the movie?"

- Comment on another's comments

- Listen to what others say

- Do not interrupt

- Use the information that they share in future conversations

We've also compared making a conversation to letter writing. You need a beginning or greeting. You need things to say in the middle, whether it's news or thoughts or feelings that you express. And then you need to end with a closing, a "good-bye." Since our Friends are so visual, we draw or show them a letter and point out the similarities.

When Asperger's kids get talking, they tend to deliver a monologue instead of allowing a dialogue to develop. They will launch into a long discourse on their favorite topic, oblivious to all signs of interest or disinterest in the listener. So we have come up with how sometimes conversation is like driving a car.

If you go too fast when you're talking, then your conversation partner can't keep up with you. You need to slow down.

If you go too slowly, then you lose your partner because their attention will drift off. You need to speed up and accelerate.

And sometimes, you need to put on the brakes and stop to change direction in the conversation. A change of topic can lead to a more interesting route or new territory.

To practice these three speeds—and the all-important eye contact, which is the basis of connecting in a conversation—we've created an activity called Zoom!

We ask the kids to sit in a circle. The designated starter looks either to the left or to the right and says, "Zoom," when he or she makes eye contact with the next child. Then that person passes the Zoom on to the next person. Eye contact must go completely around the circle at least once before anyone can put on the "brakes" (they make a braking sound—"errrrrrr").

When someone puts on the brakes, then the Zoom eye contact goes in the other direction until someone else puts on the brakes.

If the person on the other side of the Zoom child also puts on the brakes, then the original conversationalist or Zoomer must do a "four-wheel drive" to someone else in the circle, going around the two on both sides who are blocking the Zoom.

The two main rules are that each person is only allowed three brakes *and* you must make eye contact before passing a Zoom to the next person. Since our Friends struggle so much with looking people in the eyes (and in waiting their turn), this game has multiple benefits.

Another approach we have used is to introduce a conversation script, which we have the children read out loud in order to help them learn how a true conversation would go. It's as simple as this:

FIRST CHILD: "I like to read books and watch some TV shows."
SECOND CHILD: "What kinds of books do you like to read?"
FIRST CHILD: "I like science, history, and comics."
SECOND CHILD: "Do you like computer games?"
FIRST CHILD: "Yes, of course. Do you?"
SECOND CHILD: "Sure. Which is your favorite?"
FIRST CHILD: "Lego Racer and Star Wars. Do you want to get together and play sometime?"
SECOND CHILD: "Okay."

Because we must appeal to our Asperger's kids' brains first, rather than their emotions, it works to let them know the formula for a conversation. First, they need to look like they're listening and learn the flow of a typical conversation. They learn to ask questions and how to express caring.

Then, the next step is to segue into real caring about how they speak, how not to drone on and on, and how to be aware of the other person's reactions. This applies to conversation and other social interactions, which the rest of us do automatically.

Another activity we use to help our younger Friends stay on topic is the "conversation tree." This strategy was developed by Michelle Garcia Winner. We show kids how one topic forms the trunk of the conversation. Then each comment related to that main topic makes the tree trunk grow.

Staying on topic is one of our Friends' biggest conversational challenges. This visual aid of the tree lets them see how comments connect and build on one another when they're related. We also show how related responses that are slightly off the main topic become branches off the trunk.

I'll often put topic suggestions in a hat for the kids to pull out, so we have a starting point. Then I'll draw parts to the tree, showing how related comments fit in. If a response is totally unrelated to the conversation tree, then I'll draw a red branch jutting out that looks absurd. This helps the group see just how an off-topic statement doesn't fit in, basically going nowhere and stopping the growth of the tree.

There are other visual cues that we use to help Asperger's children remember who should be talking and who should be listening. We've used two methods with great success.

For our older Friends, we hand out "conversation sticks" (wooden Popsicle sticks) to everyone in the group. As each one shares a point, a stick goes in the middle of the table. When our teens look around and see that others are still holding a stick, that reminds them that others want to talk, too, and that no one should monopolize the conversation. It allows them to let others have a chance, increasing the give-and-take in the conversation.

For our younger Friends, we play a game using a wand, a ball, or a "talking hat" as a visual reminder of who should be talking. Whoever has the object is the only one allowed to speak, and everyone else has to listen. Seeing the hat stops the rest of the group from interrupting. To ask for the hat, our Friends must use only nonverbal language (eye contact, gestures, etc.).

Another great source of conversation starters are Fun Decks from Super Duper Publications (at www.superduperinc.com). One of their really fun games is called What's in Ned's Head? This large, funny-looking fabric head has holes in it to stuff things into. They have rubber items to put inside, but we put topics inside as well. Then we ask our Friends to pull out a topic or question from Ned's head to start the conversation. It's a concrete way to show how others think about things that we aren't always thinking about.

Our famous conversation rule at the Friends' Club is: "The first time is funny, the second time is not so funny, and the third time can be annoying." Our kids often repeat their favorite jokes or describe something over and over, especially if it got a laugh the first time.

We point out that in a conversation, it's best not to repeat the same thing but to bring up new ideas and observations. As one of our teens said, "I should only talk about a movie scene once to you, right? I have to remember that."

Since asking questions is a great way to launch a conversation, we use various activities to show them how. For instance, a Magic 8 Ball provides answers in its murky, inky window on the bottom. But first you have to ask it a question. One boy asked, "Will I make new friends?" while another asked, "Will I continue to be bullied at school?"

Not only does the Magic 8 Ball help them practice thinking up questions, but it also reveals their hidden concerns. This provides the group with new, and more meaningful, topics of conversation to cover.

Spotlight is a game that we created to inspire asking questions. The lights are turned off and a flashlight that is turned on is placed in the center of the circle. Each Friend gets a turn spinning the flashlight. Wherever the beam lands, that person is asked a question about himself. Once he answers, he then asks a question of the spinner.

The kids have learned that some questions can be just silly: "Have you ever jumped off a ceiling?" Other questions like "Do you like basketball?" can help you make friends. Sometimes we move on from there to have everyone take a turn saying something on the *same* topic. This helps them learn how to show an interest in what others are saying as well as how to tell when people are ready to move on to another topic.

We know that we've gotten through to these kids when, like one boy said, "It's good to ask questions because that is how we learn about someone." Obvious to the rest of us, but a revelation to an Asperger's child.

One question often asked by parents is, "Why are the kids playing two-person games? Shouldn't they be working on conversing more instead of playing games?"

The answer is that these kids have a hard time getting together, and an even harder time talking with others. To them, a board game or a game at recess is not a social activity and talking is not required. The game has a specific purpose (remember, they are concrete thinkers), and you just play it.

By having them play a game together, we're teaching them that you can learn the other person's likes and dislikes and hear their beliefs in the course of playing the game. We'll ask them, "William, you played Battleship with John. What did you learn about him?"

What we encourage them to do is to use that information as a topic in a future conversation. Our Friends need to be taught to pay attention to what the other person is saying while they play the game. They need to realize that you can learn interesting things about other people if you talk together while you're doing an activity.

Also, when children get together with a friend, they usually play a two-person game. So pairing off and playing these kinds of games during their session gives our kids some real-world experience. Since most of them have few, if any, friends, playing board games with other group members prepares them for a real playdate.

Something you can do at home to encourage your child's active listening and speaking skills is to have your child talk for two minutes about what he did last week or what interests him. Keeping it to two minutes is important, since most conversation is in brief bite-size chunks.

Next, you talk for two minutes, as well as anyone else in the family who is around, while your child listens.

Then have your child ask you one question related to what you said. After hearing the answer, have him ask the other people, too. Encourage him to respond with a simple "cool" or "really?"

Finally, you ask him one question related to what he said, as do the others.

This kind of step-by-step conversational practice is an excellent way to help your Asperger's child understand the three basics of good conversation—stay on topic, ask questions, and respond to what is said.

See also Compliance, Compromise, Letting Go and Refocusing, Obsessions and Obsessive Behavior, Perspectives and Point of View, Problem Solving, *and* Teamwork

COOPERATION

These days, in school as well as in the workplace, teamwork is encouraged and cultivated. At every grade level, group projects are assigned, which can be a particular challenge for our Friends.

Working as a group requires cooperation and, like compromise, this can be a great worry to Asperger's children. They cannot be sure that someone else will follow the patterns that they see in their mind and produce the same results. Giving up such control often causes anxiety for the Asperger's person.

We work on cooperation at Friends' Club using group activities. For example, we put a big, blank sheet of paper in front of a group. We tell them that they are to draw any figure they want. Then we pass around markers and ask each child to add one part of the figure.

Of course, each child quickly forms his own mental picture of what the drawing should look like. But, since it's a group project, they have to cooperate.

What they learn is that (1) they must wait their turn, (2) they must watch someone else draw something that does not match what they see in their own brain, and (3) they are not allowed to say, "No, that's not how you draw it." They have to accept the image that is forming in front of them and figure out what they will add as their one part.

Having the kids watch as the image evolves into something that none of them had envisioned, yet is still a fun and colorful figure in the end, gets them one step closer to understanding the benefits of cooperating with others. This activity has also served as a problem-solving exercise, since they had to watch and accept other people making a drawing that was unlike how they would have done it.

Another successful approach that we've used to teach cooperation is to offer a tub of building materials, like Legos or K'NEX or ZOOBS.

Right away, each of the boys wants to make his thing and work individually. Very soon, though, they realize that they don't have enough pieces to finish their own project. They need to ask someone else to combine their pieces to make it work . . . but that also means giving up sole control of the creation. They will have to work with someone else and cooperate enough so they can both be satisfied.

This kind of social problem-solving skill development is at the heart of cooperation. Working as a team has brought out some frustrations, tears, and even a tantrum over not getting a certain piece, but all of it becomes part of the lesson and is addressed behaviorally to cement the skill.

Something that can be done at school is to bring out a bucket of Tinker Toys or Legos for a group of kids. Give each student five pieces. Then tell the group, "We're going to build something. We don't know what it's going to be until we get all done with it. But each of you gets to put one piece in place at a time, and you'll take turns until all your pieces are used up."

This has been a terrific team-building activity that allows them to use their imagination and wealth of ideas while also improving their communication skills and abilities to cooperate.

Even though Crocodile Dentist and Tickle Toes are one-person games, you can use them to teach cooperative skills by making players wait for someone else to go first. We encourage our kids to cheer on whoever's turn it is, so they become aware of someone else's efforts.

We've also used Mighty Beanz, a game that involves building a track for the beans to slide down. We give each child a few pieces of track, then ask them to work together to assemble it. This cooperative play is challenging, making one boy say, "It's hard to do with kids." That's exactly why he's doing it!

With group projects, another challenge for our kids is keeping up. If writing or calculating comes slowly to an Asperger's child, he may be resented by the team if he cannot move at the same speed as the rest of the group.

What some of our Friends have learned is, as much as they'd like to be in charge of writing down the ideas or taking notes for the group, it is best for all if they let someone else do it. This kind of letting go and finding another task to do is at the heart of cooperation, though it's not an easy lesson for our kids to learn.

See also Apologizing, Bluntness and Unintentional Insults, Compliments, Empathy, Greetings, Manners, Phone Skills, Remembering Names, Rudeness, *and* "White Lies" and Sparing Others' Feelings

COURTESY

Courtesy is a basic consideration of others and respect for their feelings and expectations. It takes tuning in to someone else's wishes, expressed or implied, to show courtesy. It means following an often unspoken protocol that is considered good manners. Common courtesy is something most kids pick up from their parents or other adults while they are growing up.

Because our Friends are not tuned in to other people, they are often unaware of what others consider acceptable and unacceptable behavior. They may stand too close, talk too loud, arrive too late, and react too strongly to something, all of which puzzles, if not puts off, other people. Their lack of empathy makes it hard for them to discern what others are feeling or thinking, and so they seem discourteous.

We have broken common courtesy into three main elements to help teach our Friends how to become more socially successful:

1. **Promptness.** Being on time for an appointment or activity is one way that we show we care about the other person and regard their time as valuable. While the rare instance of being late is unavoidable and forgivable, chronic lateness is typical for Asperger's children who are genuinely unaware of time.

   We have role-played with our teen girls and boys to show them how their tardiness can affect other people. This helps them see the situation from someone else's perspective. It makes them aware of the negative impression others form of us when we are late and keep people waiting.

2. **Table manners.** Mealtime manners may seem like a small matter to some, but it is far more important in friendship-building

than people realize. Chewing with your mouth open, talking while your mouth is full, and grabbing food from across the table without asking to have it passed are all hard to ignore and forgive if you're the other diner. To help our Friends be more appropriate at the table, we talk about these offenses as well as how to handle the food, the utensils, and one's elbows while still making acceptable table conversation.

3. **Courteous conversation.** Children on the autism spectrum usually do not establish eye contact when they talk to someone. And they focus only on their topic of interest, with no understanding of back-and-forth conversation. This behavior seems rude to the typical child, teen, or adult. We believe that it is very, very important to work on the three key elements of conversation—eye contact, staying on topic, and asking the other person appropriate questions—to help our Friends be more socially successful.

At the Friends' Club, our strategies must begin with teaching *why* certain things happen or why they are necessary. These kids don't pick up the social niceties that neurotypical children do, so they must be explained. And, being Asperger's, they are best reached through reasoning, not emotional pleas or commands. If they come to understand the reason for doing something, then they are usually willing to do it. The more it sounds like a rule, the easier it is for them to follow.

Our kids also need to be told *exactly what to do*, not just told what *not* to do. Telling them what not to do only leaves a void in their minds—they lack the intuitiveness to know what they are supposed to do. And they tend not to look around, so they don't see and learn from what others are doing either.

As natural-born nonconformists, our Friends are immune to social conventions and conventional thinking in general. This makes them seem discourteous when, really, all they need is some training and a lot of practice to learn what the rest of us pick up automatically in social situations. The more courteous and well mannered these Asperger's boys and girls become, the more they will be able to make new friends and, later, find acceptance among their coworkers.

Some of the books that we've used with success are:

The Berenstain Bears and Franklin series for younger kids

How Rude!: The Teenagers' Guide to Good Manners, Proper Behavior, and Not Grossing People Out by Alex J. Packer for teens

Oops!: The Manners Guide for Girls by Nancy Holyoke, from the American Girl Library for the tween and teen kids

365 Manners Kids Should Know: Games, Activities, and Other Fun Ways to Help Children Learn Etiquette by Sheryl Eberly

For a more complete listing of the books that we've found helpful in teaching our Friends about courtesy and manners, please see Part Three: Resources.

See also Conversation, Greetings, Listening to
Others, Looking Like You're Paying Attention,
and Responding to Others

CURIOSITY ABOUT PEOPLE

Most of us are wired to notice, watch, wonder, and speculate about other people. Unconsciously, we entertain ourselves by people watching, especially in large venues like stadiums, shopping malls, airports, amusement parks, and at crowded beaches. We watch because we're naturally curious about other people and their behavior.

Asperger's individuals are generally not curious about people. They are usually wired to be interested in more concrete, rational things like computers, mathematics, vehicles, and science. They're wired to find the patterns in things and to be very curious about those, but not about people.

Being less emotional by nature, our Friends are rarely intrigued with the drama or vagaries of other people's lives. Consequently, they have no curiosity about how other people face their challenges. They never wonder how a difficult event in someone else's life turned out. The whole people thing perplexes our Friends, yet without making them curious about others.

That's why we work on listening skills in our groups at the Friends' Club. We keep teaching our kids how to ask questions of anyone who is talking. This shows that you're listening and that you care, as proven by having a question to ask.

We impress upon our kids that curiosity is a way of showing that we care about the other person. To show that caring, you have to ask questions. It builds connections crucial to friendships to show an interest in the other person, which increases our kids' chances for becoming more socially successful.

Can we rewire the brain to insert an interest in people?

No, unfortunately, there is no way to hardwire in social thinking and people awareness. But if we can create a motivation to connect with others, then we can teach our Asperger's boys and girls how to fake it well enough for them to enjoy more friendships.

What we can do is to help them *appear* to be curious about others. This is done by raising their awareness of social signals, asking questions, and listening well enough to stay on topic. What we're teaching is how to listen to someone else's ideas and comments, and build on those, rather than only talking about what you're interested in. It takes work, but with practice Aspies do improve.

As neurotypicals, we feel good when someone asks us about something we are doing or feeling. Most of us like talking about ourselves, but we also know how to make small talk.

By starting with small talk, we introduce others to our topic. Then they'll ask us for more information, which is our invitation to talk on.

For Aspies, being asked questions is not as important as recounting information. In fact, they don't need any questions at all. They are quite willing to deliver information right away, launching into their favorite topic without any chitchat.

Some of this is about control, since our Friends tend to be more comfortable if they are talking about what they want to talk about. They would rather not be forced into unknown territory and random topics, which could make them uncomfortable.

What we have discovered is that we can teach our Friends to talk to people via things, such as movies, books, characters, or their own special interests. If Aspies are told of a particular shared interest or experience with another person, like Legos or a computer game or wanting to travel in space, then they will ask that person about that mutual interest. Still, it is the object or activity that provides the bond and that piques their curiosity, not the person.

See also Appearance, Emotions,
Grooming and Personal Hygiene, Manners,
Peer Pressure and Avoiding Dares, Responding
to Others, and Talking with Peers

DATING AND GENDER TALK

Just because Asperger's teens are on the autism spectrum doesn't mean that they aren't interested in the opposite sex. They are, in their own naïve way. Because there is often a delay in social maturity, the boy-girl fixation doesn't usually hit as early or as hard as it does with neurotypical teens, but it still surfaces eventually.

And, as in most things, our Friends' thinking on the matter is completely different from typical kids. That's why we talk with our teens about dating and other social situations, to help them sort out the oh-so-confusing boy-girl scene.

While adolescence tends to make kids very self-conscious and caught up in how they look and what others think of them, Aspies are spared most of that. Their general cluelessness about social dynamics keeps them from being self-conscious. They don't worry about their appearance or what their peers might think. This stuff just doesn't enter their minds.

If anything, our Friends' lack of preoccupation with their looks is a problem. If basic hygiene is neglected and their clothing is too out of style with their peers, they can become prime targets for harassment and bullying.

Add this to an Asperger's teen's inability to read social signals and hidden meanings—while also taking things way too literally—and it's no wonder that Aspie teens are at a loss in handling the whole middle school and high school social dynamic, let alone the boy-girl thing.

For example, it's been a revelation to our girl teen groups to find out that beauty is more important than being smart to their peers. The fact that appearance is number one in high school absolutely baffles them.

One of the activities we do with the teen girls at the Friends' Club is to work on different hairstyles, simple ones that they could do at home. Sometimes, that means changing their hairstyle for the first time in years, since the Asperger child is averse to change and sees no need for it. We teach them that basic cleanliness is necessary and that people will accept others more readily if they are neat and clean.

We've discovered that many of our teen girls don't know what dating is or how it works. They see boy-girl things happening at junior high or high school, but they don't read the situations accurately.

So we show them clips from movies where boys are talking about girls, to familiarize our teens with the phrases and slang the kids are using and what it *really* means, instead of what it literally means.

In one of these movie clips, a boy told his friends, "That girl is hot!" One of the girls watching told the group that she overheard two boys in her class say, "The one in the red skirt is hot." She looked around and when she realized that *she* was the one in the red skirt, she became so upset that she left the class and called her mom to pick her up. She told us that she doesn't ever want to wear that skirt again!

A very valuable tool we've discovered for covering the vast array of details from hygiene to manners with our teens is a book called *How Rude!: The Teenagers' Guide to Good Manners, Proper Behavior, and Not Grossing People Out* by Alex J. Packer. This has been a terrific resource because it uses a humorous approach to important social skills that our kids need to understand and adopt.

We've had great success in using *How Rude!* with our kids ages ten years to eighteen years to help them realize that good manners are not just a trivial nuisance. They are important courtesies and considerations that people follow in order to make friends, not enemies.

Because our teens (both boys and girls) are so unclear about how to tell if someone likes them as a friend or as more than a friend— and because they have such difficulty in discerning what their peers think—we intersperse Gender Talk in our regular teen sessions, or occasionally as a special one-day session. This special curriculum discusses why people date and compares and contrasts dating with friendships. It delves much deeper into the whole topic of dating, relationships (platonic and romantic), sexual behavior as a way of communicating (flirting, kissing, holding hands, etc.), sexual pressures, and deciding what's right for you.

We feel this is particularly important for our girls, who would be very vulnerable if neurotypical boys wanted to take advantage of the girls' extreme naïveté and lack of awareness and pressure them to have sex. We share with the girls that this is a form of bullying and they need to know how to say no. Some of our younger teens are embarrassed when we talk about sex, while the older ones are more matter-of-fact and want to talk about dating to make it less confusing.

During one Gender Talk session, a girl said, "Love is like a roller coaster. When it is good, you don't want to get off. When it is bad, you just want to throw up."

As with everything you introduce to Asperger's kids, it's best to break down complex topics into small, specific steps. By talking about dating and gender topics as clearly and as unemotionally as possible, we can help our Friends better understand these perplexing social issues. The payoff is that the better prepared our Asperger's teens are about dating and sexual matters, the less likely they are to be swayed or sabotaged by more savvy peers.

See also Anxiety, Awareness, Bluntness and Unintentional Insults, Initiative, Perfectionism and Unrealistic Expectations, *and* Telling Your Child That He or She Has Asperger's Syndrome

DEPRESSION

Although it is well known that Asperger's teens and adults are prone to depression, no one knows exactly why. Whether it's constitutional or biological, inherited, reactive to their environment and the social difficulties they experience, or a combination of reasons, the exact cause is unknown.

Often, signs of depression arise in early adolescence. The great discrepancy between their high cognitive, intellectual abilities and their very low social and communication skills becomes more of an issue at this time, in middle school and high school. They are aware of how different they are, yet they have no idea what to do about it.

And, unfortunately, Asperger's kids and adults are unable to see how their behavior is the cause of their rejection. It's just a big blur, where they know that something is not right but they can't pinpoint what they've done wrong. This perplexes them and adds to the likelihood of depression.

Also, there is a tendency for Asperger's folks to carry their past mistreatment with them. Once they've become aware that others are making fun of them, at school or in the community, they tend to assume later that people are talking about them, although this may not be the case.

When Asperger's kids become aware of their different nature, and if left untreated with no diagnosis or social coaching, they tend to have four main ways to compensate, according to Tony Attwood, an expert in the field. The good reactions are imitation and imagination. The imitators absorb or copy other people's behavior. The imaginers create pretend friends and other worlds, preferring fiction and fantasy.

The more difficult reactions are depression and arrogance. Those who become depressed and defeated by their condition are plagued with thoughts like "I'm useless" or "I'm a failure." Those who overcompensate and adopt a totally authoritative attitude become quite critical of others and see themselves as superior. They deny they have any problems, yet they have pronounced anger management issues.

The depressed person puts people off by being so negative and not fun to be with. The arrogant Aspie is particularly difficult because not only are they all-knowing, but they tend to think everyone else is an "idiot" and say so. They consider others "stupid" for not knowing what they know and not thinking how an Asperger's person thinks.

Neither of these two groups attracts friends.

With such a profound inability to connect with others, most Asperger's kids feel very alone. It troubles them to see others get on so well and to seem so at ease socially. This kind of loneliness can plunge an Aspie into more than a mere funk. Tony Attwood says some Asperger's kids are prone to "depression attacks" because their emotions kick in at such a high volume.

What do we do when we see signs of depression in our Friends, whatever age they are? If you, as parents, have suspicions but aren't sure, what should you do?

First and foremost, it must be determined whether the child or teen has suicidal thoughts. If there's the slightest inkling, it's best to get a referral and take your child directly to a child psychiatrist for a thorough evaluation.

If it's determined that the child is not at risk, then it's advisable to seek out whatever treatment is suggested by a trained professional.

If your child keeps complaining about being friendless, please know that all it takes is *one* friend to help our kids feel less alone. If there is any child in your neighborhood or at school or church who is of a gentle, patient nature, that child may be a perfect person to ask over to play, just as a first step. Your Asperger's child won't usually think to call or invite another child over to play, so it will be up to you as the parent to make the call and to put the ball in motion.

One of the gratifying things about hosting the Friends' Club is that some of the new kids are down and, according to their parents and my observations, on the verge of depression when they first join us. Then after a few months, sometimes longer, parents report a gradual yet noticeable difference. Friends' Club seems to have a therapeutic effect, if only in that these kids do not feel so alone.

When our members connect well enough to want to get together outside of our weekly group sessions, that makes their parents and us very happy. It is the first time that many of them have felt understood by others who are much like them. They feel safe with someone of their own "species," as one of our girls put it.

But like all humans, our kids have their own tastes and interests, and we can't force a friendship. Neither can you. However, being proactive and taking the first step for your child to invite someone over is welcome, since Asperger's kids struggle with taking the initiative and trying to work out details. If they are going to make a friend, they will need help setting it up and getting it going.

As for the all-knowing, harshly critical, authoritative attitude—how can you help tone it down and increase your child's chances of winning over a friend or two?

It's only when the group first meets at the beginning of our year when we sometimes see this critical attitude. It seems to be out of anxiety, because once the group gets going and the child or teen realizes he's in a safe environment, it goes away. We've had parents tell us that their child sounds so different in the group than he or she does otherwise.

Much of the problem is that Aspies don't hear how harsh they sound. They really are unable to hear their own tone of voice and bluntness, just as they can't detect sarcasm in others' voices. But that only explains it, it doesn't excuse it.

For the group to function well, we need to keep it a safe, accepting environment. So when one of our new Friends becomes overly critical, we treat it individually in a behavioral way. We challenge them nicely.

First, I'll pull the boy or girl out of the group and let him or her know that his or her tone of voice or choice of words is overly harsh.

Then I'll tell them that they must catch themselves and be willing to be more kind if they want to stay in the group. Confronting them gently about this is the only way to help them become more aware of their offensive behavior, so they can try to soften it.

One of our older boys was very critical and put down the other boys when he first joined the group. After a session or two, seeing that it wasn't getting better with exposure to the leaders and other kids, I pulled him aside. I told him how much his comments and tone of voice were hurting other people's feelings. He desperately wanted to stay in the group, so he was motivated to make an effort to try to stop himself before he blurted out something belittling or harsh. He did learn to soften what he said, and was allowed to stay. But such bluntness and critical attitudes must be addressed if these kids are ever to have friends.

If your child or teen makes a nasty remark to you at home or elsewhere, don't recoil even though that's a natural first reflex. Also don't ignore it and hope it will go away. The best thing is to treat it as a teachable moment.

Stop and ask your child, "Are you trying to sound mean?"

If she says "yes," then say, "You're feeling angry," and try to get to the source of your child's frustration. But most of the time, our Aspie Friends are not mean-spirited at all and only sound that way.

If she says "no," that she wasn't trying to sound mean, then you can say, "That tone is how it comes across. Let's try to say the same thing in a different tone of voice."

There is no instant fix. But you can help them to understand how harsh they sound and how much they need to soften what they say.

And again, please watch for any suicidal thoughts and *always* take such talk seriously. Seek out an evaluation from a mental health professional. While the suicide incidence rate seems to be low among Asperger's children and teens, it is important to be vigilant and take action when necessary.

See also Anxiety, Compliance, Fear,
Letting Go and Refocusing, Meltdowns,
Parental Sainthood and Your Need for Support,
Perspectives and Point of View, Rudeness,
Sensory Sensitivities, *and* Writing Things Down

DISCIPLINE

Two of the first things that parents and teachers ask me about Asperger's kids are "Why do they say and do such strange things?" and "Why doesn't my usual discipline work?"

The short answer is that our Friends are quirky and different. Because they think differently and act differently, a different approach is needed.

But the more important answer is that Asperger's children and teens don't need conventional discipline to define boundaries and to keep them safe. They don't even understand *why* they're being considered rude or difficult or uncooperative most of the time.

Usually, their "misbehavior" and "stubbornness" are due to their lack of social awareness, sensory sensitivities, or an inability to let go of their unique perspective. They dig in and insist on having things their way, which means it won't be your way, which leads to trouble.

Just know that they don't need louder voices to make them "behave." They need calm, unemotional voices to reach them.

They don't need stricter rules or deprivation. They need to have the rules spelled out, logically and clearly, so they can follow them. Writing them down is even more effective, so they can actually see what you are saying.

And, most important of all, they need to be asked *why* they are behaving this way! Often, something that you would never think of is bothering them—a scratchy shirt, too-loud music, a personal vision of what a group project should look like that some other kids are "ruining." If you ask why, they will tell you, and the situation can either be remedied or put into perspective for them to be able to move on.

What most people don't realize is that Asperger's kids need to have any activity, and especially social events, broken down into bite-size steps so they can understand exactly what they are supposed to do.

Why? Because they really don't know what the rest of us know and take for granted. They don't know what to do next. They need help.

Our Friends lack the intuitive skills to discern what someone else is thinking. They lack the empathetic abilities to sense what another person is feeling. They don't know how to read the subtle body language and subtext messages that the rest of us consider obvious, so they miss a lot of the clues about what others want them to do.

This is exactly why they get into trouble over very basic stuff, because of their social blindness and inability to pick up the subtle verbal and nonverbal messages—they just don't catch them.

So Asperger's kids' misbehavior is really a neurological wiring issue, not a rebellion or behavior issue. Their brains are wired differently, so they need to be approached and treated in a different way.

Asperger's boys and girls continually surprise us with the atypical, not the typical. They have a completely different perspective than the rest of us, which they cling to for security, as they get bounced around this unpredictable, confusing, ridiculously emotional world of neurotypicals.

They cannot see from someone else's perspective, so they don't always agree with your requests. They will resist doing what you ask unless it is explained to them.

Does this mean that you give up on discipline altogether?

Of course not. Discipline provides order and an environment where many individuals can get along and progress.

At Friends' Club, we follow certain procedures that incorporate our understanding of these unique individuals, but which also allow us to have our group meetings and to accomplish our goals without erratic behavior taking over or spontaneous resistance getting in the way.

First, we view discipline as being about guidance, not punishment. True discipline is supposed to alter unproductive behavior so that it becomes more productive. Discipline is about coaching and improving results, not about inflicting pain or humiliation on the individual.

We've found that Asperger's kids are more than willing to be productive, as long as it makes sense to them. And when one of our Friends is not willing to do what's best for the group, we take measures to help him make that adjustment.

Sometimes we will move the group to another room, leaving the one disruptive individual behind with a leader. This gives the child an opportunity to realize that he will miss out on the activity by not being with the group. The one left behind usually becomes cooperative and rejoins his Friends.

Or we will ask the disruptive child to come outside or into another room, to calm herself down or to talk about what is bothering her, one-on-one, with a group leader.

Remember that ideas and knowledge are more important than feelings and emotions to these guys. If you can appeal to their intellect, and not their sense of shame or desire to please, then you can usually gain their cooperation and willingness to follow the rules.

That's the one ace that all parents and teachers hold with Asperger's kids—they are natural-born rule followers.

Again, if the rules that you want them to follow are logical and clear, you will gain their trust and cooperation. If you write down what you want them to do so they can see exactly what you mean, that's even better.

As for the conventional discipline method of time-outs, you need to know that this is not usually much of a punishment for Asperger's kids. It's a treat! They like nothing better than spending time alone in their room, so to send them off is not exile. It's coveted playtime and welcome alone time.

Again, if your child has been inappropriate or difficult, please don't be hard on him. Please count to ten or do whatever works for keeping your frustration in check. The more emotional you are, the more stressed your child will get and the less he will hear you.

It's best to explain in a calm voice why what he did was not acceptable, no matter how obvious it seems to you. Give him overall instructions of how you want him to behave. Then spell out step-by-step exactly what you expect him to do.

Each episode is a learning experience. It may or may not be repeated, depending on how long it takes for the lesson to be learned.

Such great understanding and patience on your part will pay off because Asperger's kids will eventually learn not to do or say that again. But there will be new episodes, other trip-ups, and plenty of social gaffes, which will require clarifications and cluing in more than discipline. The less you blame your child for not knowing better and the more you can help put our confusing people world into perspective for him, the more he will thrive and be more appropriate in any setting.

See also Homework, Initiative, *and* Time Blindness

DISORGANIZATION

As with all people with Asperger's syndrome, the source of these children's chronic disorganization is rooted in their brain. Their inability to be organized is not a behavior issue. It is not a conscious plot to bug you or their teachers. It is not a matter of being lazy or uncooperative.

Asperger's kids' disorganization is mostly from frontal lobe deficits, which means it is a neurological issue. And they're not alone—individuals with attention-deficit/hyperactivity disorder (both inattentive and hyperactive-impulsive), Tourette's, and anyone on the spectrum also struggle with personal organization and time management.

Suffice it to say, if Asperger's children could be organized, they would be, but they can't. Not naturally, and certainly not easily. Their frontal lobe won't let them. Tony Attwood has said that people with Asperger's, children and adults, basically need executive assistants to keep them on track and to keep track of their schedules, assignments, projects due, and other details of life.

Parents are an Asperger's child's first and most important executive assistants. Your child needs your help to function, let alone succeed in school and in daily life.

The good news is that there are ways to train your child to develop their organizational skills. It takes time, constant reminders, and consistent practice to get there, but Asperger's kids can learn to use agendas, notebooks, etc.

Many of our parents have said that putting finished homework in the same place every day works. If there is a front pocket in your child's notebook, that is a perfect place to put the daily homework to be handed in. As soon as she opens her notebook, the day's homework is facing her as a reminder to give it to the teacher.

For so many Asperger's kids, anything out of sight is out of mind. Unless it's right in front of them, it is too easy to forget to hand things in.

What often sabotages their ability to follow through and hand in assignments is their perception that once the work is done, it's done. Why worry about it? The fact that teachers need to see the finished work for the student to get credit doesn't really register with Asperger's kids. That final step of handing it in just doesn't occur to them without training.

Some parents swear by color codes to keep their child's work organized—a different color for each subject or class.

Others have had success using planners and/or folders to separate their student's work. The folders divide the work that's been done from the work left to do.

A powerful tool is the school agenda. Even though it seems impossible for your child to use it at first in elementary school, as with anything, practice makes all the difference. The more the Asperger's child uses an agenda, the more it will eventually sink in.

One of our boys had a very hard time remembering to write assignments down in his agenda from fourth through seventh grade. This was in part due to the fact that it took a long time for him to write anything. While other kids could jot down a few quick notes and dash out of the classroom, our Friend had trouble looking at the board and then transferring that information into his agenda on his desk. Sometimes a teacher helped write it down, sometimes another student.

Our Friend started devising his own cryptic code, a sort of shorthand, to help him write the information faster. And his parents kept reminding him how important it was to write his assignments down. Finally, by the middle of eighth grade, he was doing it all by himself and accurately, and has continued to do well in high school.

The increase of teacher Web sites makes it easier to double-check that your child has written the assignment down correctly. But there are still many times when teachers don't update their Web site or they change the assignment in class from how it's listed in the preplanned homework schedule.

Keep building your Asperger's child's awareness about listening for such changes in class and to write them down in an agenda or on a homework assignment page. This is crucial to their future independence and their ability to function on their own at school or in the workplace.

If your child can get in the habit of asking a couple of students in each of his classes for their name and phone number, that's a terrific tool, too. Then if the homework doesn't get written down *and* the teacher's Web site doesn't list it, your child has some "study buddies" to call to double-check assignments in an emergency.

And finally, some of our teens have found it easier to take down messages and information via e-mail rather than writing things down. If e-mailing themselves reminders or sending text messages helps keep our Friends more organized, then all the better!

See also Anxiety, Apologizing, Bluntness and
Unintentional Insults, Courtesy, Fear, *and*
Perfectionism and Unrealistic Expectations

EMBARRASSMENT

People and social life baffle Asperger's kids. All of the unpredictability, unspoken signals, surprises, and rule breaking can be perplexing. Aspies are often awkward around others and say the wrong things or do something inappropriate, completely unintentionally. As one of our Friends told his mom, "I have a knack for saying the absolute worst thing at the worst possible time."

As their parents, you've experienced some embarrassment, probably when you least expected it. The key is to remember that it's not intentional. They are not trying to insult people or reflect badly on your family. This isn't a discipline issue. This is a case of chronic social blunders, which requires your understanding and guidance.

Damage control is what is needed. What we've found helps the most is to teach our Friends an exit strategy when they've said or done something inappropriate. We teach them a simple plan to minimize the faux pas and lessen the humiliation.

While apologizing is usually a first step for any blunder, it's a particularly hard one for Aspies. They don't see what they've done wrong. If they broke something, it was an accident, so why apologize? If they spoke the truth as they saw it, why should they apologize? Still, we work on apologies as the magic key to help smooth over the episode.

We've noticed that people's reactions seem to depend on our Friends' age. Our younger Friends are forgiven more readily because other kids and adults just sort of write off their awkwardness to youth and immaturity.

Still, when they've done or said embarrassing things, we've taught the younger kids to just say "sorry" and leave. Or, if they won't apologize, at least to say "excuse me" and leave, rather than extend the episode.

In our sessions with teens, we have gone over what to do when faced with a public embarrassment. We've learned that it's best to keep it simple.

For example, one of our girls had the habit of stating loudly (and usually in public) when she needed to go to the bathroom for a bowel movement. When it was pointed out to her that others didn't need (or want) to hear that information and how such an announcement would be perceived, she was so embarrassed that she became very upset.

When our Friends become upset learning about a social blunder it isn't always a bad thing. It means that the new information has a higher likelihood of sticking. Being upset seems to show that it's registered with them and they are more likely to remember that they shouldn't do that the next time. We explained to this Friend that all she should say was "excuse me" and leave. She need say nothing more.

We have discovered that, in general, many Asperger's kids are picky eaters, usually because of taste, smell, or texture sensitivities. Some have gastrointestinal issues for reasons yet to be determined.

One boy in our group has been teased relentlessly by his peers because he has a chronic gas problem. Although his mother tried changing his diet and tried natural remedies, nothing worked. The boy was so embarrassed by the reactions of his peers that he decided to explain the problem—scientifically! This set him up for further ridicule.

In the end, we decided that an adult needed to get involved. By explaining this boy's condition to his classmates and how it couldn't be helped, the adult helped the children become more understanding.

It's not only our Friends who feel embarrassed by their blunders and inappropriate behavior. Often parents feel even more embarrassed for their child because they are more aware of the mistakes being made. They may also feel embarrassed about their child.

One way to handle such embarrassment is to pass out special cards offered by the Autism Society of America. These printed cards discretely inform people about autism and help others to make sense of your son's or daughter's quirky behavior without you having to do it out loud in front of your child.

It's important to remember that adults are the ones who model the behavior for all who are dealing with the embarrassing moment. It's how adults react that will influence how younger folks react. We recommend striving for patience, understanding, and a healthy perspective.

Whenever I meet new Friends in my office, I'll ask them, "Do you have any questions for me?" They often ask, "How old are you?" while their mothers cringe in the background. My reaction becomes a model for how to handle such a social blunder.

I'll respond, "That's a good question; however, it's not one that most adults want to answer because they don't like getting older." This lets the child know that, while their question is valid, age is not something most people like to think about. If you help make sense of the embarrassing question by explaining the unintended offense, then the child can learn why they shouldn't do it.

Barbara Doyle, an autism specialist from Springfield, Illinois, talks about "making sense" of the child's behavior for others who are witnessing it. This means translating Asperger's behavior, in subtle ways, for other people so they can better understand it.

For example, a social coach was with one of our Friends on an outing to a restaurant. The waitress was standing at the table as the boy was trying to decide what to order from the menu. He became more hesitant and more and more anxious. Making decisions is not easy for Aspies, from fear of making a wrong one and being imperfect.

The more anxious he became, the more he stuttered. The waitress was growing impatient and the situation uncomfortable, so the social coach made sense of the boy's behavior for the waitress without addressing it directly by saying to the boy, "You know, looking at all the choices makes it hard for me to decide. Must be hard for you, too."

This statement allowed the boy to realize that he was not alone. He became less embarrassed and more relaxed. Then he was able to say to the waitress, "I need more time. Can you come back, please?"

To make sense of your Asperger's child's behavior is a way to decode your child's actions for others. This can reduce social stress and embarrassment for all.

Just remember that a calm tone and logic go much further and are more soothing to our Friends than any shrill and emotional reaction.

See also Eye Contact, Literal Language, *and* Sensory Sensitivities

EMOTIONS

So much of human emotion is conveyed in the face. And of all our facial features, the eyes express the most information. Guess who rarely makes eye contact? Guess who misses the critical messages?

Studies at Yale University and elsewhere have proven that Asperger's kids, like anyone else on the autism spectrum, not only avoid looking in people's eyes, they often avoid looking at someone's face altogether. The slower neural processing speed of autism makes it hard for Asperger's individuals to take in such fast information as a moving mouth, wrinkled brow, and disbelieving eyes. People's faces change too fast and too much, which confuses our Friends, so they avoid looking.

When Asperger's kids do look at a face, they mostly zero in on the mouth and part of the nose. This means that they miss many clues about how the other person is feeling. In fact, they are very unaware of feelings, period, their own and others'. Being concrete thinkers, facts and thoughts rule while feelings are unfathomable.

What can be done about this?

With our younger kids at Friends' Club sessions, we begin our therapy with pictures of faces from magazines—the more expressive the eyes and mouth, the better. We have the group cut out eyes and mouths. This makes them focus on the expressions in the rest of the face, not just the mouth.

Then we have them paste a pair of eyes and a mouth on a paper plate and hold it up to show to one another. Based on the image, we ask them, "Which face would you approach to ask to play with you and which one would you *not* ask to play?" We try to make them aware of how much the eyes reveal about a person, as opposed to the mouth.

Another option is to use the Emotion Cards in Fun Decks from

Super Duper Publications (at www.superduperinc.com), which show a wide variety of faces and expressions. We play the What Is He or She Thinking? game. It helps our Friends practice reading faces for the meaning.

We also use movies to coach our kids. We play the DVD or video and then pause at random to ask the group to read the face of the person on the screen. We ask our Friends to not only read the emotion on the actor's face, but also to guess what the person is thinking. The two, as you know, don't always go together.

We also explore which feelings we want to show others, and those we'd prefer to keep to ourselves. But first, our young Friends have to become more aware of their own feelings, so we discuss the wide range of emotions that one can feel.

Using Roger Hargreaves's entertaining Mr. Men and Little Miss book series about a large array of emotions, we ask our younger groups to choose a character, like Mr. Grumpy or Little Miss Shy, that reflects their feeling at the moment. One boy said he feels most like Mr. Daydream because he daydreams at school a lot. Another boy chose Mr. Forgetful because he forgets things so often. We get the whole group talking about a wide range of emotions and what they feel like, to help them recognize such feelings in themselves.

With our older Friends and teens, we go into more depth about how people "put on" different masks, depending on the situation they're in. Being literal-minded, our boys naturally think and talk about physical masks. But after we move them away from the idea of tangible masks, we talk about the many faces or "masks" that people wear to hide their true feelings. This also allows us to teach that people change their personas depending on the situation—usually a social situation.

One boy asked, "Why do people wear so many faces when I have only one?" Asperger's folks are born to be such truth-tellers and are so guileless that they truly have only one face that they show people.

Since it is hard for them to understand why someone would want to make their face anything other than genuine, we explain that sometimes people feel the need to protect themselves, or someone else, by either hiding their true feelings or showing a false feeling. This is a tough concept to get across, and it takes lots of different activities and discussions to help our Friends learn to "read" others.

One concrete way to help them understand different emotions is through playing Charades. These kids can name an emotion, but they often don't recognize it and are unable to express it on their own face. Charades offers a chance for them to act it out, teaching them to express it consciously. Then, through practice, it can become unconscious.

We highly recommend enrolling your Asperger's child or teen in drama classes. This allows them to keep working on a range of emotions through the characters that they'll portray. And the good news is that Asperger's kids rarely suffer stage fright because they don't care what others are thinking. They don't worry about delivering their lines, and they enjoy the audience's reaction.

Often when I ask my clients to tell me what their body feels like when they're angry or sad, they'll tell me, "I can't describe it." As surprising as it sounds for such sensory sensitive people, our Friends are not in touch with their own bodies and their emotional reactions. They need to be taught the kinds of expressions used to describe such feelings.

"My body felt like it was going to explode" conveys anger. "My face felt like it was on fire" conveys embarrassment. Providing examples of how to express physical feelings of an emotional reaction will also require you to make the meaning clear, since such expressions are not literal but figurative.

We've played a game called Sensory Mystery Box to help our Friends tell us how their body feels when they're having an emotion. We put a hot or cold or bristly item inside our mystery box—any box that lets you put in two hands, but you can't see what's inside.

Then we ask each Friend to put their hands in and touch that item and tell us how it "feels" to them. We ask them about their bodies and how they feel when they are angry or sad, etc. "Is it like the hot item? Or the cold or the bristly one?" What we are doing is helping them make a connection between a physical sensation and an emotion. It's a lot of fun and the kids love it! Who can resist a mystery?

This activity also forces these kids who are so visual to rely on only their sense of touch. They feel the object and then find a feeling word to go with it. They also learn that there are more meanings to the word *hot* or that a person as well as a thing can be "bristly." This helps broaden their literal language tendencies.

Finally, while we're talking about emotions, it's important to remind you that, as parents of an Asperger's child, you will not see this child form the emotional attachment to you that a neurotypical child will form. That doesn't mean that they don't love you—they do, in their own way. But it won't be the huggy-feely-sharing kind of emotional relationship that you have had with your other children.

You may need to ask them for a hug. You may need to teach them about how and when to say "I love you." Such emotional moments are likely to be awkward at best, nonexistent at worst. All we can say is, please, keep encouraging them to express their feelings and to show their emotions. It may never occur to them to say "I love you," because they figure that you should just know that already, so why should they say it?

Be patient. Be persistent. Be kind. There is hope.

See also Emotions, Intentions, Listening to Others, Literal Language, Perspectives and Point of View, Responding to Others, Selfishness, *and* Sensory Sensitivities

EMPATHY

Empathy varies widely among neurotypicals, but the inability to show it is one of the most obvious traits of an Asperger's individual.

Empathy is about being able to put yourself in someone else's shoes. To see through someone else's eyes. And to feel what someone else is going through. It's a matter of feeling, thinking about, and experiencing what is happening to someone else without going through it yourself.

Some people are far more empathetic than others—nurses rate at the high end of the scale, while botanists are at the lowest end. Showing empathy builds bonds and helps others through tough times. It is considered the basis of morality. Empathy requires self-awareness and recognizing others' perspectives, things our Friends struggle with.

The bottom line is that Asperger's folks do care about others, but are incapable of reading subtle emotional signals or discerning the intentions of others.

Current research attributes this inability to express empathy to a malfunctioning of their mirror neuron system. These nerve cells in the brain enable us to perceive someone else's intentions and to feel empathy toward others. However, in people on the autism spectrum, the mirror neuron system is deficient.

The good news is that a form of empathy can be cultivated. Through training and over time, Aspie kids can be taught to *think* about others, which is close to but not the same thing as getting them to *feel* what another person is feeling, which is true empathy.

For example, one of our Friends' mothers told me how the family was driving to the veterinarian's office to put their old dog to sleep. Everyone was crying, except for her Asperger's son, who was smiling. His reaction upset her until I explained that he didn't know what putting a dog "to sleep" meant—being literal-minded, he didn't know that it meant the dog would die. And he wouldn't know what emotion to show because he had never been through this experience before.

Part of what we do at the Friends' Club is to cultivate our kids' understanding that different people are going to have feelings based on their experiences. Those feelings might be similar to what our Friends have felt before, and if so, we teach them to speak up and say things like, "I'm sorry you're going through that. The same thing happened to me."

What's interesting is that since our Friends can be very sensitive about a lot of things, people often misread such sensitivity as empathy. It's not. It is really very different and not related to feelings and emotions. Instead, it is related to their physical and sensory sensitivities.

When B. J. Freeman, Ph.D., was at the University of California, Los Angeles, she studied typically developing children. She found that the understanding of empathy and perspective-taking occurs between two and a half and four years of age. However, for children on the spectrum, such an occurrence does not take place, which seems to be due to their impaired mirror neuron system.

What Asperger's kids need is for you to explain *why* people feel the way they do. Once our Friends hear the reason behind such emotions, then they often become more accepting and understanding.

This happened with one of my teen Friends when he came into my office very upset. His mother had been quite involved in organizing a memorial service for one of his classmates. This teen couldn't understand why his mother would care about a boy she didn't know or spend so much time and effort helping the other mother plan the memorial.

Once I explained that his mother, having a son herself, empathized with the other mother over her loss, then the boy's anger went away and he became more comfortable. But he still said, "Okay, she gets three days to get over this and then she should stay home!"

You can see why it's easy for people to think these kids are selfish when it's really their inability to fathom the emotional situation.

We have found that while we feel empathy for our Friends with whom we work, such feelings are not returned in the same way. Some children develop a special attachment to us and can express it, but others do not.

What is gratifying is to see the increase in our Friends' abilities to consider someone else's perspective. When they demonstrate sensitivity or an altruistic behavior like asking, when someone is hurt, "Are you okay?" then they will become more socially welcome. They only have to *look* like they have empathy to win people over.

See also Looking Like You're Paying Attention *and* Sensory Sensitivities

EYE CONTACT

Looking someone in the eyes is probably our most crucial social skill. We expect to make eye contact with people when we meet or talk with them. If they don't look us in the eyes, we think there's something wrong. The other person appears to be hiding something or seems disinterested or just rude.

Without eye contact, we just don't make a connection.

One of the most obvious traits of Asperger's people is that they don't look anyone in the eye. It's not that they're hiding something. They're certainly not deceitful. And they are listening, even though it doesn't seem like it since there is no eye contact. But for them, faces are confusing.

One of our Friends admitted that it was hard for him to think if he had to look at someone's eyes. If someone asked him a question, he had to look away to be able to construct his answer. If he looked at the person, he was too distracted by their face and would even forget the question! It has nothing to do with how the other person looks—the physical act of making eye contact is hard for Aspies.

Another Friend said that it was physically painful for him to make sustained eye contact with someone. It's part of his Asperger's sensory ultrasensitivity. Plus, research about the brain has shown that there is a neurological impact in looking at another person directly in the eyes. Such eye contact forces both sides of the brain to work in tandem via the corpus callosum, which is wired differently in the Aspie brain.

There is also evidence that the emotional brain, or amygdala, which helps us know how to respond emotionally to things in our environment, may have a faulty connection with the visual cortex in people with Asperger's. This triggers stress, which causes the heart to pump faster, which makes the Aspie want to look away from a person's eyes to curb his distress.

If Aspies have to look at someone, it's often easier to look out of the corner of their eye rather than straight on with both eyes. Due to this neurological difference, many of my clients have told me, "I can listen to you better if I'm not looking at you."

And as with so much of communication and social elements that we've covered in this book, the Asperger's child can't understand why the rest of us think making eye contact is so necessary.

If and when an Asperger's child does look at someone who is speaking, they look at the mouth, not the eyes. "Of course I look at the mouth," one Friend told me. "That's where the words come from."

Unfortunately, they miss many social cues because the mouth offers nothing of the person's emotions compared to what is expressed in the eyes. A single glance into someone's eyes can reveal so much, since our eyes truly are "a window to the soul." It is very difficult to hide our true intent because our eyes give us away.

If it's any consolation, though, the Yale Child Study Center and Laboratory for Social Neuroscience has concluded that it actually doesn't help if Asperger's kids make eye contact. Why? Because they don't understand the language of the eyes anyway. Even if they looked, they wouldn't know how to read and interpret what someone's eyes were saying. They couldn't tell if someone was interested, bored, irritated, or confused.

The good news, says the center, is that when Aspies focused on the mouth, it actually made them more socially successful for two reasons. First, they were focused on what was being said. And second, by looking at the mouth, at least they were looking at the person's face. This made it look like they were playing the communication game.

So kids looking at someone's mouth as the person talked were doing better than those kids who looked elsewhere, focusing only on objects in the room. Why?

Because by not looking at the speaker at all, those Asperger's kids were the most communicatively and socially disabled. They weren't even playing the game. That's why we encourage kids to "fake like you're listening" by looking in the general direction of the speaker, even though they are already listening without looking.

Eye contact is expected in school and in the workplace. Teachers assume that students are not paying attention if their eyes are not directed at the teacher. Bosses think that employees are being disrespectful and assume they are not listening if they are not looking at them when they talk. Such employees even seem insubordinate. Aspie kids need to learn to show signs of listening—they need to somehow reciprocate to show that they get the message being delivered.

In one of our sessions, the suggestion was given to hang a picture of interest behind the teacher in one of our Friends' classrooms. That way he would look at the picture, but appear to be looking at the teacher. A great idea!

When we work on eye contact at the Friends' Club, it is always within a social context and never out of that social setting. I've seen people hold the head of a child with autism and say, "Look at me." Then they measure the endurance of the gaze, whether five or ten seconds.

Not only can this be painful for the child, but it is also teaching the wrong skill. It is teaching staring and that is *not* what we want them to do. I prefer to say, "Look in my direction" or "Look this way" instead of "Look at me." It may seem subtle, but there is a significant difference.

I teach children and teens with Asperger's to find something to focus on that is behind or near the adult who is speaking. This will give the impression of looking in the adult's direction, even if it's not direct eye contact.

In our group sessions, we play a game called Silent Building. We ask our Friends to pretend to put their voices in a real box, we close the lid, and then they cannot use them. Next we ask them to use only body gestures and eye gazes to help their partner construct something with blocks. One Friend pleaded, "I need my voice!" But he got used to using his eyes, and enjoyed the game even though it was very challenging.

Another game we play is What Am I Thinking? based on the expression, "If you are looking at me, then you are thinking about me," devised by Michelle Garcia Winner. We ask the group to watch one of their Friends' expressions and eyes to figure out what he may be thinking. Asperger's kids don't think you need to see their eyes to know what they're thinking about. To encourage them, I use the prompt, "Thank you for looking at me. That tells me that you're listening to my words."

Obviously, the inability to look someone in the eyes is a major handicap when interviewing for a job. The prospective employer expects a candidate to be straightforward and direct. They expect to be looked in the eye as the job applicant is answering questions, and can find it unnerving if the interviewee never looks at them.

Practicing typical first-interview questions and answers with your teen is an important exercise before they go off to apply for their first job at a pet store (they're good with animals), movie theater, library, grocery store, or computer store (technology is their friend). The less socially demanding the job, usually the better.

Two more games that we play in our sessions to improve eye contact (and conversational skills) are Zoom! and My Ship Is Loaded with . . . (For instructions for Zoom!, see the Conversation section.)

My Ship Is Loaded with . . . is a game intended to improve our Friends' abilities to remember things someone has said, and it also improves their eye contact. By really looking at the person who is speaking, our Friends discover that it helps them make associations to what that person is saying.

Such associations help them remember the item being "loaded" on to the ship. Each person adds one thing to be carried by the "ship" and the next player must recite what has already been "loaded" and then add one more item.

Most of us make eye contact without even thinking about it and most cultures expect it. We want to make sure that the other person understands what we're saying. We watch for their reactions. We check to see what they think or feel about what we're saying. Do they agree? Disagree? Do they seem bored or upset? Then we use these clues to know whether to talk on or to change topics.

We've had success at the Friends' Club in making our kids aware that if they can't read such signs when they're talking, it's okay to ask.

One of our fourth-grade boys had a classmate over for lunch. After talking about a computer game for a few minutes, our Friend asked the other boy, "Am I boring you? Do you want to talk about this?"

The other boy was caught off guard by such a direct approach, and assured our Friend that he wasn't bored. Not convinced, our Friend asked again, "Are you sure you're not bored?" When the other boy said, "No," then our Friend continued talking about the computer game.

This was significant because this Asperger's child realized that if you can't read the eye messages being sent, then it's okay to ask. By asking, you give the other person a chance to change the topic if they want.

What Tony Attwood, who works with Asperger's children and adults, recommends is addressing their avoidance of eye contact up front.

He suggests saying, "I need to look away to help me concentrate on answering your question." At least this way, the other person isn't wondering why the person they're talking to seems to be avoiding looking at them. It solves the mystery and tends to elicit some understanding and more tolerance in the listener.

See also Admitting When You're Scared, Anxiety, Calming Down and Focusing, Further Information About Bullying, Meltdowns, Sensory Sensitivities, Time Blindness, and Writing Things Down

FEAR

We are all afraid of something, whether we are conscious of it or not. Some of us are more afraid than others. Some are afraid of more things than others.

Because of our Friends' supersensitivity to sensory stimuli, their fears know no bounds. The world is a constant bombardment to their senses, and they are easily surprised, upset, and thrown off by their environment. Why do you think they like their home and bedroom so much? A quiet, familiar space indoors is the only place they don't feel under attack from the world around them.

Anything from loud noises and bright lights to darkness and strange smells can upset Asperger's children. One important fact you must know—none of us can ever imagine how deeply and broadly these kids on the spectrum tend to feel afraid.

As one would expect, children with Asperger's syndrome are afraid of things that we neurotypicals would never consider scary. Simple things like an electric hair trimmer or a flushing toilet or hair dryer can terrify younger Asperger's children, reducing them to screams and tears.

What's a parent or teacher or sibling to do?

Is it possible for Aspies to conquer their fears, and if so, how?

The short answer is yes, Asperger's children can overcome their fear of many things, but it won't be overnight. It may not even be within weeks or months. And each type of fear will need to be addressed differently, just as every child will respond a bit differently.

One universal with our Friends is their fear of the dark. That was the #1 answer to my question, "What is something that you are afraid of?" (The #2 answer was "spiders.")

But these are the fears that pop easily into their minds. And when asked, Aspie kids will be quite honest about what makes them afraid. For better or for worse, there are many, many more fears that they forget about until the situation or object arises again and scares them.

Remember that often, Asperger's kids get "stuck" in an emotion. Fear is one of those emotions. Usually when someone admits to being afraid, it allows that person to do something about it and move on.

But our Friends can get stuck and just keep feeling the fear even after they've acknowledged it. They are unable to move past it, so they just keep being afraid.

We've found that it's best not to get into a discussion about what is frightening them. That can make the fear become even stronger, giving it more weight than it deserves.

What's best is to **acknowledge the fear**: "So you're afraid of bees." Then offer up one way to **put it in perspective** such as, "Seeing one bee does not mean that there is a swarm of bees. Plus you can move to another part of the playground to play."

What helps even more is to write down on a piece of paper what you're saying. This gives the Asperger's child a visual tool, something concrete to look at. They can see your written reassurance and reread it, as well as have a way to put their fears into perspective.

In the Friends' Club, we often **practice careful, measured breathing** to make sure that our kids know how to calm themselves when fear strikes. For older kids, we encourage "smart breathing," which is done quietly so no one else can hear them.

After a fearful episode, when your child is calm again, go ahead and **talk about what made him so afraid**. When there is no fear present is the best time to discuss ways for your child to get calm the next time they are afraid of something. It's also good to practice a strategy that they can use to get them through the next time they are scared. (And, yes, a night-light or leaving a bedroom door open is an acceptable way to address their fear of the dark.)

Carefully planned exposure to whatever is generating fear can help to desensitize the child to that object or sound or condition.

The vast majority of our Friends like animals, but one boy was very afraid of dogs. We started by having him play his favorite game near a dog that was resting in a crate in the same room.

After a few weeks, we let the dog out of the crate, starting for three minutes at a time, while the boy played his favorite game in the same room.

Once we had built up to ten minutes at a time with boy and dog in the same room, then we started having the boy walk with the dog outside with someone else holding the leash. And finally, by the end of three months, the boy was walking the dog holding the leash himself. The family now has a therapy dog living with them and the boy does not show any fear of dogs or try to avoid them outside the house.

Also realize that our Asperger's Friends don't know what's next because of their time blindness and inability to predict. They cannot see ahead to the next activity, so they often feel in limbo and uncertain, which makes them afraid and anxious. That's why telling them ahead of time what to expect and even writing it down helps reduce their fear.

See also Acquaintance Versus Friend, Conversation, Intiative, Listening to Others, Manners, Responding to Others, *and* "White Lies" and Sparing Others' Feelings

FIRST FRIENDSHIPS

Our goal at the Friends' Club is for our members to learn the skills to make new friends—some of them have never had a true friend! At our sessions, it is often the first time in their lives that they connect enough with someone to make a friendship.

Where we usually start is with a discussion about what a friend is. The most common answer is that a friend is someone who is loyal and trustworthy because that is what is most important to Asperger's people. Or they say a friend is "someone who is nice" or "someone who plays with you." Yet friends are so much more than that!

So we ask our kids to come up with more traits.

For instance, one of our girls groups listed "honest," "giving and sharing," "able to apologize," "helping," "includes others," and "creative."

We use games and books to help teach the concept of friendship. In *How to Be a Friend: A Guide to Making Friends and Keeping Them* by Laurie Krasny Brown and Marc Brown, the story reveals that friends aren't bossy and, while arguments are okay, meanness is *not* okay. Asperger's kids tend to think that anyone who is smiling must be friendly, and if there is disagreement or conflict, it is very unsettling and stressful and must be bad. With this book and others, we teach them that even among friends, there will be conflicts but there are solutions. We discuss and role-play, so our Friends can see how.

By playing games like Friendzee (available from the Speech and Language Association), our kids have to listen and answer inferring questions, which is not easy for them. There are also some problem-solving questions, and if the player is having difficulty answering alone, we encourage them to ask other kids for help. Since our Friends are reluctant to ask for help, this game makes them reach out and opens the door to forming bonds by working together.

Books like *The Paperbag Princess* by Robert Munsch and *How Humans Make Friends* by Loreen Leedy help us address what a true friend is and how you can tell how much they care. After one reading, a boy said, "The way you are friends is with your heart and your brain." To which another said, "But your heart pumps blood." A quite typical literal Aspie observation.

As we continued the discussion, one boy said, "It's the soul" where friendship takes place. "But," said another boy, "you can't open someone up and see their soul."

Alas, the invisibility and murkiness of friendship baffle our black-and-white Aspie thinkers. They wish they could push a friendship button or see some tangible signs that would tell them who is a true friend and who isn't. But there are no such conveniences, so we keep on explaining the steps and levels of friendship, and so will you.

Tony Attwood points out the similarities in the development of friendship skills and typical child development, which you can learn more about on his Web site, at www.tonyattwood.com.

What we do is to tailor our skills lessons to the age and socioemotional level of our groups. And once we've covered the meaning of friends and their understanding of friendship is clearer, then we move on to explore ways of making and keeping friends.

To make friends, we teach the kids that they have to be interested in others while also being interesting themselves. To show they're interested in others, we encourage them to ask questions, to notice what someone is doing or wearing (for instance, ask about an interesting T-shirt), to ask others about their likes and dislikes—all of these will help.

We also point out that people are attracted to interesting people. That means that you can share your special interests, but not too much. We urge our kids to **make sure that they listen as much as they talk**.

This give-and-take of conversation is a struggle even for many neurotypicals, but for Asperger's folks, it's a special challenge. Yet conversation is the first step to a first friendship, so it really matters. We prime our Friends to be aware of what they're saying. Ask questions. Listen to the answers. Say something nice. Even pay someone a compliment. These are all promising ways to make conversation.

Of course, it takes practice because our Asperger's kids would rather launch right into reporting on their weekend activities or rattle off some new facts they've learned rather than ask someone else some icebreaker like "How was your weekend?" or "What good book have you read lately?" So we practice asking questions and taking turns.

Another important ingredient to becoming friends with someone is spending time together. Going somewhere or enjoying an activity together is how friendship blossoms. We coach our kids to take that first step, which is a struggle because they rarely take the initiative. We urge them to **call (usually with a parent's help) someone** in the group **to get together and play** outside of the Friends' Club session. Many first friendships have been formed this way, we're happy to say.

Occasionally, the kids are so excited to finally have a friend that they become too enthralled to the point of suffocation. As thrilled as the children (and parents) are that a friendship has been formed, it is best to give both kids some breathing room from each other. If possible, keep working on engaging other kids as possible friends or give the new friends time apart, so that the intensity of this first, all-encompassing friendship doesn't snuff it out as well.

We have found that once our Friends make a first friend, it's a significant breakthrough. Not always, but often, they do better at making another friend and another, and learn from each relationship.

And since our Asperger kids have a hard time letting go in general, be aware that it may be hard for them to understand if a friendship is not going to work. You may have to tell them that they must "let go" of that person, especially if there is no reciprocity.

Younger and older people are usually more willing to cut the socially awkward Aspies some slack than their own peers. And often, other quirky kids make good friends for your own quirky child. It helps if you explain that not all friendships are made to last. We all learn from everyone we've grown close to, so it's okay to move on and keep making new friends because there is always more to learn and more people to like.

See also Bullying and Bullies, Empathy, Perspectives and Point of View, *and* Selfishness

GIVING AND HANDLING MONEY

Because Asperger's kids have such difficulty seeing things from other people's perspectives and they have an impaired ability to empathize, the concept of charitable giving makes no sense to them.

It's not that they're selfish in the typical way. It's a matter of only knowing their own view and seeing the world exclusively from their own perspective. This hampers their ability to see others' needs. Unfortunately, it can come across as selfishness to the typical person.

The problem with describing the needs of others is that it's too abstract to inspire or affect our kids and teens. When asked to give money for a charitable cause, Aspies struggle with understanding why this is a good idea or why it's even necessary. They can't grasp it if they can't see it or experience it themselves.

As one boy said to the others in his Friends' Club group when they were asked to contribute coins to buy a game for an abused children's home, "Well, what's in it for us? What game are we buying ourselves?"

Again, he wasn't being as selfish or as unfeeling as he sounds. He truly couldn't understand the concept of giving money or goods to others to make their lives better.

This disconnect can be gotten around through concrete experience. When an Asperger's child is involved in a hands-on, on-site activity for children or adults who obviously need help—like building a house for a homeless family or picking up trash in public places—then they seem to understand the reason for giving and helping others. But it does not come naturally and has to be nurtured.

Related to giving is their naïveté about money and the monetary value of things. Baffled by currency, prices, making change, and keeping track of money, Asperger's kids need a lot of practice and supervision when it comes to handling money and understanding what things cost and what something is worth. Our Friends are quite prone to "give away" things and seem generous although it's totally unintentional.

For example, one of our seventh-grade boys met a boy at his middle school who was interested in the new Star Wars computer game that our Friend had recently received as a gift. Excited that he had something the other boy liked, and wanting to be friends, our teen took the game to school and gave it to him.

The other boy, knowing that it was worth thirty-five dollars or more, said, "How much do you want for it?"

Our Friend said, "How about five dollars?" To him, that seemed like a lot of money, since he had no clue what the game was worth or how much five dollars was. Besides, the Asperger's child wanted to be friendly.

The other boy gladly paid him the small amount, and only after the transaction did our Friend's family find out about it. A new rule was established that this boy couldn't take anything out of the house, even his own things, without first showing his parents or older brother. He promised to tell them what he was planning to do before he took any objects anywhere.

Our kids are also often asked for things out of their lunch by other classmates. Sometimes it's just someone being hopeful, saying, "Can I have your cookie?" or "Do you want that granola bar?" But sometimes it's bullying and blackmail, as in "You can't sit at our table unless you give me your sandwich."

One of our boys was coming home from school every day with an empty lunch bag. His mother assumed that he had eaten it all. Only when the boy insisted one day that he must have a Rice Krispies treat in his lunch did she find out that for three weeks some kids were demanding that he "give" them his food.

Typical of our Friends, the boy didn't realize that he had a choice. He wanted so much to be included in the lunch group that he thought he had to agree, so he kept handing over his food.

This is just another example of why it's so important to keep asking your child about school, to listen for anything that sounds odd and to alert the school if other children are coercing your child to "give" away his lunch or lunch money or anything else of value.

See also Conversation, Curiosity About People, Eye Contact, Initiative, Manners, Responding to Others, Sensory Sensitivities, Social Stories, *and* Taking One's Leave

GREETINGS

Greeting people when we walk into a room or see someone we know comes automatically for most of us. We don't even have to think about it. We just do it. "Hi, Jason. How are you? How did that test go?" or "Hi, Molly. Are you ready for the holidays?"

If we're meeting someone for the first time, we usually offer our hand to shake. If we know the person well, we give him a hug or give her a kiss on the cheek.

But even the simplest greetings are much more complex than we realize. Such nuances as when to speak, what to say, and how much to say are all embedded in the simplest greeting. And for Asperger's kids, all greetings are fraught with pitfalls.

First, everyone expects eye contact when being greeted, yet Aspies rarely look other people in the eye. That lack of eye contact makes our Friends seem aloof or indifferent or even a bit cagey.

Second, Asperger's folks don't see the need to say "hi" because they see that as announcing their arrival. As one of our twenty-year-old Asperger's Friends told his coworkers, "I don't need to say 'hi' when I walk in the door because you saw me come in." To him, greetings have no purpose and seem totally unnecessary.

Third, Asperger's kids have a terrible time remembering names. One mom has told me that her son can't seem to learn any of his classmates' names until March or April of the school year! It just doesn't sink in before that, and even then, he gets kids mixed up. If a classmate doesn't stand out in his mind because of a distinctive look or shared interest, then that person remains anonymous to him.

Fourth, Asperger's kids rarely remember another person's interests or any details about their life in order to ask them about it (unless it has to do with video games or computers). Not only do Aspies not pay enough attention to what others say to be able to ask about it later, they also don't have the natural curiosity about people to ask such questions. This makes it seem like they just don't care about the other person.

And finally, if it's a new person they're meeting, Asperger's kids are at a loss about what to say or how to act. It doesn't occur to them to speak first or to shake hands. To take the initiative is foreign to them. And to make such physical contact is not something they would do.

Which is why, given the importance of greetings and making a friendly first impression, we start each session at the Friends' Club with greetings.

The group leader stands at the doorway as each child enters the room and waits for the child to greet him. We don't remind them because they won't be reminded in the real world. But our standing there is usually a big enough clue to make our Friends realize that they're supposed to do something.

Then, depending on the age of the group, we work on specific skills. For younger kids, we'll write a rule to give them a concrete explanation of greetings so they know what they should do and why they should do it.

For example, to teach our young Friends how to greet people who come to their home, we may embed the rules in a Social Story:

> A nice way to greet people is to look them in the face and say "Hi" along with some kind words. When Mommy's friends come over, it's nice to greet them at the door by saying "Hi" and "How are you?" and other nice words to welcome them. Mommy will like it if I look at her friends' faces when I talk to them. If I say nice things, then they will tell Mommy that I am friendly.

For teens, our lesson in greeting others starts by practicing the whole process, and then breaking down the components into each detail. For instance, we shake our Friends' hands. Then we teach them the three elements to a good handshake:

1. Look the person in the eye.

2. Use a firm grip.

3. Don't shake too long—let go as soon as the other person lets go.

If you think about it, a successful handshake comes down to the right amount of pressure for the right amount of time.

Along with greetings, we work on improving the kids' skills at casually talking to others since small talk is expected to follow any greeting. We have them play Milling to Music, a game that is a little like musical chairs—the kids wander around the room while the music plays, then stop when it stops. They turn and ask the closest group member some questions about themselves.

When the music starts again, the kids move on until it stops and then they talk to a new person about themselves. At the end of the game, we have them say something about each of their Friends in the group. This is what greetings and initial conversation are like—the ability to make superficial yet important contact among individuals, and to seem approachable and friendly to others.

With the older kids, we have them interview one another for a few minutes. Then they have to introduce the person they were talking with to the rest of the group. This reinforces what the interviewee told them, which helps seal it in their memory a bit more.

Of all the elements of greetings, eye contact is the toughest one for our Friends to tackle (please see the Eye Contact section as well).

First off, for some Asperger's individuals, it is physically painful for them to look someone directly in the eyes. It truly is a sensory issue. For others, it's just distracting and they can't think and express themselves as clearly as they can if they look away.

Others can't listen as effectively while making eye contact. I've had a client tell me, "I can listen to you better if I'm not looking at you."

Based on what we know about the brain, looking another person directly in the eyes is a neurological activity. Visual information passes to the amygdala, or the emotional brain, determining the child's response.

According to an article in the July 2007 *Scientific American* about the mirror neuron system, the connection between the visual cortex and the amygdala is altered for an Asperger's individual. This triggers a stressful reaction, which makes the Aspie want to look away from the other person's eyes. It's actually easier for them to look out of the corner of their eyes than to make direct eye contact with another person.

Of course, if we really think about it, it's not absolutely necessary to look the other person in the eyes when we're talking to him. It is a social convention, important to neurotypicals but not to Asperger's kids. Yet it means a lot to most of us to make eye contact. It conveys the impression that the other person is listening to what we are saying. It tells us, nonverbally, that they care.

If we can't achieve a straight look in the eyes with our Friends, we do urge them to at least look in the speaker's general direction. This will make it seem like they are listening, which they are, but more important, it will look like they are interested in what that person has to say.

For our kids to make friends and mix with others more easily, such skills as making friendly greetings, smiling, and establishing eye contact are worth working on.

See also Appearance, Awareness, Dating
and Gender Talk, Embarrassment, Fear,
Manners, Perspectives and Point of View,
and Sensory Sensitivities

GROOMING AND PERSONAL HYGIENE

One of the biggest hurdles faced by our Friends is how unaware they can be about personal hygiene. Granted, some of their avoidance is due to sensory sensitivities—shaving feels scratchy, brushing teeth hurts, electric hair-trimming clippers are too loud and tickle.

For some, they lack the coordination to brush, bathe, and wipe independently and need assistance.

For a few, it's about keeping things the same. A haircut, as one boy said, might make him "look different" so he refused, fearing change.

But for most, it's simply not being aware.

Also, outward appearance just isn't important to Asperger's folks. And their inability to understand another point of view prevents them from understanding why it's important to anyone else.

Yet, as the rest of us know, basic cleanliness is critical to making a good first impression. And a good first impression is critical to making a new friend. And if you want to make friends, you have to think about other people and make concessions, even if, as with good grooming, you don't think that it is important.

What our Aspie Friends prefer is comfort over fashion, practical over appropriate. And they are interested in things and how they work, not how clean or attractive they are to others.

Just for the record, it is not laziness that keeps our Friends from bathing. They don't have an aversion to water or soap. Most of the time, bathing is not even a sensory issue. If Aspies are not bathing and washing their hair, it usually is because they just don't think about it. It never enters their head that they might need a shower or a bath. And to improve their appearance? Forget it. That's no reason.

The same is true about clothing. As neurotypicals, we will look into our closets and say to ourselves, "What is the right outfit for this occasion?" or "Did I wear that last time?" We'll think about different outfits and how different people will react to them.

Not Asperger's folks. While they can think about details and can be very detailed people, grooming is *not* the kind of detail that interests or even occurs to them.

But it does occur to everyone else. And kids at school and coworkers on jobs will notice. Their comments may turn to teasing the Asperger's kid who has greasy, uncombed hair or stains on his shirt. Our Friends already do things that make them stand out socially, so any way they can look less different on the outside is a good thing.

That's why we address basic grooming at Friends' Club. We teach that it's best to establish a routine. We cover brushing the teeth, washing the face, showering or bathing every day (or at least, every other day), and wearing deodorant as necessities of life and part of their routine. Then we break these elements down into steps and reinforce them as "must-do's" for Aspie kids and teens to help them be more socially acceptable.

A visual schedule is a good tool because it shows our kids what is expected of them and when. Verbal directions are often not enough with Asperger's kids—they really need a visual reminder, a list to refer to.

A very valuable book that we've used a lot with our teens is *How Rude!: The Teenagers' Guide to Good Manners, Proper Behavior, and Not Grossing People Out* by Alex J. Packer. It has a wonderful chapter on personal hygiene, and loads of other great advice presented in a conversational, humorous way.

With our teens especially, we've worked hard to make them understand that the impression they make on others *starts* with their appearance, even if they don't think it is or should be important. First impressions are formed by how we look because that is all anyone can go by from a distance, before conversation is possible.

Also, our teen Friends are made to understand how important appearance is in the job market. A first, and even a second, interview can be influenced by one's appearance. Employers won't allow poor grooming and coworkers may be resentful of body odor, greasy hair, or dirty fingernails.

With peers, appearance is the key to blending in. Our teen girls, for example, have responded well to coaching on how to fix their hair so that the style is both flattering and fits in with their age group.

One parent shared that her daughter loved the hair lesson so much that she came home very chatty and picked up a book and read the entire thing (a first for her!). Then the next day, she was willing to do something different with her hair after insisting on braids every day for the previous year. Our Friend fixed her hair by herself, sweeping it up and clipping it in the back for a whole new look. Her mood and her self-confidence improved dramatically, much to the delight of her parents.

In one of our sessions, a teen girl said, "I don't have to be a peacock when I'm really a nightingale."

"But," the leader said, "you do need to be a nightingale with clean feathers that are neat and in place."

The message got through because the leader used the girl's metaphor, a good thing to do when it applies to the situation.

See also Anxiety, Calming Down and Focusing, Change and "Change-ups," Leaving the House, Meltdowns, Self-regulation or "Stimming," Sensory Sensitivities, Social Stories, *and* Writing Things Down

HOLIDAY GATHERINGS

Holidays are filled with sights, sounds, smells, and festivities. The average household hums along at a busy, frantic pace filled with the excitement and energy of the holiday season. It also becomes a more difficult setting for any child on the spectrum to handle for exactly the same reasons.

As sensory-sensitive individuals, Asperger's kids can be easily overwhelmed by too much noise, laughter, and the typical convivial confusion at family get-togethers. What is socially stimulating and fun for neurotypicals is often excessively stimulating and extremely stressful for Aspies. And they can't help it. Their brain is wired with barriers that make it difficult for them to adapt to their surroundings.

During the holidays, routines are usually tossed out the window, yet routine is exactly what Asperger's kids depend on to help them function. The regular world is tough enough for them to figure out, so they depend on doing the same things and seeing the same people in order to cope. The holidays tend to bring new activities and new faces into our household or we go to other people's houses full of strangers, and this rocks an Aspie's boat.

They may become frightened and confused from too much newness or strangeness or the unexpected. They feel comfortable in known situations with familiar people because they've learned how to deal with them. But when anything or anyone changes, then the Aspie has to relearn and get their bearings all over again, which is very, very hard for them. Suffice it to say, holiday time is a minefield for Asperger's kids and teens.

You can make it easier for your Asperger's child by not making them dress up in stiff, starchy clothes that chafe their skin more than the average person's. Or by not forcing them to sit for long periods of time, visiting or eating.

What else can we do to help them navigate these trying times for them, but fun and festive times for everyone else?

There are five areas we've identified at the Friends' Club that are particularly troublesome for these kids around the holidays:

1. **Before your company arrives.** At times, Aspies seem very bossy and controlling because that is how they try to shape the world that is very hard for them to figure out, so that they can fit into it. When new company is about to arrive or a new activity about to start up, it is best to prepare your child by talking about who is coming and what you will be doing. It's also helpful to keep reminding your Asperger's child that the holidays last a short time, only a few weeks. Then things will go back to normal after the season is over.

2. **New activities.** If they start to become anxious and upset by all the new things and overstimulating activities, we teach them to "breathe and count." It's a simple trick of slowly breathing in while counting silently to five or eight, then slowly breathing out to the same count. We've also found that humming can help— either humming a tune they know or simply humming, which gives them a continuous sound to calm themselves.

3. **Too many people and too much noise.** If your child is getting overwhelmed by crowds and noise, it's best to find a quiet place where he can spend some time alone, away from all of the hubbub. Bringing along a favorite object or toy to play with is always helpful in calming him down.

4. **Holiday foods.** There are so many senses involved with food— sight, smell, taste, and touch—as well as the chewing and swallowing (which can be troublesome for some people with autism), that it is a challenge for Asperger's kids to eat familiar foods, let alone new ones. It's best to serve very small amounts of the new food first, and have them try eating it. Then give them their preferred food or something close to it.

5. **Change of routine**. Any kind of visual cues explaining the holiday schedule will help your child see the order of activities. This helps reduce anxiety about the unexpected. Writing out a schedule is effective. If you can't write it out, then counting on your fingers the different activities will give a visual total of the number of activities planned.

As for those times when your child self-regulates through physical stimulation, or "stims," to calm himself down, we've learned it's best to let him do it in order to make him feel more comfortable.

Whether it's rocking or humming or flicking fingers or flapping his arms, these repetitive movements are actually soothing to the Asperger's child, even if such actions seem weird or disruptive to the rest of us.

If everyone is gathered in one room, it's okay to lead your child off into another part of the house to let her continue stimming. These motions will eventually calm the child enough for him to return to the hard-to-figure-out world of the neurotypicals. While the stimming behaviors are usually seen as socially inappropriate, just remember that your child can't help it. It's his or her way of coping with overly stressful situations, and Aspies' unique way of releasing their anxiety.

Asperger's children are not trying to be disruptive.

They're not seeking attention.

They'd stop their spontaneous singing or flicking or flapping if they could, but they can't.

It's not the parents' fault or the hosts' fault or the Asperger's child's fault if the social gathering becomes too much for the Aspie to handle. It's best not to assign any kind of blame to anyone, because it's no one's fault. There is no fault. Finding a quiet place for the child to regain a sense of calm is often the best solution.

What helps many of our Friends is to have a Social Story written about where they are about to go, what they can expect to do, and how they are expected to behave. Seeing in writing what a holiday gathering may be like will help your child be less surprised and better able to predict what is planned. This should make it less upsetting.

Asperger's kids crave predictability, and since social situations are full of people who can be so unpredictable, a written story about the event will help calm them. For example, one of our holiday scripts goes like this:

Holidays are special days when we do things in a different way. Holidays can mean that people who we don't usually see may come to visit. We may eat special foods that we don't eat at other times. Thanksgiving, Hanukkah, Christmas, Easter, and Halloween are called holidays. Usually there is no school on a holiday. Holidays are usually change-ups. This means that we do something different. Change-ups can be okay but I may not like them because they are different. I can try to understand that it's a different day or that I will do something different. Mom is a good person to ask because she can explain what it is that we will be doing. If I have company staying at my house, it means that my schedule will most likely change. Mom or Dad will help me by writing out my new schedule. Fun things can happen with holidays. It can mean presents. I will try to be flexible when there is a holiday.

Please understand that, depending on your child's challenges, Asperger's kids should not be left alone when visiting. An adult should stay nearby to keep an eye on their stress level, which in any big gathering can fluctuate *radically*.

The less familiar the people, the more stressful it is for your child. Taking along books, puzzles, handheld games, and other things from home is wise, to keep him occupied and to offer a comforting diversion.

See also Alone Time, Asking for Help, Compliance, Disorganization, Meltdowns, *and* Sensory Sensitivities

HOMEWORK

Most of our Friends' parents plead with us for any help we can give them on how to motivate their Asperger's child or teen to do their homework. The struggles are endless and the resistance sometimes fierce.

Since most Asperger's kids are bright and interested in facts and learning, the difficulty is rarely from a lack of intellect. What seems to make homework such a challenge really comes from residual stress about school and its social traumas, either real or perceived.

Also, unlike neurotypical kids who need more repetition, Aspies get the information the first time around. Most Asperger's kids have solid rote memory skills. This makes homework seem like a waste of time to them, since they don't understand why they need to go back over things that were already covered in class.

Our Friends also figure out a lot in their heads, so they don't show their work in math or their writing strategies. This backfires because teachers assume that the student is cheating if there is no work to show how they arrived at that answer.

As Tony Attwood has often stated, **the most important educational accommodation for these special needs students is to determine what, if any, homework is truly necessary**. "While homework is tolerable in limited amounts to these children, when time spent begins to exceed an hour, the stress it causes in their mind is much worse than any educational benefit that the studying or homework would have."

Especially when we account for other issues that are involved. Our kids often struggle with more than just their Asperger's. As many as 60 to 70 percent of Asperger's kids have been diagnosed with attention-deficit/hyperactivity disorder (ADHD), either the inattentive type or the impulsive-hyperactive type.

Asperger's and ADHD greatly hinder one's ability to concentrate in class, let alone after school. Doing homework is even harder once the ADHD medicine has worn off, if the child is taking medicine. Written expression difficulties are also common among Asperger's individuals.

No wonder homework is so time-consuming and challenging for many of our Friends! This is why modifying the amount of homework is often the best solution—doing some of it is better than doing none at all.

Unfortunately, homework may be perceived by some Asperger's student as an invasion of their private sanctuary—their home. School is a stressful, sensory-overloaded, socially challenging place for our students. Home is the one place where they can escape the social stresses of the world at large, and especially the school world.

An Asperger's child's bedroom is often his special place, the only place where he can retreat and decompress. By leaving the stresses of the social world outside, he can unwind quietly in his own way at home. To bring schoolwork into that inner sanctum just reminds him of distressing events that may have occurred at school. These events tend to replay in an Asperger's child's head like a video recap of the day, often disturbing and stressing the student all over again.

What can you do to help your child manage their homework?

One thing I've seen work is for the Aspie student to be allowed to do their homework during a study skills period at school. This keeps schoolwork at school and will allow downtime at home for the student.

Allowing your child to spend the first half hour at home after school playing alone in his room before tackling homework also works well for many of our Friends. They need the break. They need the quiet. Teens may want to listen to music and younger kids to play with Legos. A break helps them let go of the day's stresses and feel calm again.

Here are a few other strategies that I recommend to our Friends and their families, but remember that every student is different and any approach should be customized to your particular child:

- During your child's Individualized Education Program (IEP) meeting, when goals and placement options are discussed with your child's teacher and a school administrator, see if you can get the accommodation of no homework or at least modified homework, whether it's every other problem or a few select questions out of the whole assignment.

- In middle school and high school, it is usually possible for the student to sign up for one period as a resource class or study hall. If that's not an option, then taking one less class at the end of the day will allow for extra time to get a jumpstart on homework at home.

- Of the homework assigned, see how much of it is practice on skills that the student already demonstrated that she can do at school. If it is a lot of repetitive or redundant work, then ask the teacher about reducing the number of problems for your child.

- The goal is to be sure that the value of the work outweighs the stress and anxiety of having homework invading the safe place that they call home. Again, communicating with the teacher and working together to come up with what absolutely needs to be done is the best solution. Most teachers are understanding, especially once they see that Asperger's children are interested in learning and know the material—as proven on quizzes and tests (which they may need extra time to finish, an accommodation that should be in their IEP).

- Whether a community or four-year institution, college is within reach for Asperger's teens who enjoy learning and who want to enter a particular field of interest or chosen career. By all means, use college as a motivator for them to do their homework. It provides a logical reason for them to make the effort. Homework, modified or otherwise, will be expected in most subjects, and doing high school homework is good preparation for the even greater academic demands at the college level.

- Your Asperger's child is naturally disorganized and unlikely to ask for help. This double whammy means that you will need to provide backup. Go to the teacher Web sites to make sure that the assignment directions are correct. Send teachers an e-mail or note if anything is unclear. Establish routines to help your child get in the habit of handing in his homework, bringing home new handouts, and writing in his agenda about future class projects and due dates. Repetition and practice help build study habits, making homework less of a chore and more automatic.

- For standardized testing, extra time is usually available to students with an IEP as part of their accommodations. However, for college entrance exams like the PSAT, SAT, and ACT tests, you must make a formal request for extra time that is submitted to the State Department of Education. Since approval can take a few months, you'll want to ask well in advance of the exam date. For such a request to qualify, it requires previous psychological-educational testing and evaluations like those done for an IEP. Ask your child's education specialist for assistance.

When Asperger's teens' test scores and grades are strong enough to gain college entry, that doesn't mean they no longer need support. These students will usually continue to need accommodations and various types of academic and life skills support throughout their college career.

Many campuses offer tutorial and special education services but the students need to know how to ask for them. These teens must advocate for themselves or get help from a counselor to stay on track and to keep up with their studies.

See also Annoying Behavior, Bullying and Bullies, Literal Language, Perfectionism and Unrealistic Expectations, Sarcasm, *and* Teasing

HUMOR

The concrete thinking associated with Asperger's syndrome, as well as the tendency to take everything literally, tends to hamper the development of a sense of humor—at least, the sort of humor that we neurotypicals enjoy and expect.

Where we can see the irony, sarcasm, and the underlying meaning in what others are saying, and thus the humor intended, that is usually lost on our Asperger's Friends. They have difficulty reading between the lines.

Sure, what's funny to one person is not always funny to another, but at least the intent of trying to be funny is obvious to most of us—but not to Asperger's kids.

Humor is a tough thing to explain. What makes it so hard to understand for Aspies is that humor is often about shared outlooks on life. We laugh at universal perspectives being voiced because it's what we've all thought about or noticed, but haven't dared to say.

Such shared insights are validating. They make us feel less alone, less like we're the only ones bothered by that or that we're the only ones thinking those thoughts.

Asperger's kids have a unique perspective on things. As out-of-the-box thinkers, they see everyday life differently than we do so they often don't see humor in the same things that we do.

Seriousness is rampant in this population because that is how their brains are wired. They take life at face value. They respond to it as best they can, but it's hard for them to navigate. It takes such serious effort just to get through the day that life is not a laughing matter.

One of the first things we do at Friends' Club is work on *smiling*. Just to get some of these kids to smile is a huge achievement, but an important one. A smiling person is much more approachable and can make friends more easily than a frowning one, so we work on smiling.

Laughter is also one of the great stress reducers in life. When we can get our Friends to laugh during a game or activity, that is a huge relief to them and to us. Humor loosens up all of us. It takes away some of the rigidity that often accompanies Asperger's.

When they finally crack the code on understanding jokes, Aspies can be quite funny and creative. One of our younger boys came up with his own joke: What is the first number a baby says? Goo-gool-plex.

With joke-telling can come the problem of repetition. Our Friends like to tell their joke so much that they repeat it over and over again. We have a big rule that we use in groups: "The first time is funny, the second time is not so funny, and the third time can be annoying."

The next level, if possible, is to show them that it's okay to laugh at themselves. This is especially hard for Asperger's individuals because, so often, they think they are always right. They don't like to make mistakes or to be told that they're not as perfect as they think they are. So how could they possibly laugh at themselves?

But to be able to admit being human, and to laugh at themselves, not only reduces some of the burden of their perfectionism, it also makes them more approachable and likeable. This opens the door to new friendships.

To help loosen things up in our groups, we've borrowed Michelle Garcia Winner's "rubber chicken moment." This tactic encourages our kids to laugh at themselves and their mistakes. Whether it's truly a rubber chicken or some other funny-looking object, we make it available to kids during our sessions. When they know they've made a blunder or said something they shouldn't have, they take the chicken and tap themselves on the head, saying, "It's a rubber chicken moment," which makes everyone laugh.

If someone else goofed up, then they tap that person lightly on the head. Turning a mistake into a humorous incident helps the kids realize that the world won't end if they do something wrong. This is an important concept for them to learn.

When it comes to practical jokes, we teach our Friends that it makes a big difference depending upon *whom* you play the joke. One person might think it's hilarious while another might be offended and get very mad.

More often than not, our Asperger's kids are the butt of a practical joke, not the perpetrators. They make very easy targets since they rarely see anything coming. In our bullying lessons, we teach them the difference between a joke and harassment. If someone is smiling when they say something, that fools our Friends into thinking that the person is saying something kind and means well. It's difficult for our kids to know when people are truthful or sarcastic, or when they're laughing *at* them or *with* them.

Friendships are usually based on a shared sense of humor, so being able to laugh and make others laugh is a valuable skill. It keeps friendships going, through good times and bad.

Finding the humor in situations is also critical for those who raise or work with Asperger's kids. As serious as it can get sometimes, and as frustrating, being able to laugh lightens everyone's load and restores hope.

As with anything, modeling the behavior you want your child to adopt is the best way to teach it . . . so keep the humor flowing!

See also Bullying and Bullies, Disorganization, Perfectionism and Unrealistic Expectations, Perspectives and Point of View, Problem Solving, *and* Writing Things Down

INDECISION

"What would you like?"

"I don't know."

"What wouldn't you like?"

"I don't know."

As strange as that exchange sounds, it happens all the time with Asperger's folks. Deciding what they like and don't like means that they have to tap into their feelings, and that doesn't come naturally to them. With Asperger's, thoughts come first and the rational brain receives messages before the emotional brain, where the feelings reside.

You'd be surprised how many decisions are based on feelings, not logic. Every day, we need to consult our emotions to figure out what we want to do.

But it's more than that. Other factors besides feelings contribute to an Asperger's child's inability to make decisions. Part may be from perfectionism and the fear of making the wrong decision, so they make no decision (which is a decision in itself). They may be paralyzed because they can't picture an answer. If they can't picture what's being asked of them because it's too abstract or beyond their personal knowledge, they are at a loss for making a decision about it.

For example, one mother took her twentysomething Asperger's son to the grocery store. They had company coming over that night and she was looking for appetizers to serve. "What should we have for hors d'oeuvres?" she asked him.

Her son just stood there in the deli section with dozens of options of cheese, dips, meats, and so on in front of him, and said, "I don't know." He was devoid of a decision, being bombarded by too many options, too blank of a slate, and with no guidelines to follow.

Seeing that he was stumped, but wanting him to practice making such a decision, the mom rephrased the question. "If you were at someone else's house, what would *you* like to see for appetizers?"

Ah, now that was different. He knew what he'd eaten before and liked. He could picture the kinds of grazing food that he'd enjoyed. This kind of question appealed to his personal experience instead of the more blanket, sweeping question, "What should we have?"

Since Asperger's folks see things from their point of view, it's best to start there—their point of view—before asking them to think about others.

Being indecisive can be more debilitating than you think. Our Friends end up stuck, unable to move forward, which usually frustrates and may even anger whoever is waiting for an answer. It's just one more way that our Aspie kids are misunderstood in a world that expects everyone to hurry up and keep up.

One of our teens remembers how in first grade, his teacher told the class to "Draw a picture of anything." While all the other kids set to work, picking up crayons and filling their blank paper, our Friend just sat there for twenty minutes, totally stymied. He had no idea what to draw. The teacher's general statement was too abstract. Nothing came to mind. If she'd said, "Draw an animal" or "Draw a person" that would have been different. But he had no idea how to decide what to draw without more specifics.

Looking back, he realizes that it was at *that* moment when he knew he was different from all the other kids. In first grade, he became aware that the other kids all knew what to draw and what to do next, and he didn't.

To help our groups, we incorporate decision making into our activities and conversations at Friends' Club. We always have a general schedule written so that the kids can see what to expect: "Activity: SPLAT!" "Book: *Tacky the Penguin*," "Snack: Goldfish crackers," and "Good-byes."

While playing an activity, there are always decisions to be made—what color playing piece you want, who goes first, who will you pair up with, whether to have teams, etc. If it's a building project with Legos or blocks, then there are even more decisions to be made—where do you start building, who will help whom, what will you make, etc.

We always have a predetermined curriculum and have chosen the books and games ahead of time to reinforce or practice a certain social skill. But once that routine is well established, we've discovered that it's good sometimes to not fill in the schedule and to leave that for our kids to decide. This helps them learn to make up their minds and to work together. We call it "Build a Schedule" and it's good training for real life, when they'll have to learn to schedule their own time.

For the younger kids, we still prewrite the general categories: "Activity," "Book," and "Snack," and then we let them choose. This requires them not just to talk to one another but to listen to what the other kids want. Then a fair way of deciding must be agreed to.

With our older Friends, we leave the whiteboard completely blank. It's up to them to decide what to do with the hour. They need to suggest activities, books, discussion topics, and snacks. They need to listen, cooperate, and compromise. Inherent in the planning is decision making.

The most challenging thing is to figure out how to decide as a group what to do—vote and have majority rule? Do it one way this week and agree to do it the other person's way the next?

What our Friends don't always grasp is that life moves on and whether you make a decision or not, people and time keep going. Stronger personalities, savvier and more conniving characters could persuade an Asperger's child to do something if the Aspie hasn't decided how to act. Ideally, our kids will be around people who won't take advantage of their inability to decide and their paralysis in the face of choices.

What you can do to help is to keep offering them opportunities to make choices, small and large, so they can practice this important life skill.

INITIATIVE

Reaching out.

Taking the first step.

Picking up the phone and calling someone.

Going up to someone to ask if they want to come over to play or go out to a movie.

None of these actions would occur to an Asperger's child to do because all of these actions require taking the initiative. Being the first one to make a move, especially a social one, is foreign to them. It is something that does not come naturally to Asperger's children or adults, not even to those who say they wish they had friends.

Partly it's because Aspies are unaware of the give-and-take necessary in any healthy friendship. Partly it's because they have no idea where to start, or what to say, or that it takes someone reaching out to make an activity happen.

Mostly, though, it seems to be from their impaired mirror neurons. According to research done by Vilayanur S. Ramachandran at the University of California, San Diego, dysfunctional mirror neurons are what would cause language deficits, poor imitation abilities, and an absence of empathy. This condition means they lack mindsight, the ability to sense someone else's feelings or thoughts, a term that was coined by Simon Baron-Cohen, an autism expert at the University of Cambridge in England.

Mirror neurons are special nerve cells in the brain that appear to be the basis for learning, empathy, and compassion. They allow us to sense other people's feelings and deduce their thoughts, even when they're not expressed out loud. This ability is at the heart of empathy, and these mirror neurons seem key to our being able to form connections with other human beings.

Researchers are convinced that without functional mirror neurons, the urge and ability to reach out and form connections with others is compromised. This inability to take initiative is a big reason that Asperger's people can feel so isolated and unconnected to other people.

To counter this social skills disability, we work with our Friends' Club members on everyday tasks that you and I take for granted but that will build their social connections. And the good news is that they can learn by rote, from having the skill broken down into each small step and then modeling them.

For example, in helping them plan to get together with someone else, we start with their own group. We have our Friends in the room ask for another child's phone number and have them write it down.

Then we tell them to call that person before the next meeting, just to say "hello." This is actually quite foreign—and hard—for our members because they see communication as strictly for information sharing. To be expected to make small talk and share vague pleasantries is baffling.

When someone at the other end picks up the phone, our Aspies often forget to say who they are because they think the other person should just know it. They blurt out what their idea is but, if it involves setting a time and place and transportation details, they're at a loss.

Planning is not their forte. Scheduling is beyond them. Blame the frontal lobe deficits affecting all Asperger's kids for their inability to be organized and their lack of time management and sense of direction. But these challenges shouldn't stop them from trying to reach out and plan activities with friends.

So we rehearse various scripts of how to set up a playdate, knowing that the parents will need to be involved for the actual execution of the event. And we urge parents to help their child follow through in making the calls and making the arrangements because, as in anything, practice makes perfect . . . or at least, in this case, practice makes possible.

As many of you know, it's the same in the classroom. Our Friends are good at absorbing facts but may be confused by the whole lesson.

Even if they have questions about in-class assignments or homework, do they ask for help?

Of course not. That means that they would have to take the initiative.

Our Asperger's Friends need encouragement, reminders, and prodding to speak up to ask for help. A step-by-step written script is helpful for specific requests, to give them the words and visual cues to look for when speaking to a teacher: "I will go to my teacher. I will say, 'Ms. Wilson, I don't know what will be on the test. Please tell me which chapters to study.' I will write down what she says in my notebook."

And if you know that your child is coming home from school confused and with questions that he didn't ask, please contact his teachers to let them know. Ask them if they would please go to your child in class and ask if he has questions, until he learns to do it himself.

While some teachers may think this will make more work for them, it's actually going to make their job easier! If a student is less frustrated and less confused, he will be better able to do the assignment.

Finally, here's a classic example of our Friends' true inability to take initiative. One of our six-year-olds goes to Chess Club for an hour every Friday after school. Then his mother picks him up to come to Friends' Club.

One Friday, he had a substitute teacher who didn't know that she was to send him to Chess Club when school let out. While the other kids headed to chess on their own or headed home, this boy left the class and sat out in front of his school for the whole hour, waiting for his mother.

Even though he was waiting a long time, it never occurred to him to take the initiative to go ask the school secretary to call his mom. It also didn't occur to him to look in his lunch box for a snack since he was starving or to go inside and ask to use the restroom, even though he needed to go.

When his mother finally came, he wasn't angry. Having no idea how much time had passed, all he said was, "I thought you forgot me."

Being unable to take initiative or ask for help means there are lots of missed opportunities for our Friends. It's not that these kids don't want to initiate and communicate with people. And it's not shyness. It's that they don't know how to make that first move and they are very awkward when they try.

Our Asperger's Friends lack the bridge-building ability to reach out slowly to get to know others and to get known themselves. They want friends and want to initiate with people, but their awkward attempts tend to put people off.

Teaching them to take the initiative is an essential communication skill that will serve them well throughout their lives. It won't be easy, but it's worth the effort.

See also Bullying and Bullies, Dating and Gender Talk, Peer Pressure and Avoiding Dares, Sarcasm, Slang and Idioms, *and* Teasing

INTENTIONS

What people say and what they mean can be very different, especially if the person is trying to mislead or trick someone.

Detecting the intentions of another person is one of the greatest challenges faced by our Asperger's kids. Learning to read between the lines of someone's spoken message to discern their true intention is something we work on all the time at Friends' Club. Our kids are so easily deceived by dishonesty and teasing, we want to open their eyes to what's really going on.

One way we do this is to teach the kids that a person with a bad intention will often disguise the suggestion with nice words. And if our Friends do what that person suggests, they'll get in trouble. We clue them in that even with the nice words, the true *intentions* are far from nice. In other words, the person with bad intentions will not always use mean words, which would tip off our Friends about what's really up.

Research has shown that in any spoken message, 55 percent of the meaning comes from body language, 38 percent is in the tone, speed, or way it's being said, and only 7 percent of the meaning comes from the words. Aspies don't look at the speaker, so they miss the body language. They don't pay attention to the tone of voice or how it's being said. They only hear the words, and those they take literally.

No wonder that they miss all the clues to the true intentions behind the words, and are easily duped. Our Friends often become the butt of a joke or get in trouble for doing something that "seemed" okay.

Fortunately, our kids are visual learners. We show them clips from movies to provide concrete examples of bad intentions being disguised. The movie *Never Been Kissed* is a valuable teaching tool. It's best for seeing and identifying the intentions of the characters. We stop the film and point out the difference between looking out for one's best interests and malicious motivation. We also replay scenes to reinforce the lesson to make our kids more aware.

We're particularly concerned for our girl members as they enter the socially charged environments of middle school and high school. With our tween and teen girl groups, we go into greater depth about the difference between what is being said and what is really meant by it.

The subtleties of everyday conversation, let alone slight flirtations and blatant come-ons, are too much for our Friends to grasp, making them easy targets.

One of the best things that parents can do is to talk with your kids about their school day *every* day. Ask specific questions about whether anything was said or done that they didn't understand or thought was odd. Ask if it happened in class or, more important, out of class. If you wait for your child to tell you without prompting, it may be too late to intervene or to keep the troublesome situation from festering and escalating.

We also advise you to make sure your child has a point person at school to go to when they are upset or having a meltdown. Whether it's a teacher, school psychologist, or librarian, your child needs to have a trusted adult who will be understanding and helpful until the matter is resolved or you are called.

Our Friends feel isolated and uncertain among their peers. That means going to another student is not the answer in a crisis. If your child thinks that he is getting taken advantage of by another student with bad intentions, he needs to go to an adult for help.

And finally, we have a Golden Rule that we tell our Friends to remember whenever they're in doubt about someone else's suggestion:

If it seems like a bad idea, *it is.*

If it doesn't sound right, *it's probably not.*

If you don't think you ought to do it, *then don't!*

Ultimately, it's better to err on the side of caution since our Asperger's kids miss so much of the meaning behind the message.

See also Anxiety, Change and "Change-ups,"
Fear, Letting Go and Refocusing, Meltdowns,
Moving On to New Things, Sensory Sensitivities,
Travel, *and* Vacations and School Breaks

LEAVING THE HOUSE

So many parents have come to me and asked, "Why does my child always want to stay home and never go anywhere?" or "How can I get her to go someplace with us without a fuss?" Then, with a mix of despair and exasperation, "Will he ever leave home and live on his own?"

All of these highlight the Asperger child's preference for the comfort and sanctity of home. Asperger's kids are inclined to stay indoors where they're not bombarded by the too-bright sunlight. Or the too-loud noises of trucks, planes, and blaring car radios blasting by. Or the chaos of pedestrians hurrying every which way or the struggle of trying to cross busy streets with unpredictable traffic.

Staying home means that an Asperger's child or teen can avoid sensory overload, upsetting surprises, and much social discomfort.

It's not easy for them to contend with the real world, but as we all know, the real world isn't going away either. What we strive for at the Friends' Club is to prepare our kids for stepping out of their protective shell of home life. We want them to function as well as possible at school, social events, and later, in the workplace.

We work with our older kids, and especially teens, in having them be more open to going out in public with family and others. It's not easy for them, but it's not impossible either. If we can lure them out by dangling something fun, then it will increase their tolerance and flexibility in leaving the house and, ultimately, enrich their lives.

As with so many new things, our Friends balk at first. But once they actually try it and get over their initial worry about change and a new experience, then they discover that they enjoy the outing. This, in turn, makes them more willing to go out the next time.

Of course, we break it into small steps. We talk about an outing to a local store or coffeehouse or restaurant within walking distance. Then we tell them what to expect when we get there—whether it's noise from video arcade machines at the pizza parlor or karaoke at the restaurant. We remind them that they may need to wait for change after buying something at the convenience store.

Then we tell them to expect to go during the next week's meeting. And as always, facing one's fears is the best way to conquer them.

After encouraging our Aspie boys and girls to venture out like this and face new situations, with a few adults to monitor and guide, we've seen them relax more in public. They do become more at ease in new settings, and even more animated and talkative. When they return from these outings, they're still talking about the shared experience.

So, to recap, why your Aspie child is most comfortable indoors and at home is because it's the least stressful place for them in their sensory and socially sensitive state.

You can get your child to be more willing to leave home for outings by talking about or writing down where you're going to go, what will be going on when you get there, and how long you will be staying. It's important to reassure them that you will be close by to help them adjust to the new surroundings. This pretalk for the outing is important, to give them time to get used to the idea and to give them a mental picture of what to expect. If you have real pictures of your destination, do show those, too.

As for the big question, whether your child will ever be able to live on his or her own? It all depends on the individual. Unlike more severe autism, Asperger's syndrome is surmountable to a degree. Many Aspies are able to finish high school, go on to college if they work hard enough to get good grades, and later to find jobs that cater to their strengths (or sometimes, obsessions).

Remember that Albert Einstein, Hans Christian Andersen, and Andy Warhol are all considered by many to have had Asperger's. So instead of worrying and seeing your child's differences as a negative, it's a good idea to look at their out-of-the-box thinking and fresh insights as a plus.

With your help or their school's help, they could easily land at an enlightened company, university, or a forward-thinking research institution smart enough to value the kind of unconventional thinkers and trailblazers that Asperger's people are. There are many places that offer our Friends the opportunity to be who they are and to be creative in their own way. They just need to find their niche.

So, yes, there is hope—we just have to get them through childhood.

See also Anxiety, Calming Down and Focusing, Change and "Change-ups," Compliance, Meltdowns, Moving On to New Things, Obsessions and Obsessive Behavior, Sensory Sensitivities, *and* Writing Things Down

LETTING GO AND REFOCUSING

Obsessions and an inability to let them go is a very common concern among families with an Asperger's child.

So many of our Friends get caught up with a particular idea or question or object. They are unwilling and truly unable to switch to something else. To keep from driving themselves and their parents, teachers, or employers crazy, our Friends need help in getting unstuck in order to refocus.

Fixating on an idea or object is called *perseverating*. Asking the same question over and over, or focusing on a detail to the exclusion of all else, is one way that many Asperger's kids counter their stress when meeting a new person or walking into a new situation. They feel more confident knowing that they know the answer to that repeated question. They crave predictability and the reassurance it gives them.

Perseveration is all too common with Aspies. Many of our Friends tell me their minds seem to run nonstop, obsessively thinking about something, even when they're trying to sleep. One of our teens says that he goes back to his birth date for comfort "because I know it will *never* change. It's an anchor." Always having the same answer is reassuring.

There are several techniques we use at the Friends' Club to help Aspies conquer their obsessive behaviors.

First is a relaxation strategy. So often the perseveration is worse when Asperger's kids or teens are anxious and suffering from sensory overload. It's very safe to assume when your child is overly focused on something, especially on an object, that he is anxious about something else. Usually, it is the social setting where he finds himself.

Social interactions constantly change, which is unsettling. So Aspies resort to fixating on something concrete that won't change. But this is disruptive to neurotypicals, and prevents sociable conversations and interactions.

One relaxation technique that works for our Friends is simply to breathe in, very slowly, while silently counting to a certain number, then exhale to the same count. Repeating this a few times helps calm the individual.

Another is to hum for a minute or more, which seems to calm them as well as loosen their grip on their fixation.

Speaking of numbers, this is one of the reasons that so many Aspies love math. Math problems offer finite answers that never change. The fact that one plus one equals two, and always will, is a great comfort to the Asperger's girl or boy who otherwise feels at sea in a too changing and too confusing world.

After working on relaxation, one strategy to break the obsession is to turn the repeated question or thought into something more concrete that your child can visualize. Many times, I've written the child's thought or the name of the object on a piece of paper. Then I put it in a compact disk case or drawer. When it's shut inside, I tell the child that it cannot come out until we've finished doing what we're doing. Being rule followers, Asperger's children usually obey such a command.

This technique has worked well in the group setting many times, too. When one of our members has a repetitive thought that is taking over the work we're trying to do with the group, one of the leaders will write the name of the object or thought on a piece of paper and put it into a box or CD case. The child is told that it cannot be talked about or handled until the end of the session. It's amazing how well this works.

Because of the technological leanings of our Friends, referring to computers also works. I've often told the person who can't let go of an idea to "take it off your desktop." The visual of their obsession being an icon on a computer screen clicks with these kids. They seem to accept having it "removed" and the obsession disappears, allowing us to move on to something else.

A written schedule has been effective. If you write down what is going to happen, this visual tool can make your child feel less stressed and more assured. Writing down rules that discourage an obsession can also work. We have had to make a rule about jokes because our Friends can become obsessed with telling the same joke over and over. We write down: "The first time is funny, the second time is not so funny, the third time can be annoying."

Remember though, getting angry is not going to help. Shouting, yelling, or any other strong emotion only stresses these kids out more. An Aspie child asking the same question over and over is not trying to drive you crazy, even if it does. They repeat the question because they are comforted by already knowing the answer. So the calmer you remain, the better for all.

Write down what they're saying, put it in a drawer, and tell them that they can't talk about it for an hour. The next time, make it two hours . . . then three . . . and so on.

I've learned that when a child comes into my office for the first time and focuses on an object, like a lamp or a picture on the wall, to the point of overfocusing, it's merely their way of countering the stress they're feeling over meeting me, a new person, or being in a new place. I refocus their attention by engaging them in playing a game or asking them easy questions or letting them ask me questions.

The kind of stress triggering this obsessive behavior is not the kind that neurotypical parents or teachers would experience in the same settings. But that shouldn't stop any of you from trying to help reduce these kids' stress as soon as possible. Once you do, then it will open the door to refocusing their attention on what you want them to notice or learn.

The key is to address only the bad experience or personal setback *once*, then move on. While other people may need to revisit a problem over and over in order to think through the solution and process the changes that need to be made, our Aspie kids tend to get more stuck and unable to move on if too much attention is given to a problem or hurtful incident.

Discuss a bad experience once, so it will be aired and released from the silent loop cycle going through your child's brain. Then calmly and logically state that it's time to move on. This helps Aspies get unstuck and allows you to refocus their attention on to something more current and productive.

See also Conversation, Eye Contact, Manners, Perspectives and Point of View, Responding to Others, *and* Rudeness

LISTENING TO OTHERS

Socially successful people listen to one another. As one person speaks, the second listens or at least acts interested in what the other person is saying. Being able to listen well to someone else is a fundamental skill.

It makes or breaks friendships.

It determines success in school and in the workplace.

Active listening is a lifelong skill that makes it possible to connect with fellow human beings.

That is why one of our Friends' fathers became so concerned when he was watching his son's group in action. He noticed that his son wasn't listening at all! In fact, the boy wasn't even acting interested in what was being said. This became one more worry added to the long list of worries that the father had about how his son would function in the outside world.

An Aspie's lackluster listening seems to be caused by their dysfunctional mirror neuron systems. Mirror neurons enable us to intuit someone else's intentions and to feel empathy toward others. This has been called "mindsight," or the ability to gauge what might be going through someone else's mind. Asperger's folks are mindblind.

Research has revealed those on the autism spectrum have deficient mirror neuron networks, and thus they lack mindsight. They tend to relate to and treat people more like objects than like people. Being only aware of their own perspective and point of view, our Friends don't get that others may think and feel differently than they do.

Consequently, since they're not aware of others' thoughts or feelings, they have little reason to listen.

Fortunately, there are ways to learn how to listen. In Friends' Club, we play a game called My Ship Is Loaded with . . . It teaches players to listen carefully to each other and remember what's been said. (See the Eye Contact section for instructions.)

We also play the Talking Hat game. A very valuable tool, the hat serves as a visual reminder of who is to talk and who is to listen. One member wears the hat, greets the other group members, and says a few words about his day. Then the hat is passed to the next person. Only the child wearing the hat is allowed to talk, which means everyone else has to listen.

We do variations where we give the Talking Hat member a ball. When someone has a question, she raises her hand. The hat wearer tosses the ball to her to speak. After the question, the ball goes back to the hat wearer. Our Friends have such a hard time remembering not to interrupt and to wait for their turn to talk that this visual prop makes it more fun to listen and wait to speak.

Sometimes our groups, especially the girls, can become too talkative (in general, girls are more verbal than boys, including Asperger's girls, which is also why they're not as easily diagnosed, since they appear more social). To help the more talkative girls remember to listen to the others without interrupting, we pretend to put our voices in a box. This really helps keep the group quiet. And when anyone talks out of turn, we hold up the "box of voices" and point to it. The girls respond by getting quiet again, enjoying the pretend play.

We've also talked about what a listening body looks like. We show how we look toward the person who is talking, holding our hands quiet and keeping our mouth closed. Then we practice it during role playing. One boy said, "Look, my eyes are listening!" as he made extremely wide eyes at one of his Friends.

After we've had a conversation in a group, I often go back and ask the members what one person has said. This helps reinforce the importance of listening—you won't know the answer unless you paid attention and really listened.

And when we play games like Apples to Apples, Cranium, or Whoonu, I teach them a strategy that will help them win—concentrate on how others think about things and listen to what they choose. In Apples to Apples, listen to how the judge makes her selections. If she has a sense of humor, she'll choose the funny answer and not the serious one. Listening to what someone chooses in Whoonu is also the key to winning.

It is a struggle, but Asperger's kids can learn to be better listeners. With lots of practice and lots of encouragement, they can interrupt less and pay attention more to what is being said. All of this will reduce their social and communication disability and make them better friends.

See also Humor, Listening to Others, Perspectives and Point of View, Slang and Idioms, Talking with Peers, *and* Teasing

LITERAL LANGUAGE

Have you ever read one of the Amelia Bedelia books for children? The main character is a well-meaning lady who takes *everything* literally.

Asperger's children are Amelia Bedelias. And while neurotypicals can see the humor in Amelia's misunderstanding of idioms and other common expressions, Aspies would side with her strict interpretation until they learn otherwise.

Born to be literal-minded, our Friends take language at face value. Research shows this may be due to deficiencies in their mirror neuron system. Mirror neurons seem to enable us to guess what others are thinking or feeling and to be empathetic.

Unfortunately for our Friends, who are concrete thinkers, language is not always straightforward. Some words sound like they mean one thing when, really, they can mean something completely different.

How do we help Asperger's kids understand idioms, metaphors, and slang, which are such ambiguous and abstract parts of our language?

I've found that the best approach is the most direct approach. In our Friends' Club groups, members learn exactly what the idiom means. Using stories like *The King Who Rained* by Fred Gwynne and other similar books, we teach the meaning of those tricky idiomatic expressions.

With our teens, we use a book on slang called *The Slangman Guide to Street Speak 1* by David Burke. At this age, it's especially important for our Friends to know current phrases and their meanings to keep them from being targets of unscrupulous schoolmates.

When it comes to inferential language, our Asperger's kids also struggle with that. In elementary school, the curriculum requires students to learn how to infer or guess what will happen in any given story. Their ability to do that is measured as part of their reading grade.

Asperger's kids do not infer. They do not try to predict or guess what will happen next because they see no reason to. To them, the story is written, so why rewrite it when someone already has finished it?

When a teacher asked one of our Friends to "give us a different ending to this story," the boy had an anxiety attack. He was convinced that no one could change what was already stated or written. Taking such liberties is totally foreign and even offensive to our kids, causing them stress.

One way to break through this kind of resistance is by finding the right books to show that a story can have different endings. I've found two books to be particularly effective: *Milo and the Magical Stones* and *Milo and the Mysterious Island*, both by Marcus Pfister. Each offers two different endings, one happy and one sad ending. When the reader reaches the middle of the book, he must choose between them.

Our Friends can accept this because the multiple options are pre-written. They are published. They are concrete examples of a story having more than one ending. With two paths already laid out in the story, Aspies see that it is possible and they take the next step to apply it elsewhere. It transfers to the classroom, too, where they are able to guess at endings to new stories they read.

Any books with strong patterns in them such as *If You Give a Mouse a Cookie* by Laura Numeroff and *It's Not Easy Being a Bunny* by Marilyn Sadler also help our Friends learn how to predict what could happen next. When I've modeled making a guess, the kids are willing to try.

As might be expected, these children not only struggle making inferences in literature. They find it just as difficult to make inferences about people. This requires the ability to see things from different perspectives and to accept other options.

In their mind, our Friends assume others think the same way as they do. Their single-mindedness prevents them from taking another view. They are stuck in their own perspective, as well as unable to recognize the cues on someone's face or interpret someone's speech to know what that person is thinking or feeling.

This is why we work so hard on showing our Friends different faces with many expressions. It is possible for them to learn how to recognize what someone else is feeling or thinking with practice.

A final thought on Aspies' literal approach to language: it can make them seem disobedient, confused, and even "bizarre" at times to the neurotypical parent or teacher. Yet, with Asperger's kids, it's best to assume nothing. Hold off on getting angry until you find out what they're really thinking and why they're doing what they do.

We've learned to give them the benefit of the doubt when they don't follow our requests, and to dig deeper. We've learned to ask, "What's wrong?" or "Why aren't you doing what we asked?" instead of assuming that they're being uncooperative. The answers often surprise us.

For example, one of our Friends had to go to a specialist's classroom to print out work from his laptop computer. This room was separate from his classroom. When he came back, he told his teacher that he was told that he could no longer go into that other classroom.

When his teacher asked the specialist about it, she was baffled. She had never told him not to enter the room. A school administrator asked me to find out what was going on.

When I entered the specialist's classroom, I immediately spotted a small sign on the door. It said, "*No* noncredentialed persons may enter this room." It was intended to stop volunteers and aides from using her classroom as a passageway to other rooms.

Well, to the Asperger's boy who came to use the printer in her classroom, this meant that he wasn't allowed to enter the room since he was noncredentialed.

When I pointed this simple thing out to the specialist, she was relieved that a sign had "told" the boy not to enter her room, and it was not her fault. But she was still befuddled.

It took some time for her to understand the black-and-white thinking of the Asperger's mind. There are no deviations. No exceptions. Those on the autistic spectrum do as signs and the people who they believe to be in charge tell them to do, unless told otherwise.

While there is no single solution for undoing their literal take on words, it is possible to teach Aspie kids on a case-by-case basis not to believe everything they read. Being such major rule followers, they are hard to convince that they are exempt from some of the rules posted all over. But it's possible. Case by case, it's possible.

See also Conversation, Eye Contact, Listening to Others, Manners, *and* Sensory Sensitivities

LOOKING LIKE YOU'RE PAYING ATTENTION

When we talk, we expect the other person to look at us. We pick up clues from their eyes. Are they interested in what we're saying? Have we struck a chord? Or are we getting boring?

Asperger's kids find it too distracting or stressful to look people in the eyes, so they look away. While they appear not to be listening, it's not true. They *are* listening. It just doesn't look like they are.

When we expect our listeners to look straight at us, and make eye contact, it bothers us when they don't. It's unnerving. We assume the worst: they are disinterested, discourteous, and disrespectful.

But since Asperger's kids *are* listening, and it just looks like they're not, how do we remedy this situation?

What we've devised are several ways to teach our kids to *look* like they're paying attention, even if they can't look that person right in the eye. Some of our ideas came from Richard Lavoie, a well-known learning disabilities expert. He's taught students how to look like they're paying attention in the classroom by keeping their eyes facing forward, even when they're not interested.

Several techniques work. One is to **do the hit-and-run**, where they just glance at the person and then can look aside. Then, after a few moments, glance again and then go back to looking wherever it's more comfortable for them.

The hit-and-run technique gives the speaker the satisfaction of having been looked at, but also gives the Aspie the freedom from the stress and distraction of looking directly at the speaker's eyes for a length of time.

Another technique that we've taught our Friends is to **look in the general direction of the person speaking,** if not at them. Pick a spot over the speaker's head or shoulders. This way their eyes are pointed in the right direction, which gives the appearance of paying attention without having to actually lock eyes.

A third technique is from Michelle Garcia Winner's social thinking strategies. Michelle teaches her Asperger's students to **tell themselves, "I'm looking at you, so I'm thinking about you."** The act of looking is to remind the Aspie to direct his attention and thoughts to that person.

In teaching our Friends to look in the right direction, we don't want to encourage them to stare at people. Again, with their literal interpretation of language, when we say, "Look at the person who is talking," some of our Asperger's kids do just that—look at the person in a full-on stare. This isn't good either. Staring creeps people out even more than not being looked at, so we don't want to cultivate staring.

Again, we encourage them to look just past the person, or to glance up and then look away at intervals. Both of these strategies are acceptable. However, staring is not.

Once we had to explain to school administrators that one of our Friends was not trying to intimidate a girl in his class by staring at her. We worked with the boy to help him realize that he mustn't fix his gaze on anyone for long periods. It was offensive. Of course, he had no idea it was a problem. And, fortunately, he did stop staring after we talked to him.

See also Acceptance, Anger and Frustration, Meltdowns, Perfectionism and Unrealistic Expectations, Perspectives and Point of View, Social Stories, Sportsmanship, *and* Teamwork

LOSING GRACEFULLY

None of us like to lose, but for Asperger's kids, it can be particularly devastating. It's not that they're hypercompetitive. They're not competitive by traditional standards at all. But it's very difficult for them to lose at a game, any game, whether it's a board game, sports, or a video game played all by themselves.

Why?

For one thing, they don't see the gradations of losing. It doesn't register with them that to lose (or not be first) in some things is not that important, while in other things, it is more important. They don't understand there is satisfaction in playing well, even if you lose.

Another thing is that Aspies, especially our youngest ones, don't understand that the main purpose of playing a game is to have fun, not to win. Even if they know this, they need constant reminding because they forget that the process is more important than the outcome.

Some of our young Friends get so discouraged when they don't win that it overshadows any fun that they could have, and did have, in the playing of the game.

Remember, kids with Asperger's have a strong need for perfection. They dislike being wrong, and losing at a game feels like they've done something wrong. It can be so upsetting that an otherwise nice, gentle Asperger's child turns into an angry, frustrated, tantrum-prone child when faced with a loss.

Because losing—or winning—gracefully is such an important component of a friendship, we keep having the kids in all of our Friends' Club groups play games and practice being graceful losers and winners (and practice taking turns, another challenge for this crowd).

We have found that with steady reminding, our Asperger's Friends do learn that they are supposed to have fun first and foremost, and not worry about winning.

If they become frustrated as the game progresses, we gently remind them why we're playing the game in the first place—to have fun! This helps to defuse their mounting stress.

In some cases, we've needed to write a Social Story for individuals who can't accept defeat. This is a short script that spells out what is going to happen and what behavior is expected. The child reads it before the game, or it is read to him, to put the activity into perspective. One of my favorites is this:

> When I am playing a game with my friends, we will each take a turn. We can count our dice and we can move our pieces in the game ourselves. My friends will like it if I let them take their own turns by themselves. This means that I am being a good sport when I am playing a game. My friends won't like it if I tell them what to do when they are playing. If they want my help, they will ask me. We will play for fun. It does not matter if I win or lose. What matters is if I am a good sport and my friends and I have fun playing the game.

As you can see, a script like this takes a positive approach. It emphasizes what the child *should* do, not what they shouldn't do. This is the kind of help our Friends need. They need to have things spelled out. They need to be told why that kind of behavior is so important—"So that your friend will want to keep being your friend and will want to play with you again."

Losing gracefully is within our Asperger's kids' grasp, as long as they receive help seeing the bigger picture. Our Friends are so locked into their own perspective, they need help seeing how it's not the winning and losing that counts, but how you play the game that makes friendships possible.

See also Apologizing, Bluntness and Unintentional Insults, Compliments, Conversation, Courtesy, Greetings, Grooming and Personal Hygiene, Phone Skills, Responding to Others, Rudeness, Taking One's Leave, *and* "White Lies" and Sparing Others' Feelings

MANNERS

People appreciate and welcome anyone with good manners.

Social situations go so smoothly when guests greet each other warmly, shake hands, pay compliments, say "How are you?" and "Please" and "Thank you," and show consideration in all sorts of small ways.

Conversation flows when everyone takes their turn sharing ideas and insights, and listens well enough to add to the subject at hand.

Dining is delightful and people bond whenever basic table manners are observed—not talking with your mouth full, asking someone to pass you a dish instead of reaching and knocking something over, using utensils and napkins properly. All of these are signs of good manners.

Throw an Asperger's child or teen into the mix, and things rarely go as planned.

Not that Aspies are intentionally ill-behaved or ill-mannered. These children are truly unaware on the one hand, and do not understand the need for niceties on the other. While they can seem rude and unfeeling, they are usually inappropriate without even realizing it.

As purveyors of truth, Aspies often state exactly what they are thinking as they think it, whether it's socially acceptable to say out loud or not. This makes them too truthful by conventional standards. And while their bluntness is not meant to sting or hurt others' feelings, it can have that effect.

Do they apologize? Not automatically. Not without some coaxing. Usually, they don't see the need. They were just telling the truth. What escapes them is that the truth can hurt. So they often need someone to point out why their statement offended the other person, and that the kind thing to do is to apologize.

The good news is that by being born to follow the rules and by appreciating structure, Asperger's kids can learn and remember good manners, if taught properly with continuous reminders.

At Friends' Club, we start with logical reasoning about why each social skill is important to learn. We break the skill down into step-by-step components. Then we ask each Friend to role-play the social situation with the group.

By practicing the new social skill with another member, our kids become comfortable using it and are more likely to remember it.

For instance, we go over what to do if you ask someone at school, "Do you want to play with me?" The answers are scripted as follows:

- Sometimes the person will say, "Yes." That means we can play.

- Sometimes the person says, "No, thank you." That means I say, "Okay," and walk away and play something else.

- Sometimes the person doesn't say anything at all. I can ask one more time. If they still say nothing, then I walk away and find something else to do.

This kind of spelling out of what to say, what the response may be, and how to react to the other person's response is the best way for our Friends to understand how to become more well mannered.

Ironically, I've found that some of our Aspie rule followers can cling too tightly to the good manners they've just learned. Once they've accepted that this is a rule to follow, they may scold their classmates or peers who are misbehaving and not being well-mannered. Our Friends have a hard time understanding that some of their peers think it is uncool to use good manners and that they want to be rude intentionally.

We have made up quizzes on manners, giving our Friends a variety of social situations to solve.

One question, for example, that the leader asks is, "Your friend's mom gives you a ride home from school. When you get out of the car, do you say 'See ya later,' or 'Good-bye and thanks for the ride,' or nothing?"

While the answer is obvious to you, it's not at all obvious to our Asperger's kids. Most of them would say nothing as they left the car.

Why? Because they know the mom can see them get out, so "good-bye" is unnecessary.

And of course they appreciate the ride, so "thanks" is unnecessary.

And they will see their friend and his mom again, so "see ya later" is not necessary.

So saying nothing makes the most sense . . . to our Friends. Case in point of why good manners need to be taught.

One time, in a group session that was working on manners, one of our leaders pretended to be rude by bumping into people and sitting too close. Finally, one of the boys said, "You need to say, 'Excuse me.'" So you see, there is hope.

That same group listened to a series of scenarios about rude behavior. The boys were to put their thumbs up if it was an episode showing good manners, or turn their thumbs down if it was an example of bad manners.

This kind of visual cue with the thumb to indicate good or bad manners is very effective. Aspies respond to and remember visuals. It also lets the kids see what the rest of the group thought, which can be validating.

Surprisingly, a group of our younger girls realized that it was bad manners to pick your nose or pass gas in public *and* it was bad manners to comment on it if someone else did, even though some of our older groups did not know that.

What was funny was that when we asked for a volunteer to act like she was picking her nose, so we could role-play the scenario, no one was willing to do it. Some became very upset. It took us a few moments to realize that they were refusing because they all knew it was bad manners to pick your nose. Only when we made them realize that it was just *pretending* did they change their minds and then they all wanted a turn.

As we've mentioned in other lessons, an excellent book about manners for the tween and teen audience is *How Rude!: The Teenagers' Guide to Good Manners, Proper Behavior, and Not Grossing People Out* by Alex J. Packer. This book is conversational, funny, and packed with great advice for adolescents about the whole range of mannerly behavior.

Many picture books for younger kids have manners, good and bad, embedded in their stories, so we pull from a large selection to highlight particular skills. For the younger kids, the Berenstain Bears series and the Franklin the Turtle series cover many topics about manners. The

"Goofus & Gallant" feature in the monthly children's magazine *Highlights* offers a contrast of good and bad manners.

For tween and teen girls, the American Girl Library publishes *Oops! The Manners Guide for Girls* by Nancy Holyoke. Also effective with many of our groups is *365 Manners Kids Should Know: Games, Activities, and Other Fun Ways to Help Children Learn Etiquette* by Sheryl Eberly.

What's important to remember is that it's better not to work on every social misstep. If too many mistakes are pointed out, your child may feel too self-conscious and too flawed, which leads to hopelessness.

Consider your belief systems as parents and what's most important to you—your social, political, or religious views—and use those as guidelines to decide which skills to concentrate on. Prioritizing will help you know what to ask specialists or other parents, all in the quest of improving your child's ability to relate to others and to be more socially accepted.

See also Anger and Frustration, Anxiety, Depression, Emotions, Fear, Further Information About Bullying, Literal Language, Obsessions and Obsessive Behavior, Perfectionism and Unrealistic Expectations, Perspectives and Point of View, Self-regulation or "Stimming," Sensory Sensitivities, Staying Calm, *and* Writing Things Down

MELTDOWNS

The sudden, unexpected meltdowns of children and teens who have Asperger's syndrome are probably the trickiest to handle of all their quirky behavior. Meltdowns are certainly the most explosive and upsetting.

A meltdown strikes like an earthquake, fiercely and without warning, shaking up everybody who's around. These emotional outbursts blindside the child as much as they blindside parents, grandparents, babysitters, teachers, or whoever is with the child.

Because meltdowns come out of nowhere, there's no way to know how long they will last, what will calm your child this time, or when they will be over.

An Aspie's meltdown is no mere tantrum. This is *not* a behavioral issue. This is *not* a battle of wills. The source may be sensory, but it could just as easily be from the child's expectations being dashed and his inability to cope with the disappointment, or from unexamined emotions.

Meltdowns go beyond sobbing and shouting. There can be head rubbing and hair pulling, whacking pillows over and over, knocking things down, slamming doors, or punching walls. Meltdowns turn a rather docile, gentle child into an absolutely inconsolable, raving, quivering wreck.

If you're lucky, the meltdown is from an overload of sensory stimulation. Once the source is figured out, it can be addressed. If it's too noisy, go to a quiet place. Too many people? Leave to find a less crowded spot for you and your child to regroup.

Too hot? Find a cooler spot. Too cold? Give him a sweater.

Feed your child if he is having a hunger-induced meltdown. Sometimes the solution is as simple as giving him a small snack.

Let your child nap if he's too tired or overwhelmed.

Dealing with a meltdown from sensory issues is a matter of deducing the source of irritation, then doing your best to eliminate it to make conditions easier for your supersensitive Aspie child until they learn to cope with it. It seems with age, many of these sensitivities fade or are less extreme.

When younger children have meltdowns, it might be for very simple yet unexpected reasons. For example, one of our third-grade Friends melted down during a math test and refused to take it. When asked what part was so hard, the boy said, "This is not a spelling test. This is a math test."

One of the test questions asked the students to write out the numbers in words, not numerals.

The boy's expectations of math tests were to only work with numbers. His expectations were shattered by being asked to write words. Once his teacher explained that there are times when numbers need to be written out in words, like on checks or contracts, then the boy said, "Oh." And he took the test.

So often, when Aspies refuse to do something, it is because what is being requested does not match their expectations or make sense to them. So they get upset and dig in, refusing to cooperate. But if they are calmly given the logic behind a request or activity, that usually defuses their resistance and ends the meltdown.

However, as our Friends get older, social confusion and unexamined emotions may cause meltdowns. Those emotions lie buried in the murky depths of their unconsciousness. Once these emotions work their way up to the surface, they may become too much for an Aspie to bear, and a meltdown erupts.

The slightest thing may ignite an outpouring of anger, frustration, self-loathing, and unhappiness from a normally quiet, content child.

As you'll read elsewhere in this book, understanding and managing emotions are very difficult for our Friends. They also have a hard time coping with change because change is not what they expected. They need your help to put things into perspective, which is one of their biggest challenges.

What's so hard about meltdowns for everyone is that they are so random and seem to come out of nowhere.

On a seemingly average day, when you ask how school went, your child says, "Fine." But homework takes much longer than usual. He seems more lost in thought. You ask, "Is anything wrong?" At first, he says, "No."

Finally, if you're lucky, he starts to talk about how he said the wrong thing to someone in his class. And now he's convinced that the person is avoiding him.

Then how someone called him "stupid" or "retarded" or worse in PE class, or threw food at him at lunch.

Maybe he was slow to finish a test, which grows into his conviction that he's *always* too slow in writing things down or he *never* says the right thing. Such negative absolutes make your child feel all the more upset, defeated, and hopeless.

Just by listening and asking more questions, you'll find out that two days ago someone laughed at him. Two weeks ago, he accidentally insulted a "popular" girl in math class by being too truthful. Then a few months ago, another student pulled your child into the gym for the innocent reason of watching the cheerleaders practice, but that made him really uncomfortable. That was months ago!

If it's a big meltdown, *all* the slights come out, recent and ancient history, going back many years because there is a video that replays incidents in their heads. The memories have been lurking in your Asperger's teen's unconscious mind, festering, and now they're surfacing and rattling his spirit.

The perfectionist in him is embarrassed and becomes angry. Despair kicks in, too. You may hear such plaintive statements as "Why am I so different?" or "No one likes me" or "I hate school."

At some point in elementary school, our Asperger's Friends realize they are not typical. They know they don't notice or understand the subtle social signals that other kids seem to get.

This inability to understand and get along with their peers leads to major frustrations that pile up out of sight. Then, if our Friends don't tell someone who can give them a reality check, it leads to a sudden eruption and total meltdown.

What's a parent or teacher to do?

When these outbursts happen at Friends' Club, we stay calm, do not match their anger with anger, and take action.

First, we remove them from the group if we believe that they would do better without an audience. However, sometimes the group can help by offering suggestions, since they've struggled with meltdowns themselves. What our Friends need is a fresh perspective on what they cannot see for themselves.

The main thing is to *not* talk about feeling or emotions. Leave emotions out, even though meltdowns are so emotional.

What's best is to present the logic in the incident. Address their memories based on the experience itself, not the emotions of the experience. In a cause-and-effect manner, go through whatever happened and put it in perspective that way.

A rather extreme case was with one of our teens who loves going to the fire station. He expected to visit it on the way home from an afternoon appointment, but the session went longer than expected. So his mother said they had to go straight home because it was dinnertime.

Our teen Friend melted down. He cursed at her and threw a pen from the backseat while they were riding in the car.

When they got home, he slammed the front door on his younger brother. Then, in the kitchen, the boy grabbed a knife and waved it around.

The boy's mother did the right thing. She remained calm. She spoke to him about something unrelated, like what they should have for dinner. As he started to calm down, his tutor showed up for their usual session.

The tutor also had experience in special education. He sat the boy down and started writing a cause-and-effect chart of what had just happened. Visuals are very powerful for the Asperger's crowd, even simple ones like a piece of paper and pencil or a whiteboard and felt pen. The tutor wrote out:

CAUSE	EFFECT
Left appointment late	No time to stop at fire station
Threw pen at Mom	She's driving a car—dangerous
Slammed door	Could have hurt little brother
Grabbed a knife	Could have hurt someone—dangerous

When he saw the knife episode written out, the teen said, "But I wasn't going to hurt anybody."

"Your mom didn't know if you would hurt her," said the tutor, "or if you'd hurt your little brother. Knives are dangerous."

Once the teen saw his actions spelled out in black and white, he could see how such actions were illogical. He became aware of the possible dangers of his emotional outburst. No punishment was necessary. The important thing was that this boy saw how, in the end, these behaviors did not get him to the fire station. So he learned they were not worth repeating.

With some of our groups, I've used poster board and drawn a circle at the center representing the meltdown's source. I write in the behavior, "screaming," and not the emotion, which would be "frustration."

Once I've written "screaming" in the center, then I draw concentric circles out, like ripples in a pond. With the group's help, I write within each circle a logical, concrete action or effect of the original cause. I do not try to address the emotions. We stick to the facts and logic.

In the first circle, it may say, "Hurts people's ears." In the next circle, I'll write, "Distracts other people." And then in the last circle, I'll write, "Gives the impression of being a baby because babies scream."

Overall, you need to understand that our Friends really cannot figure out what may seem to you like very simple social problems. They take things too literally and are hurt by teasing that other kids could shrug off. They need reassurance, coaching, and ways to adjust their perspective when it comes to people situations and learning what to do.

It's also important to know that these kids are easily overwhelmed from too much happening too fast. For example, if it's time to leave the house for school and they hear a bunch of directions all at once, that could cause a meltdown. If you call out, "Get your shoes on, comb your hair, grab your lunch, and find your coat," that is too much information too fast for them to process. A better approach is one calm direction at a time, preferably no shouting, to avoid morning meltdowns before school.

During a meltdown with younger children, it can be best for you to sit close by and listen while they cry and spill their stories. A hug may or may not be welcome. Sometimes physical contact can irritate Aspies more than help because of their sensitivities to touch. You might want to ask first, or try giving a hug, but be ready to let go quickly if your child gets more upset.

Please, never take such a refusal personally. He would like a hug if he could tolerate it at that time, so please try not to feel rejected.

When they seem to be running out of steam, you may want to point out their strengths like "You're smart" or "You're kind and gentle and very good with animals" or "We love you for your honesty and original thinking."

Again, it's so important to put things into perspective for these kids. You could point out that maybe the other child wasn't telling a lie, but simply exaggerating to get kids to laugh. (People telling lies can upset Asperger's kids very quickly, since they believe so strongly that the truth should always be told.)

For teens, letting them talk is also best. If they call themselves "lame" or "worthless" or "stupid," don't counter them! It may only make them more upset. But you don't have to agree either. Often it's best to listen and wait for an opportunity to offer a different way of looking at the situation and see if they understand.

One of our teen Friends, after melting down and venting about whatever is bothering him, finds the best way to calm down is by going to his bedroom and listening to his favorite music. He may play with his Legos.

Yes, even into their teens, many Asperger's kids find it soothing and relaxing to play with Legos. As one of our moms proudly points out, Legos are used at the Massachusetts Institute of Technology and at NASA (National Aeronautics and Space Administration), so why shouldn't Aspie teens enjoy their Legos? There are worse ways to handle stress, and at least the Lego way is creative and therapeutic.

Just keep in mind that there is no one "right" way to handle your child's meltdown. You'll need to customize your approach each time, tailoring it to the incident and probing for the underlying cause with a new set of questions.

Remember to always ask your child *why* they are getting upset, once they've calmed down enough to talk. You can't assume it's the same reason each time, especially as they get older and teen angst may kick in.

So often, they're upset about something that would never occur to you. Just as often, it's easily remedied, as with the boy taking the math test, when someone asked, "What part bothers you?" It's usually not the whole test, not the whole day, or not the whole anything that is bothering them—just one small part that sets them off and upsets them, and it's usually something you'd never suspect.

The bottom line is that meltdowns are most often caused by unmet expectations or sensitivities to the child's environment. Meltdowns are best handled with calm, cool logic and patient understanding.

See also Change and "Change-ups,"
Compliance, Letting Go and Refocusing,
Sensory Sensitivities, Taking One's Leave, *and*
Writing Things Down

MOVING ON TO NEW THINGS

When our Asperger's Friends are playing a game or talking about a certain topic, it is often hard for them to let go of what they're doing and change to a new activity or topic. This kind of change is called *transitioning* in behavioral psychology lingo. You may know it as "switching gears" or "changing course" or "moving on."

Why is it so hard for Aspies to accept change?

As we've explained in some of the other lessons, the real world is fluid and unpredictable. People and activities and time are ever changing. All of this is unsettling for our Friends on the autism spectrum.

Asperger's folks prefer the tangible, fixed, and predictable. They feel sideswiped, even ambushed, by sensory stimulation the rest of us don't even notice. The world feels like one constant assault on their senses, which is stressful and distracting. Whatever they can latch on to, they cling to tightly to feel more secure in a confusing world.

Since it usually takes Aspies quite awhile to embrace a new thing—anything—it is difficult, even outright upsetting, for them to hear that now they are supposed to move on and leave the familiar behind.

It's like asking them to cross a new bridge. Your child knows and is comfortable with the side he's on. Why would he want to go to a side he doesn't know and is not sure he'll like? That's just too much of the unknown, in both the crossing over and the final destination.

If they sense that someone understands them, then Aspies tend to cooperate more easily. With understanding comes trust. With trust comes more willingness to let go and move on to the next thing.

One strategy that should become standard for you with your Asperger's child is to offer a verbal or written schedule for the day. A schedule is a concrete explanation of what will be happening and gives your child a preview, a plan to hang on to. This makes things seem less random and makes for easier transitions.

Writing down each step is the best way to help your child move on to something new. It's a tangible, visual cue. Write on a notepad or on a whiteboard with felt markers. Use short, clear sentences or phrases, writing exactly what you want your child to do: "Put on your shoes" or "Say good-bye and go out the door." It sounds absurdly simple because it is, but it works. It really works!

Another good technique to help your child move from one particular activity to another is to set a timer for the amount of time that the first activity should take. Let the child know how long that is. When the bell or buzzer goes off, then it signals the end of that activity or conversation. It is time to move on to something else.

See also Anxiety, Change and "Change-ups," Compliance, Fear, Letting Go and Refocusing, Meltdowns, Moving On to New Things, Perfectionism and Unrealistic Expectations, Sensory Sensitivities, Strengths and How to Cultivate Them, *and* Writing Things Down

OBSESSIONS AND OBSESSIVE BEHAVIOR

Yes, Asperger's kids are like so many children on the spectrum and prone to obsessive behavior. They cling to ideas, things, or actions that provide comfort in an unpredictable, confusing world.

Trying to loosen their grip on favorite objects, or favorite phrases, can be a challenge for parents, teachers, and professionals alike. But turning these obsessions into improved behavior is a trick that can work well.

For instance, one of our boys kept saying, "You're fired," whenever he was upset with someone and wanted them to leave. It became his catchall phrase, repeated obsessively, to express his frustration and anger. We spent time working on lessening his use of the phrase, with good success.

Then, during a one-on-one social coaching session at the boy's home, our leader accidentally hit the boy in the face with a tennis ball that they were throwing outside. Even though she apologized and let him know that it wasn't intentional, the boy became more and more upset. "You're fired!" he kept yelling.

That's when she remembered one of his other obsessions—professional wrestling, which he watched on television. She said, "Now pretend that you're a WWE wrestler who's been hurt in a match."

The effect was immediate. His face switched from anger to fascination. "Wow, do I have any blood?" he asked excitedly.

That's how quickly a difficult situation can be defused. If you can use another interest of the child to help him refocus, then he will let go of the obsessive behavior.

Note that it's important to recognize the hidden intention *behind* the words. In this case, "You're fired" was another way for this boy to say, "I'm really, really mad at you." It's best to acknowledge whatever is upsetting him, and tell him that you know he is frustrated, rather than object to the words themselves.

Sometimes, when our Friends have a favorite topic or phrase that they keep repeating, the perfect solution is as simple as limiting the number of times they can say it or the amount of time they can talk about it.

One of our Friends loved to point out patterns in things . . . all day long! So I told him that he could only talk about or point out patterns twice a day. That was it. Two times was his limit. And I told his mother to remind him that, if he had already talked of patterns twice in a day, he was done.

She later reported that it worked beautifully. With a finite limit to this obsession, the boy knew what was acceptable and the family was relieved of the crazy-making repetition.

Sometimes, just telling a child that he can't talk about his obsession right now is enough to stop him. The important thing is to speak in a calm, unemotional voice.

In one of our groups, an eight-year-old boy loved to talk about emergency vehicles, such as ambulances, fire engines, etc. When told that he couldn't talk about it anymore during What's *Up?* when everyone is supposed to share one bit of news or information, the boy groaned and said, "My head is going to explode if I don't talk about emergency vehicles!"

The leader nodded and calmly said, "That's okay. We can clean up the mess afterward, but we need to talk about something else right now." This worked because he was acknowledged in a matter-of-fact way. No additional details were needed, and the conversation moved on beyond ambulances. The boy quickly got over it.

Much of the trick to decoding these Asperger's kids is to see what they see. It means trying to understand their obsessions and unique perspectives on things, then figuring out a way to tone down the extremes and increase the appropriateness. It also means that I have to give up my initial responses as a behavioral psychologist, and meld these kids' perspectives into mine so that I can meet them halfway and still make progress. It takes some creativity, but then, I'm working with original thinkers, right?

For instance, one mother warned me that her son needed to take

something away with him whenever he left a new place. It didn't matter what—a sticker, a business card, even a leaf from a tree—but something. Otherwise, she said, he would not be happy or successful in the
group.

Well, the behaviorist in me said, "We'll change this habit." I didn't
tell the mother, but I decided that we would not be handing out stick-
ers every time. That would be ridiculous, since that would not happen
in the real world. And the purpose of the Friends' Club is to help our
members function better in the real world.

However, after a few weeks, the leaders of that boy's group came to
me. They said that he was getting out of control and that they weren't
sure that they could keep the others in the group safe with this boy's
behavior.

Perceiving that he was anxious and needed something concrete, I
came up with a new approach. I made a little box and called it the
Choices Box. Then I wrote "choices" on a piece of paper and cut it into
four pieces, like a jigsaw puzzle.

Then, on a separate piece of paper, I wrote down our expectations of
him when he was in the group session so that he had a visual way of
seeing what he should do. I told him that in every session he followed
the group's rules, he would get a piece of the puzzle. And when he had
all four pieces that spelled out "choices," then he could choose something from the Choices Box.

The results were dramatic. The very next session, he did so well that
not a single issue occurred. And after only four weeks (meeting just once
a week), his obsession went away and he no longer needed the box!

For another boy, machines were his obsession and vacuum cleaners
in particular. When he visited the bathroom one night and saw a couple
of vacuums that we had stored in there, his voice got loud and he vio-
lated personal space even more than usual during the group session.
This frightened the other boys. (Besides his obsession, this boy had difficulties with self-control as well.)

So I used his vacuum cleaner obsession to create a positive change in
his behavior. I drew a picture of a vacuum and cut it up into four puzzle
pieces. He was told that he could earn a piece by keeping his voice down
and not invading the other boys' space. When he had all four pieces, he
could use the vacuum cleaner to clean up after the session.

Again, the results were dramatic. This boy earned all four pieces that first night and was allowed to use the vacuum cleaner. But he chased all the boys out of the room before they even had time to put their shoes back on!

So we rewrote the rules to make it clear when he could vacuum and when he would have to wait. And we changed the reward system: when his Friends caught him talking appropriately, then they could give him a vacuum puzzle piece. This was an opportunity for his peers to see him positively, instead of just an adult acknowledging his progress.

If only school could be like this for our Friends. If only their peers could recognize and appreciate the positive things our Asperger's kids do. Wouldn't it be great if their strengths and good behavior were the main focus, instead of all the blunders and social missteps?

See also Awareness, Bullying and Bullies,
Dating and Gender Talk, Embarrassment, Emotions,
Further Information About Bullying, Grooming
and Personal Hygiene, Intentions, Slang and
Idioms, Talking with Peers, *and* Teasing

PEER PRESSURE AND
AVOIDING DARES

Asperger's kids often consider anyone who will talk to them as being a friend, even if the "friend" may be taking advantage of them and their lack of social awareness.

One of our younger boys was dared to do something by a "friend" at school. It wasn't really a bad thing, but our Friend didn't want to do it. Yet he didn't know how to get out of it without being called a "chicken" or some other name. Even Aspies don't like to be labeled "chicken," or to be seen as weak or afraid.

That's why we often talk with our kids about what to do to get out of a dare without being teased. The best response, we decided, was to tell the person making the dare, "That's boring," and just walk away.

Research about bullying has shown that some kind of response is needed to satisfy the aggressor, or else their pestering will continue and even escalate. In the past, we've taught our Friends to just ignore the bully, but now we know that this causes more bullying.

So whether it's to deflect outright dares or just mild peer pressure, it's always better to say something rather than nothing. It can be as simple as "I'm not interested" or "No, thanks" for a quick way to get off the hook, while also addressing the dare.

The main thing is to have our Friends be able to refuse to do something and stay safe.

Of course, peer pressure is much more than just dares. Peer pressure involves what you wear, how you talk, what music you like, what toys or video games you play, how hip and "cool" you seem. This is where the great divide resides between Asperger's kids and their neurotypical peers.

Asperger's kids and teens see intellect and knowledge as the most important thing. They don't think it matters what you wear or how your hair looks. They only care whether someone is on the same intellectual plane as they are and if they have something interesting to say.

Conversely, most typical kids consider outward appearance to be hugely important, especially in the middle school years. Most judge each other by their looks and how they act, which has nothing to do with intelligence. Tweens and teens especially want to look like their peers and fit in, all in a desire to bond, to connect with their age group and feel part of the pack. They don't want to stick out. Acceptance is paramount.

Our Asperger's Friends don't feel that same need to fit in, and thank goodness! Born out-of-the-box thinkers, they are revolutionary discoverers. They are the ones who will come up with innovations and new ways of thinking or doing things to benefit society, as a whole, precisely because Aspies don't think like everyone else and they don't care if they're like anyone else. Bottom line, they were born *not* to fit in, and it's okay.

For the most part, they don't care if they're popular. The good news is that they won't be worrying about their image or their status. It does fall on you or an older sibling to help them look fashionable enough to blend in, just so they are less of a target visually for teasing and bullying by their peers. But popularity isn't a big issue.

Good grooming is important, even though they're oblivious to it or avoid it for sensory sensitivity reasons. You do need to make sure they bathe regularly, wear clean clothes, and comb their hair each morning, so at least they start the day out well.

What's tougher to tackle is their lack of social awareness, which makes them easy marks for other kids who are looking for someone to pick on. Unfortunately, our Friends rarely have peers willing to stand up for them to stop such abuse. That's why, as a pediatrician who specializes in ADHD and Asperger's kids told one of our parents, "We just have to get them through childhood."

Meaning, we just have to help them navigate and survive the pressure cooker of peer pressure in elementary and middle school years, when tolerance is low and the need to feel superior and popular is high.

The same doctor said that once our Friends reach high school, it tends to get a bit better. There's a bigger population of students and greater likelihood that Aspies will find others like them, out on the fringes, minding their own business and thinking deep thoughts. Then, as adults, there's an even bigger population to blend into and adults, in general, are less harsh and more forgiving of people's differences.

The difference between true autistic kids and Asperger's kids is that all of the Asperger's kids whom I've met—at the Friends' Club and outside of it—want very much to have at least one friend.

That's not to say that kids more impacted by autism do not have a desire to connect with other people. They do. But because they are unable to do so on their own, more severely autistic kids require someone's help to make connections for them. Someone else paves the way for making their social contacts.

That is where our Asperger's kids get into trouble with their peers. Many are so desperate to connect with kids their own age, they are willing to do anything to make a friend. They will take dangerous dares and stupid risks, leading to injuries, which they never thought of. Their deep desire to forge a friendship makes Aspies overly susceptible to peer pressure. This condition is what we strive to alleviate in our groups.

Unlike other social skills groups, Friends' Club only includes Asperger's kids. This means our kids meet others like themselves with whom they can relate and share interests. Our Friends feel a connection that they haven't felt elsewhere. Once they don't feel so alone anymore, it reduces their desperation.

As one teen girl said on her first night with us, "It's about time you put this together for my species." And that's how many of them feel—like a separate species from their peers. Some even say they feel like aliens.

While all of us know we are individuals and different from one another, there is still much that binds neurotypicals: our emotions, interactions, humor, and relationships. Asperger's folks, on the other hand, know they are different and a breed apart.

So, to make it through their school years, Asperger's children do need to fit in enough that they can find other kids who are interested in similar things, or who value intelligence over appearance. As much as they enjoy being alone and need quiet downtime, Asperger's kids and teens don't want to always be alone. They enjoy company, too.

The important thing for parents or teachers to do is to keep talking to them about what's going on at school. Make sure your Asperger's child or teen knows that you are interested in their school life. Make sure they tell you what's happening, and not just in the classroom. Trouble springs up more often during the less supervised times, like recess, lunch, and PE.

And keep asking how it's going, because sometimes you won't hear about something that is bothering them the day it actually happens. Sometimes a week, a month, or even months can pass by before an upsetting episode finally surfaces and your child tells you about it.

Again, the important thing is to keep asking. Keep probing for how they're feeling. Look for signs of agitation or pent-up anxiety. The sooner an upsetting event gets out in the open, the better.

A bad experience tends to get trapped and replayed in Asperger's kids' minds over and over, making it seem much worse than it really was. When they finally tell someone about it, that stops the replay and relieves their stress over the incident. So, talk is good.

See also Acceptance, Anger and Frustration, Compromise, Depression, Letting Go and Refocusing, Meltdowns, Perspectives and Point of View, Social Stories, Staying Calm, *and* Writing Things Down

PERFECTIONISM AND UNREALISTIC EXPECTATIONS

Like all good perfectionists, Asperger's kids suffer from the notion that life should be perfect and people should be perfect all the time (not necessarily them, the Aspies, but everyone else).

They have literal minds.

They prefer precision and exacting results.

They expect everything and everyone to do as we're supposed to, with no deviations or mistakes.

Can this be more unrealistic? As you know and I know, we spend our whole lives coping with the imperfections of everyday life. The real world—our imperfect world—is full of imperfect people.

This reality is a constant source of frustration and disappointment for our Asperger's Friends. Human error is rampant. People's emotions get in the way of logic and reason. Things don't always go as planned.

So what do you do if you're seeking perfection?

Well, the worlds of computers, science, and mathematics are certainly attractive. They're filled with precision and concrete formulas and numbers. There is nothing vague about numbers. They have a set value and only mean one thing, unlike those pesky words and idioms and slang, which can be interpreted all sorts of ways and have multiple meanings.

Some of the most famous scientists and mathematicians are now being recognized to have been on the spectrum, based on the array of sensitivities and quirky traits that they displayed—Sir Isaac Newton, Thomas Edison, Charles Darwin, and Albert Einstein.

This is not to say that Asperger's precludes any interest or ability in the arts. Some of the most famous trailblazing musicians, writers, and artists are now believed to have had Asperger's: Mozart, Beethoven, Erik Satie, and Glenn Gould in the music world; Jonathan Swift, Hans Christian Andersen, Herman Melville, Lewis Carroll, Sir Arthur Conan Doyle, and George Orwell in the literary world; Michelangelo, Leonardo da Vinci, Vincent van Gogh, and Andy Warhol in the art world.

A by-product of perfectionism is unhappiness, of course, and even depression. And depression is a common companion to Asperger's, where the individual feels disconnected, down, and joyless. If your child displays severe symptoms of depression or even hints at suicide, please take him or her immediately to a children's psychiatrist for a professional evaluation.

We are conscious of our Friends' perfectionist tendencies. We remind them weekly—just as you remind them perhaps daily—that people are not perfect. Life is not perfect. We let them know that we're all works in progress. Ideally, people do the right thing in the right way at the right time, but there are no guarantees.

We coach our Friends to realize that the other group members, as well as their own family members, are probably doing their best. We urge them to *encourage*, and not criticize, others if they want to help make things more "perfect" and achieve certain results.

Because group projects are so frequently assigned in schools, we use games, building projects, and other group activities to loosen up our Friends. Instead of letting our kids work alone, which they would prefer to do, we make them team up. In pairs or as a whole group, they tackle various creative projects. This helps them to learn to let go and accept other people's ideas and efforts. We've been pleased to hear from parents and teachers that they have noticed improvements on this front.

It's best to keep reminding your Asperger's child or teen that perfection is a fleeting moment to be enjoyed, but not something to be expected on a constant basis. We should all do our best. High standards are admirable. But perfection is not a permanent condition.

As the famous French artist Eugène Delacroix once said, "Artists who seek perfection in everything are those who cannot attain it in anything." When one of our Friends heard this quote, he said, "That applies to me!"

Naturally, as perfection-seekers, Aspies hate to make mistakes. So we use humor to make light of things that go wrong. We have borrowed the "rubber chicken" technique from Michelle Garcia Winner to lighten the moment for these born-to-be serious children.

The girls or boys sit in a circle and take turns talking about a certain topic. If they make a mistake of some kind, then another member holding the rubber chicken gently bonks them on the head. Being bonked or getting to bonk others is funny to the kids and takes the seriousness out of whatever mistake they made.

We've also seen this activity increase the kids' attention to others because they want to catch a "rubber chicken moment." Anything that helps them listen harder and pay more attention to a speaker is valuable.

I was asked to help one of our Friends who hated making mistakes. He would get so frustrated and angry in school that he would erase his mistakes so hard, he tore holes in the paper. Spelling was his special interest, so he was hypervigilant about correct spelling.

The way I handled this was to create a Social Story script for him to write out while we videotaped him. But the script had a spelling mistake, which he made as he copied it. Then we watched the video and he saw himself make the mistake *and the world did not end*! That really is the issue about mistakes—the seriousness with which they view errors of any kind, and their skewed perspective.

Tony Attwood has said that Asperger's folks have a pathological fear of making mistakes, while their supreme delight is in being right. Their need to be perfect and not make mistakes throws off their ability to keep things in perspective. Mistakes are blown way out of proportion.

The good news for this Friend was that, by watching himself make the mistake over and over, he became much more flexible from then on. The key was using visual tools—the written script, the video of him making the mistake—to show him how mistakes are livable. Visuals are always a powerful way to reach this group. Put it in writing. Show them pictures.

We teach our Friends that, ultimately, it's up to each of us to choose— the more unrealistic one's expectations, the more disappointed one will be. Lowering one's expectations to be more realistic will raise one's chances at happiness.

These kids will need continual help in understanding this. They will need reminding that people are not perfect most of the time. And since perfection is elusive, our Friends need to know that it's unfair to expect it all of the time of everyone and everything.

See also Change and "Change-ups,"
Compliance, Compromise, Letting Go and
Refocusing, Manners, Reading Minds and
Faces, Selfishness, Social Stories, *and*
Teamwork

PERSPECTIVES AND POINT
OF VIEW

Every day with every age group at the Friends' Club, we work on perspective-taking, or seeing from someone else's point of view whether we intend to or not. This is one of our Asperger's kids' biggest stumbling blocks with other children—not being aware of someone else's point of view and not accepting their right to have it.

Using what Simon Baron-Cohen called "theory of mind," or "mindsight," most of us realize that other people have thoughts and feelings that differ from ours. This doesn't occur to anyone with Asperger's. Our Aspie Friends know of only one point of view—their own. Their brain is truly different, preventing them from picking up and understanding someone else's perspective.

Consequently, because they are trapped in only their perspective, Aspies can come across as ill-mannered, even downright rude. They reject others' suggestions or ideas and insist that only theirs are right.

Our Friends unintentionally offend others because they do not know how to compromise. Rigid and inflexible, they cling to their own singular, and often unconventional, perspective and refuse to let go. This makes group work or teamwork very difficult.

Being able to see only from their own perspective makes Asperger's kids focus intensely on what interests them, but they have no grasp of the Big Picture. They're unable to see things in a greater context, often noticing the obscure and hyperfocusing on mere details.

For example, on a playground at recess, a young Asperger's child will notice a red ball and run to grab it. He doesn't realize that it's part of a game being played by a whole group of children, who are now mad at him. They are annoyed and think his behavior is selfish and rude.

This doesn't win friends. And it makes enemies. This mindblindness—that inability to see from someone else's perspective—can get Aspies into real trouble.

One of our constant goals is to teach our kids that people look at the same thing but see it differently and that's *okay*! We teach them that it's important to acknowledge someone else's perspective, even if you don't agree with it.

We're not trying to change Asperger's children's minds about their own firmly held beliefs and opinions. The goal is to have them realize that other people may think differently and they are entitled to those beliefs and opinions. We teach them that there are other sides to everything, and it's important to listen to the person and hear their side.

Since this is such an abstract issue, we turn to books, games, and other tangible learning tools to make perspective-taking more concrete.

For younger kids, we use books like *The True Story of the Three Little Pigs* by Jon Scieszka because it takes a well-known children's tale and turns it around. It startles the kids to have to think of the wolf as the victim and the three little pigs as the bad guys. There are other children's books based on famous fairy tales where the point of view has been altered. These make great teaching tools, providing a concrete way to teach inferential reasoning skills (which our Friends struggle with).

Or we'll bring up how different Harry Potter's story would be if told from Draco Malfoy's or Voldemort's point of view. As one of our boys said, "Voldemort would probably say that Harry is such a pest and he just won't go away." Now that Friend got the idea completely!

Award-winning children's book author-illustrator David Wiesner has many wordless picture books that help our kids learn how to see the Big Picture. The stunning images appeal to their visual nature. Having no text, books like *Flotsam* and *Sector 7* don't distract our kids with words while forcing them to figure out what's going on in the story by looking at the whole thing, not just bits and pieces.

With nine-to-eleven-year-olds, we play What's Wrong with This Picture? We show simple drawings called "absurdities" that portray illogical scenes. Then we ask our Friends what doesn't make sense in that picture. For example, a man is walking in the rain with his umbrella resting on his shoulder even though the rain is slanted at him. Our kids have to look at the whole picture, not just the umbrella or the sidewalk or the raindrops, to figure out what's wrong.

Sometimes conversations can get in the way of the "work" that our groups need to do. But other times, such detours become a valuable teaching point that we incorporate into our lessons on social skills.

For instance, one of our younger boys was telling another that his dog was really seven years old, in dog years, not one. The other boy disagreed and they became stuck in their black-and-white, entrenched positions. As a group, we took the time to talk with both of them to work through their opposite points of view. Finally, one boy said to the other, "Okay, I see what you mean, but I don't have to always agree with you."

When we heard this, then we knew that what we'd taught had sunk in. We love to hear this kind of tiny shift in our Friends, which is really quite huge. Accepting someone else's right to an opinion is an enormous breakthrough for our kids.

A game we play with all of our groups is called Apples to Apples. In this game, one person is the judge while everyone else draws five cards about a wide range of things—animals, food, TV characters, toys, nature, famous people.

The judge lays down an adjective card. The players then choose the card in their hand that they think is most applicable to that adjective. The judge chooses the best match.

What's so terrific about this game is that players make decisions based on their perception. Then there's a judge who will decree the winning card based on his or her point of view. For example, if the adjective is "cool," the judge may have to decide among a refrigerator, my friends, or water guns. There is no right answer, it's what the judge thinks is the coolest choice.

This leads to wonderful discussions about why someone chose to play the card they did and why the judge chose a particular card as a match. We get to reinforce the phrase, "That is my opinion," over and over again. The kids get to practice getting unstuck and letting go.

Playing Apples to Apples also gives us a chance to teach our Friends about the difference between assertiveness and bullying. We've seen some of the kids walk a fine line between the two, and then we need to mediate. On one of the judge's turns, a girl was told her card was a stupid answer. The girl then told the judge, "I don't like what you said to me. It hurt my feelings."

How wonderful it was for the girl to be able to express herself that way and stand up for herself! Working through this became an important part of our lesson on point of view. We are always looking for more opportunities to teach our Friends to advocate for themselves and speak out about their feelings. It's a huge step for them, and crucial at home, at school, and later in the workplace.

See also Conversation, Curiosity About People, Initiative, *and* Remembering Names

PHONE SKILLS

Most of us talk on the phone without giving it a second thought. You pick up the receiver. You dial a number. You listen to the ringing. If someone answers on the other end, you say "Hi" and converse. If no one is home, the answering machine comes on. You leave a message and hang up. What's so hard about that?

Everything, if you're an Asperger's kid.

First, you don't really think of calling anyone because that requires initiative and reaching out.

Second, you don't know anyone's phone number. And usually you don't know their last name to look them up in the phone book.

Third, the longer the phone keeps ringing at the other end, the more likely you are to forget what it was that you were calling about.

Fourth, without being able to see to whom you're talking, it's hard to know if it's your friend or the mother or father or brother saying "Hello" at the other end.

Of course, after the greeting, whoever answered expects you to make small talk, which is always awkward. All you want to do is find out whether your friend can come over, or meet you somewhere, but the other person wants to talk.

And finally, if you do talk with your friend and he does want to come over, it's way too complicated to figure out the details. You haven't thought through the when, where, how to get there, and how long the activity will go on. So you need one of your parents to talk to your friend's parent to work it out.

Now, if the answering machine goes on, that's even harder because you have to talk without anyone asking questions to guide you. It's so disorienting to talk into a void that you may hang up without leaving a message or you leave a confusing one because you're flustered.

Yet, if these Asperger's kids are to make and keep friends, they need to know how to use the phone because it is such an essential socializing tool. Even in this age of e-mails and instant messaging, telephones and voice mail are here to stay. Decent phone skills are especially important in the workplace. So phones are not to be avoided but figured out and mastered.

This struggle with phones comes from our Friends' deficient frontal lobe and the lack of executive skills, which is what also makes them very disorganized and unaware of time so that they're chronically late.

What's the best remedy?

Practice. In small steps. With your help.

At Friends' Club, we have them practice phone skills as homework. First, usually with our nine- or ten-year-olds, we encourage them to take down the number of someone they like in the group. We ask them to call each other, even if it's just to say "hello."

Then, when they've done that, we ask them to call their Friend again. This time, it's to get together to play or go to a movie. But we tell them, first, they should think about what they want to do, when and where it is, and how they will get there.

We make this preplanning into a group activity, since it does not come naturally to any of them and they can all use the practice.

Once they've gotten together with one Friend, we encourage them to call each other during the vacation breaks and weeks when the group is not meeting. But they don't have to call that same Friend again the next time. Mainly, we urge them to call anyone they want, just as long as they use the phone again soon.

Such practice not only makes them more comfortable with dialing phone numbers and talking into that faceless mouthpiece, it also makes them take the initiative, reach out and plan a get-together.

Your help will be required for your Asperger's child to master the phone. She will need you to tell her which number to call, and you may need to read it aloud so that she can concentrate on dialing.

She will need prompting through the call, because the other person is bound to ask questions or say things that throw off your child. That's okay. Your child needs to learn how to say, "Excuse me while I check on that," when she doesn't know the answer.

And once the other child has said yes to getting together, your child will need to hand you the phone to cement the details with the other adult. It's just beyond them to sort out who's going where and how.

Sometimes even teens need help with the details. Still, the more they practice telephoning and inviting and setting up details, the more possible it will be.

The good thing is that they are calling someone, and reaching out beyond their usual home and family sphere. Mastering the phone will expand their world and make them feel more connected.

See also Leaving the House, Perspectives and Point of View, Self-regulation or "Stimming," Sensory Sensitivities, Sportsmanship, *and* Teamwork

PHYSICAL INACTIVITY

In general, Asperger's kids have an aversion to getting physical. Or let's just say they're not the most physical kids in the world.

First off, they're usually not very coordinated and many are quite clumsy. This lack of athletic ability, coupled with their noncompetitive nature, tends to make them reluctant or even totally disinterested in sports.

Many struggle with gross motor skills—running, climbing, hopping, skipping, catching balls, balancing, bike riding. Coordination has to do with body-space awareness, which for Asperger's kids is an issue. For some reason, they may be unaware of their body to the degree that they feel the need to flap their arms or rock back and forth. These repetitive motions are called "stimming" and help them know where their body is.

Couple this lack of coordination with hypersensitivity to sensory stimuli, and you've got the main reasons that Asperger's children really prefer to stay indoors. At home, it's calmer and quieter than the great outdoors. Being cocooned in their room is soothing to their ultrasensitive senses. It's also less physically demanding.

This doesn't mean that Aspies can't be physical. Some excel at sports, becoming star baseball or basketball players or terrific golfers. If the sport requires great precision like becoming a great hitter or super free thrower or a particular kind of runner, then some of our Friends who are athletically inclined do very, very well. If it's a sport like baseball, which is really individual performances that masquerade as a team sport, then Aspies can participate surprisingly well.

Otherwise, the best sports for this crowd are individual ones like jogging, rock climbing, karate, swimming, bowling, golf, track and field, and tennis. These pursuits allow them to be active and get exercise, but not be overwhelmed socially.

With very young kids, we recommend simply taking them to a nearby park with jungle gyms and swings or the local fast-food place with a play structure. These are perfect spots for your child to climb, crawl, and slide, and will help improve their motor skills and strengthen their muscles. Anything that gets them out of the house and moving is good!

Be alert, though. You should definitely stay close to your child and keep an eye on him the whole time. Asperger's kids usually need more help than you'd expect until they master the apparatus, and remember—they won't ask. It doesn't occur to them to ask for anything, in general, so needing rescuing on a jungle gym is no different.

From time to time at the Friends' Club, we will take younger groups outside to play a game of tag or to throw a ball around. This has two benefits. It exposes them to the kinds of outdoor games they might not play, or tend to avoid, at school. And it familiarizes them with team or group play.

The main challenge that team sports presents for our Asperger's kids is that they only see things from their unique perspective. They do not understand or embrace other people's points of view automatically. This makes it all the more challenging to think and act as a team player.

But if you want them to try a team sport, then soccer is one of the most inclusive and forgiving. With eleven players on the field, there's a place for everyone and there are plenty of players to help each other out.

Those who want to run a lot do well as forwards or midfielders. Those who are not interested in running or who are less clued in to the whole back and forthing of the soccer ball make great defenders.

One of our Friends played as a defender from the time he was in kindergarten through fifth grade on recreational soccer teams. He was so good at stopping the ball from coming near the goal box that his coaches dubbed him "The Wall."

Over and over, this boy was able to stop any oncoming ball immediately. Then he would give it a big kick and send the soccer ball in the other direction, to his own team's delight. He had no idea how to dribble it up the field or score a goal, but he was terrific at keeping the ball away from his team's goal. And with the goalie to back him up, there was always another line of support to take the pressure off.

With our upper elementary kids, sometimes we'll walk or jog around the block toward the end of our session. The activity burns off some excess energy, but it also allows the boys or girls to talk (and complain) with other group members, which forms stronger bonds.

Basically, the more you expose your Asperger's child to physical exercise, the more comfortable they'll become with their bodies and the stronger their muscles will be. Since they won't take the initiative or ask for such activities, you'll need to put it on their "to-do" list so it becomes part of their routine. If you turn exercise into a regular activity, or even a rule, then it will be sure to happen.

See also Acceptance, Asking for Help, Change
and "Change-ups," Compromise, Cooperation,
Letting Go and Refocusing, Listening to Others,
Perfectionism and Unrealistic Expectations,
Perspectives and Point of View, Teamwork, *and*
Thinking in Pictures and Patterns

PROBLEM SOLVING

What comes up in almost every session, for issues big and small, is problem solving. We work on it all the time.

Why? Because problem solving affects individuals and groups. It's about immediate issues and those in the future.

Let's face it—life is full of problems or "challenges," as some folks prefer to say. Obstacles and difficult situations, or difficult people, afflict neurotypicals just as much as they do Asperger's people. But while neurotypicals, or Tippies, can put things in perspective, and allow some give-and-take to solve things, Aspies often hit a wall.

It's never an issue of power. Their inflexibility is not a matter of being unwilling to yield to someone else's authority. It is an issue of control, order, and, most of all, vision.

Asperger's kids get such a strong picture of how something should be or how it's going to come out that it makes it very, very hard for them to let go of that vision. They are programmed to pursue what they see in their mind, so they become rigidly attached to it. So attached that they are reluctant, or even refuse, to accept other ideas or modifications.

To ensure that their vision materializes, they insist on total control. They are convinced that things must follow a certain order.

This makes it very difficult for anyone else to contribute an idea or to improvise. Group projects crop up all the time at school or in child care, but the Asperger's child can become quite agitated and upset the more his idea is challenged. He can't accept other kids' suggestions or changes of any kind.

Such problem-solving difficulties add another barrier to friendship for our Asperger's kids. No one wants to be friends with someone who only clings to his idea and won't listen to anyone else's. Who wants to build something with someone too inflexible and unwilling to adapt their plans to fit other people's suggestions?

That's why we play so many games. And draw group pictures where everyone contributes a partial element. And build group structures out of Legos or K'NEX or ZOOB Tubes.

Such group activities force our young visionaries (and perfectionists) to loosen their grip on their idea. It forces them to cooperate with others. Targeted group play forces them to realize that while their idea is special to them, other people's ideas are worthwhile, too, and need to be taken into account.

Group activities also make them realize that their point of view and perspective is not the only one, and that other kids have their own perceptions that need to be considered.

The better our Friends become at letting go of control and the need for order, without losing sight of their vision, the better they'll be at problem solving and making new friends.

Increasing their flexibility and lessening their rigid adherence to their ideas will also make them better equipped to make their way in the real world and workplace. Our Friends will have fewer people problems if they seek input and solutions from others, instead of resisting them.

See also Awareness, Emotions, Intentions, Literal Language, *and* Perspectives and Point of View

READING MINDS AND FACES

We've talked elsewhere about how difficult it is for Asperger's kids and teens to read the emotional expressions on someone's face or their body language. In fact, the whole social situation confounds them. They are simply unaware. And this cluelessness about people is a neurological condition, not a psychological or intellectual inability.

Those of us without Asperger's—also called neurotypicals—can decode voices, posturing, and human interactions fairly accurately. We can tell what the subtext of a conversation is. What the hidden meaning might be behind the words spoken and the gestures made. It's almost like we can read someone's mind by watching and listening to them—but we can't. And we know we can't.

The irony is that while anyone with Asperger's cannot read someone else's facial or physical expressions, they *do* expect other people to be able to read their minds. Aspies can even become quite upset if they have to tell you their feelings or thoughts because, to them, you should just know it.

They just assume that what they are thinking or how they are feeling is not only known to them, but is obvious. Thus, it should be known to anyone around them. Even though they give few clues as to their thoughts or feelings, they become frustrated and outright angry when we don't do what they want . . . without them telling us what they want!

Yes, it's a catch-22. They won't say, so we don't know. They get angry, we don't know why.

When we try to find out what's upsetting them, they get more upset because we're making them put into words what, to them, we should already know. It's hard for them to express their feelings in the first place because feelings are slippery things, not concrete, not black and white.

Also, Asperger's children have an ongoing monologue in their mind where they *think* that they've said something, because they've heard it in their own mind so many times. In actuality, they've never said it out loud.

Their unexpressed feelings get caught in a replay cycle the same way that an episode of being bullied can replay in their minds, over and over again, multiplying it, and making the one incident seem much worse than it was. The unexpressed feelings get amplified as well.

And while Asperger's folks know that something is bugging them or that they feel bad about something, they have trouble figuring it out. Often, it takes something else to set them off and force what's bothering them to the surface. Only when a trigger event happens will they speak up.

Of course, it's not healthy for upsetting thoughts or feelings to stay trapped in one's mind on replay. That's why it's important to get your Asperger's child or teen to talk.

But how? How do we get them to tell us what's on their mind?

At home, it's best to start by being with your child. Go into his room or wherever he is, turn off the TV or music, and ask specific questions. Something that tells him what you see, like "Your face and body look upset. Is something wrong?" is better than a vague "How was your day?"

For some kids, it's better not to ask but to draw it out for them. For instance, if they were at school, you could draw a chart of boxes showing the separate periods or subjects of the day. Then you could ask what happened in each class to narrow the trouble down to one particular time.

When Asperger's kids get in trouble, it's important to look at the steps leading to the outburst or misbehavior. By studying what led to what they did, you'll find it's usually a misunderstanding or someone tricking them.

For instance, one of our middle school boys was asked by a boy in his music class to point out which girl he would want to have sex with. Our Friend said, "That's gross!" So the bully said, "Just point to a girl." When the Asperger's boy did, then the bully went up to the teacher and said, "Jessie said he wants to sleep with Rebecca." And our Friend was punished by the teacher.

It took us a long time to unravel exactly what had happened because this boy doesn't see the Big Picture, and didn't remember the exact sequence of events until it was pulled out of him. Breaking it down into small steps is the best way to ferret out the details and figure out what happened.

At the Friends' Club, where we only have one hour each week, we start by playing games or role-playing. Whatever activity will open up dialogue and lead to awareness, we pursue it.

For instance, one of our leaders invented the group game Impersonations, Jeopardy Style, for our older boys. Taking turns, each boy impersonates an actor in a scene from a movie or video game. The rest of the boys write what they think the impersonation is meant to be.

Now there are two things that make this more challenging than it sounds. First, an Aspie style of impersonation is to give as little help as possible to the viewer. Second, the Aspie impersonator assumes that others can read his mind, so few clues are needed anyway.

This becomes part of the exercise, to teach the impersonator that the rest of the group needs more clues in order to make good guesses.

And, of course, our Asperger's kids' minds latch on to the obscure and not the mainstream. It's the lesser-known ideas, facts, movies, books, etc., that capture and hold our Friends' interest, not the more conventional things that the rest of us would notice and remember. So we needed to make a new rule that you can only impersonate an actor or a movie scene familiar to "most people" since other people cannot read your mind to know the obscure.

What the acting out does is to give our kids the opportunity to express feelings. This is a first step for them to be able to show their own feelings later, at other times. We often tell our Friends that it's okay if they pretend or act out feelings that they may not have right then, but that the other person may need to see. If they act out the feeling, then later, the feeling will be more familiar to them.

As for reading other people—understanding their faces and trying to determine others' thoughts or feelings through their expressions and body language—we've made up games like the one that uses Polaroid photos of people's faces showing different expressions. We tape the pictures around the room, and then ask our younger boys and girls to go "catch" that feeling. This means they have to recognize the feeling first, and then they are to act it out. The kids love it!

We also turn to games like Uno and especially poker, which involves bluffing. During each hand, we have the kids pay attention to the other players to "read" their faces, to determine how good their cards really are. As one Friend commented, "It would just be easier if they wrote what they were thinking on their head."

Showing certain films with complex, subtle communication scenes, and then pressing the pause button to talk about what's really going on, has proven quite effective and enlightening for our kids. Having a visual example makes it much more obvious to them.

Remember the Titans is wonderful for its scenes of misunderstandings and the true meaning of a look or a glare. *Never Been Kissed* has many scenes of very important social communication that our girls take literally, listening only to the words. They don't pay attention to the tone of voice or intention of the words, nor do they read the facial expressions or body language properly. They believe a smiling face and only hear the nice words being used, without hearing the disguised, cruel intent behind the nice words.

By stopping the movie, scene by scene, we can point out the nonverbal and verbal subtleties. The girls learn over time, with practice, to spot what they couldn't see before. Their awareness is raised.

During a group session, we talk a lot about what "most people" know and notice and care about for good reason. When we give these kids a clearer picture of how the general population sees things, our Friends get a glimpse of conventional thinking.

Our out-of-the-box thinkers benefit from this awareness of the conventional so they can relate more easily with others. But don't worry. It doesn't taint their ability to be unconventional and original. Our Friends will still be just as creative and just as able to see the world differently, even if they better understand a neurotypical viewpoint.

Being aware helps them to be less baffled and to feel more connected to their peers. This is so important in making friends, whether you're five or twenty-five years old.

By the way, one time I asked the teen girls to "read my mind." One girl looked at me and said, "Now, Cynthia, you know we can't read your mind." This literal thinking prevents Aspies from being able to interpret feelings, but at least the question made her more aware that if she couldn't read my mind, then how could she expect me to read hers?

Awareness. It's the crucial first step for all of our Friends. It's what will help them to form friendships, which they want. No one wants to feel all alone, not Asperger's kids, not anyone. The more aware they are, the better their chances of making friends, which is so important . . . even if it's just one.

See also Acquaintance Versus Friend, Asking for
Help, Awareness, First Friendships, Greetings,
Responding to Others, and Writing Things Down

REMEMBERING NAMES

As you've undoubtedly noticed, your Asperger's child has a really hard time remembering names. Granted, there are a few who learn and use names quite well, to the point where it's almost an obsession. But the vast majority of our Friends really struggle to connect a name with a face.

Why? Well, to start, it requires paying attention to the kinds of details that our kids just don't notice. Faces are confusing so they don't really look at them. People are kind of a blur so no one really stands out in their minds as individuals, and neither do their names.

Also, our Aspie Friends don't care as much about being called by their name as neurotypicals do. They know their name. You don't have to tell them it. While acknowledgment by name is important to the rest of us, it's not to them. Someone not using our name bothers us much more than it does Asperger's folks.

Yet, one of the key differences between a mere acquaintance and a friend is that friends *always* know each other's names!

That's what makes it so hard for Asperger's kids to look like they really want to be someone's friend. If they can never seem to remember the other child's name or get it straight, what kind of friend are they?

One boy's mother said that her son has no idea what the names of any of his classmates are until March or April of the school year. It just doesn't sink in until the seventh or eighth month! He can't make the names connect to the faces and stick.

So we practice strategies at Friends' Club for learning someone's name and remembering it. One is to look at the person's face or what they are wearing for visual cues. Do they have a distinctive nose? Are their eyes blue and their name starts with a *B*? Do they wear glasses? Anything that will make that person distinctive in the child's mind.

Of course, most of the time, our Friends don't really look anyone in the eye. They look at the mouth because, as one of our Friends said, "That's where the words come from." Consequently, they miss many obvious clues of hair color, freckles, teeth, etc., unless it's pointed out to them. So, to learn names, we teach our kids that they must look at the person for at least a few moments so that the face can register in their mind's eye.

We also teach them to listen for clues to what that person is interested in or for their sense of humor. If a person has a title, like "Doctor" or "Principal," that seems to help. In my case, "Doctor" is easier for them to remember than "Cynthia."

During our sessions, we have activities that require using the name of each person in the group to reinforce the label in our kids' minds.

For instance, the kids love to be helpers. So when we ask someone to pass out materials, we ask him to use each person's name before handing out the piece of paper or pencil. We also write everyone's name on the whiteboard or on the schedule, so the names are in black and white for our younger Friends to see. **Writing things down for this crowd is very, very important.**

Another very successful activity with the younger Friends is our version of Duck, Duck, Goose, which we call Name, Name, Goose. We have the group sit on the floor in a circle. Then the child who is It gets to go around and tap each Friend's head, but instead of saying, "Duck," the tapper says each boy's name as he goes around the circle.

When he finally says, "Goose," that person leaps up to try to catch the member who is It. Very quickly, it becomes apparent who has learned the other members' names and who still needs to work on it.

The bonus to the whole group taking a turn is that everyone hears all the names a lot, which reinforces them in their minds. Repetition more than anything else helps our kids learn each other's name.

We also teach our Friends that if they forget someone's name, it's a good idea to ask someone else for help. We show them how to quietly lean over and whisper their question, "Do you know her name?" These kids are not inclined to ask for help for anything, so this is a twofold lesson in admitting you don't know everything, and learning and remembering a name.

Every session, we reintroduce all the members to one another until we hear them use their new Friends' names on their own. All of us can have trouble learning a new acquaintance's name, but the more you use it, the more you are going to remember it.

The rule "Use it or lose it" applies in remembering names as much as it does in anything else. So we use names every session to make sure the boys and girls connect with their group and truly feel recognized as friends.

See also Conversation, Listening to Others, Rudeness, *and* Taking One's Leave

RESPONDING TO OTHERS

Many times, a boy or girl in one of our groups speaks up to share an idea or experience. No one responds. There's just silence.

As unnerving and rude as it seems to the rest of us, this is not unusual for Asperger's kids.

They assume that you know that they are listening and that they heard you. So they see no reason or need to respond. (Of course, they may well have been spacing out and really didn't hear you. But they assume that you will repeat something if it's truly important.)

One of our goals is to make our Friends understand the importance of acknowledging what someone has said. It really is crucial to let the other person know that you were, indeed, listening. Responding to a speaker not only helps build friendships, but it's critical in school and in the workplace. Everyone who speaks expects a response of some sort. Silence will not do.

Since our kids don't grasp this behavior intuitively, we teach them what to say and then practice it weekly. A response does not have to be much. Something as simple as "That's cool" or "Me, too" works fine. Even "Good" and "Yes" or "No" are sufficient, and better than no response at all.

Then we practice by starting conversations and asking members to share their thoughts, feelings, or experiences. We wait to see how the listeners respond. If the kids don't say anything, we model what the appropriate response could be, by saying "Really?" or "Okay." Then we ask more questions and keep giving the kids a chance to respond.

The bottom line is that *any* response to someone's thoughts or ideas is better than silence. Not acknowledging the speaker's comments is interpreted as the listener being rude or uncaring. Responding is a basic code of conduct that cannot be broken if our Friends are to become more accepted and appreciated by others.

Fortunately, making a response is such a simple thing to do—one syllable ("Fine") or two ("Uh-huh") is sufficient to let the speaker know you heard them. The more an Asperger's child or teen practices responding, the more successful a listener they will seem. Do your child a favor and make sure they respond when you converse. Practice may not make perfect, but it will make a response more automatic.

See also Annoying Behavior, Awareness, Bluntness and Unintentional Insults, Compliments, Courtesy, Greetings, Manners, Perfectionism and Unrealistic Expectations, Responding to Others, Sensory Sensitivities, Taking One's Leave, *and* "White Lies" and Sparing Others' Feelings

RUDENESS

On a rudeness scale of one to ten, Asperger's folks can quickly reach seven or eight without saying a word, and then hit nine or ten once they do.

It's never intentional.

There is no cruelty or malice behind their behavior or comments.

Nothing they say or do is meant to hurt or offend other people. But it does.

Our Friends' rudeness stems from their unawareness of others. They don't realize that it's not okay to be totally honest about what they think or feel. They see, they speak—they do not filter. They do not have the intuition to figure out the code of conduct that dictates good manners. This can be a social nightmare.

Unaware that, to spare someone's feelings, you wouldn't say something that way or perhaps you wouldn't say it at all, our Friends hurt their parents', siblings', and total strangers' feelings by saying exactly what they think. To them, the truth is the truth—why shouldn't they say it?

For example, one mother told us about an episode while she was volunteering one morning in the library at her son's middle school. Lots of students were milling about before the bell rang. She was standing next to her eighth grader when a girl came up to her son and said, "You're the one who called me and my friend stupid the other day in English class."

Mortified, the mother said to the girl, "Well, I'm sure he didn't mean it. He apologized, right?"

"No," said the girl.

The mother turned to her son. "You need to apologize, right now."

"Why?" said her son. "They are stupid."

Cringing even more, the mother sternly told her son, "That is rude, and you need to apologize because you've hurt her feelings."

Unmoved, the son stood there, looking confused. "But they didn't even know that more questions were on the back of the worksheet."

The mother shook her head. "Not everyone knows the same things you know. That doesn't make them stupid. You need to apologize right now."

While her son did say he **was** sorry, and the girl moved on, it wasn't until after school that the mother could really talk with her son. She made him realize how much it hurts people's feelings to be called names, even if it seems to be the truth to him.

Once he understood what he had done, and remembered being called names himself and how much it had hurt, *then* her son felt terrible about it. He went back to school the next day and apologized again, more sincerely, to both girls.

This is very typical for our Asperger's Friends—they are purveyors of truth. Their truth. So they do not understand how bad their comments sound because it's just the truth to them. They have no inkling of their rudeness. And it's only *after* the fact that they can be made to understand how much words can hurt, which is surprising since they have been called names before and been hurt themselves.

Sometimes such episodes come out in Friends' Club sessions. We welcome these unplanned opportunities to talk about being too blunt and hurting others' feelings. We teach them a catchphrase: "Stop and think before you speak."

We have also dubbed such moments of making a mistake or saying something that we wished we could take back as "rubber chicken moments." This is based on a humorous prop used by Michelle Garcia Winner with her groups. It's a lot like when we hit ourselves on the forehead with our hand after a blunder.

A toy rubber chicken (or any funny-looking substitute) is tapped on the head of the Friend who made a mistake. Everyone laughs, including the boy or girl who made the mistake. This helps them see the humor in blunders and that the world does not end if they are not right or perfect all the time.

Just as important, we talk about how that person can "repair" the error that was made. Is an apology enough? Is an explanation in order?

How much should they say about what they said or did? Would a compliment be appropriate to soften things? All of these are unknowns to our Friends. They need help figuring out how to mend the damage, if possible. They also need to know how to get over having made the mistake so it doesn't replay in their head over and over, which such blunders are prone to do.

As one of our young men said, "I just have to try to forget it or I get angry." This was great insight from one of our members! Anger is an issue because Asperger's kids expect perfection of themselves and others. The best way to avoid getting angry is to apologize and explain the unintended mistake, learn from it, and then *move on*.

If they've made an unintentional insult, it often takes a long conversation to pierce their rigid view that they are right. It takes even more effort to get them to see how socially unacceptable their comments can be, but it does sink in eventually. Repetition and practice are the keys to all the social skills training that we do at the Friends' Club.

Asperger's social cluelessness also makes it tough for them to learn even the basic manners of polite society. They don't think burping, nose picking, sneezing without covering your mouth, and talking with your mouth full is a big deal or offensive really. They just don't think about it at all. The importance of good manners, personal grooming, and good hygiene is lost on them.

Facts and truth are what are paramount, not the niceties of acceptable behavior. But for other people to want to be their friends, these kids need to learn the basics. That knowledge comes from being taught and practicing.

One very effective tool is the book that we've used with our tween and teen groups, *How Rude!: The Teenagers' Guide to Good Manners, Proper Behavior, and Not Grossing People Out* by Alex J. Packer. With hefty doses of humor, this practical book covers so many of the social skills and relationship questions that our kids have that it always stirs up lively conversations.

I highly recommend getting your own copy of *How Rude!* for your tween or teen to read or for you to share with them. It covers all sorts of social situations that your child will encounter, public and private, whether she's with family or out in the real world. The book satisfies our Friends' craving for rules, offering invaluable facts and guidance to help our Friends understand social intricacies. The humorous approach makes them more receptive to the message.

Most of all, though, what works best is explaining the behavior that you want your child to learn. Remember, they don't learn from being told what not to do. They need someone to **tell them exactly what they should do**.

For Asperger's kids, even the simplest social skill must be broken down into small steps for them to understand it. What the rest of us do unconsciously and intuitively is what they need to be made conscious of and taught in small pieces. Spell it out. It's okay. They need clarity and specifics.

The good news—there is hope! They can become less rude, eventually. As you know by now, every Asperger's person is different and there is no fixed timetable, no guarantees, but there is always hope.

See also Acceptance, Compliance, Cooperaton, Moving On to New Things, Obsessions and Obsessive Behavior, Perspectives and Point of View, Sensory Sensitivities, *and* Writing Things Down

RULES

On the whole, Asperger's kids are rule followers. That's the good news.

Oddly enough, though, they may refuse to follow rules that they don't understand or that seem illogical. That's the bad news.

Although born to be rule followers, children with Asperger's are also born to be out-of-the-box thinkers. Their very unconventional view of the world makes it hard sometimes for them to accept conventional thinking. That is, the kind of thinking that creates rules believed necessary by the neurotypical population.

If there are rules that they don't agree with, or rules that don't make sense to them and their thinking, then they challenge them. Our Friends have no qualms about questioning authority or rule makers or the rules themselves. We should be glad. This is exactly how innovation and inventions are born.

As George Bernard Shaw once said, "The reasonable man adapts himself to the world; the unreasonable one persists in trying to adapt the world to himself. Therefore, all progress depends on the unreasonable man."

Some famous "unreasonable" men who are now thought to have had Asperger's based on their quirky behavior and obsessions are Albert Einstein, Thomas Edison, Sir Isaac Newton, Thomas Jefferson, Charles Darwin, Beethoven, Hans Christian Andersen, Gregor Mendel, H. G. Wells, and Vincent van Gogh. We shouldn't be surprised.

An Aspie's brain is wired for truly original thinking. Born to be unconventional thinkers, they are more likely to be rule breakers, instead of rule makers.

But how do you help them to be rule followers?

Even Aspies need to follow rules, for their own safety, for group concerns, or for social reasons.

Again, the good news is that as long as the rule makes sense to them or they trust you that it's necessary, then they'll follow it. Once they've questioned it, and been given a satisfactory, logical, *unemotional* explanation for why they should follow certain rules, then they will abide by them . . . sometimes too well.

In fact, that's the irony. Once they accept the rules, they tend to latch on to rules too tightly. Rules are concrete and certain. They become their comfort zone, to hang on to in an ever-changing, puzzling world. Couple that with an Aspie's natural inflexibility and it can make it very hard for them to adjust and bend the rules to have fun when the rules become too binding for everyone else.

We address rules both ways at Friends' Club. We are always prepared to have a logical explanation for why a rule is necessary and why our Friends need to follow it. We are also prepared to tell them when to loosen up and when not to be too worried about the rules, for the sake of having more fun when playing with friends or playing games.

Please know that their objection to certain rules is purely an intellectual challenge. This is not about power or control. Unfortunately, an Asperger's child's refusal to follow rules is often misperceived as being disrespectful or spoiled or a discipline problem. It's not true.

Give an Aspie a logical, acceptable explanation for the rule he's being asked to follow, and he will usually obey. Something as simple as "It's for your safety" or "It's the school's policy" or "It's the law" should work. Spoken clearly and calmly, this approach usually gets results.

That said, there are occasions when our Friends' sensory sensitivities or special interests or obsessions get in the way of them being able to comply. If they're put off by too much noise, too-bright lights, too cold or hot an environment, then they may balk at following the rules.

Or if the rule somehow encroaches on or conflicts with one of their special interests, and they are obsessed with doing something or not doing something, then they may not cooperate. These are the times when Asperger's kids just can't follow the rules. What can you do? How can you gain their cooperation?

Again, it's not about power or control, as it may be with a neurotypical child. To find out what is holding them back, ask them questions. Lots of questions. And be prepared for some surprises.

At Friends' Club, we help them over such hurdles by talking about what's stopping them. We ask them why they are refusing to do something. If it's easily remedied, we handle it. If not, we explain why they need to follow the rule that we're presenting and we calmly explain until we reach an understanding.

If an obsession is in the way, we put it "in a box" to remove it as an issue. We literally open a small box, act like we're dropping something in, and then close the lid. As simple as it sounds, it works.

One technique we've used when the opposite happens, and our Friends become too rigid and too focused on precisely playing a game so that it's not fun, is to change the rules to that game. This gets them used to the idea of accepting new rules and new ways of playing.

Some of our Friends break rules on their own, but as usual, it's in an all-or-nothing kind of way. They ignore all the rules for the way a game is supposed to be played and instead, they use the pieces or cards to come up with their own new game with a new set of rules. For instance, using Apples to Apples decks, one boy came up with "Battle Apples." Borrowing heavily from Yu-Gi-Oh card rules, he used certain Apples cards to summon combatants, power them up, and attack his opponents.

As we say over and over, "Expect the unexpected" with these girls and boys.

And that's the thing. Going along with their black-or-white, either/or personalities, *either* they follow the game precisely and adhere to all the rules *or* they make up their own game with completely new rules and ignore what existed before. What we strive to teach them is that there is a middle ground. Shaded areas abound where everything is not black or white. The real world is many shades of gray, and it helps our Friends to be aware of this.

Working with anyone with Asperger's means that you will gain a fresh perspective on everything. They continue to surprise and often delight us with their originality and unusual observations.

We urge you to embrace their differences.

Encourage their outlook.

And nurture their strengths because you may be fostering the next groundbreaking, "unreasonable" innovator to help push our society forward.

See also Bullying and Bullies, Conversation, Humor, Intentions, Literal Language, Talking with Peers, *and* Teasing

SARCASM

Being the literal-minded folks they are, Asperger's kids tend to take what anyone says at face value. They miss innuendos. They have no tongue-in-cheek detector. They can't tell when someone is being sarcastic, or ribbing them about something to get a laugh or a rise out of them.

Even self-deprecating humor is lost on this group because it sounds like the person is putting themselves down by admitting how bad they are at something, when really they're making fun of themselves to find humor in a stupid mistake or lack of talent.

The problem with sarcasm is that it's not self-inflicted, like self-deprecation. Sarcasm is aimed at others. Asperger's folks make good targets because they don't hear the true, underlying meaning. They only catch the surface words.

People can laugh at our Friends twice as hard for two reasons: first, because they're being made fun of, and second, they don't even know they're being made fun of.

That's why we teach a technique of being direct with whoever is speaking. Addressing the sarcasm outright defuses the situation and deflates the power of the other person's words.

For example, one of our seventh graders was walking by a girl in his class and she said, "Nice shirt."

Our Friend turned to her and said, "I don't understand sarcasm, so were you being serious or sarcastic?"

This caught her off guard and, without saying another word, she wandered off. By questioning her motives, our Friend took the fuel out of her potential laugh at his expense.

What we also teach our Friends is to listen for the meaning, not just notice the words or delivery. Since our kids are easily fooled by a smile or laugh when someone says something, they need to be more aware of how mean kids can laugh even as they hurt feelings. Making our kids conscious of another's true intentions—the true meaning of what they're saying—is what will help them in the long run and help them deflect sarcasm.

A final reason this brand of humor is particularly painful for our Asperger's kids is that sarcasm zeroes in on people's imperfections. Our perfectionist-prone Friends would be ultrasensitive to having their mistakes or flaws pointed out, so this kind of humor is even more hurtful to them and best nipped in the bud.

Given that sarcasm is often embedded in teasing or bullying, it's not something that should be ignored altogether by our Friends. Research has shown that bullying will intensify if the child being targeted says nothing. So we teach and practice responses to any bullying and teasing, sarcastic or otherwise, so that our Friends will know what to do if the occasion arises.

Simple phrases like "If you say so" or "So what?" or "That's boring" work well, being generic enough to fit most situations. Be sure to remind your child or teen that if they are ever being teased or bullied, they should say *something*—"Yeah, right" or "So you say" or "Be nice"— and then walk away and find an adult (see Further Information About Bullying in Part Three: Resources for more ideas).

See also Bullying and Bullies, Depression, Embarrassment, Perspectives and Point of View, *and* Strengths and How to Cultivate Them

SELF-ESTEEM

This won't come as much of a surprise, but Asperger's kids are different from neurotypical children when it comes to building their self-esteem.

Their natural, built-in arrogance and conviction that they are right (and others are wrong) provides a solid base of a type of brittle self-esteem. No one has to convince them to believe in and trust their own opinions. If anything, we're trying to make our Asperger's Friends realize other people have worthwhile ideas, too, and that they should listen to and respect others' opinions.

What we do find is that because our Friends are often bullied and laughed at, such negative behavior does deflate their social self-esteem. To some degree, our Friends know that they are different and don't always fit in. They know that they are socially out of step with the other kids. This can make them feel more isolated and even depressed, dampening their opinion of themselves.

What's also hard for them is that they need so much extra help just to make it through the school day.

With the frontal lobe deficits sabotaging their sense of time and ability to organize, our Friends need help getting started on tasks, staying on task, collecting their work, making sure it gets into their binder, and handing it in at school. Their inability to prioritize and get organized can undermine their self-esteem because it means so little will get done without outside help. Plus there are so many opportunities for them to mess up and make mistakes.

The opportunities to build themselves up through tackling challenging endeavors on their own are fewer and farther between than for the rest of us.

At Friends' Club, we ask the kids what makes them like themselves. One girl said that she liked herself when she shared her toys with her sister. Another liked herself when she had done all her chores. Do you hear the pattern?

The best method for self-esteem building with Asperger's kids is to focus on what they do themselves, and not what they can't do or what is done for them. By focusing on the thoughtful or productive things they've done, our Friends realize that they are worthwhile and that they can make a contribution.

Gail Heyman, a professor of psychology at the University of California, San Diego, once said, "Self-esteem really comes from mastering something difficult, not from being praised all the time."

For our Friends, just getting through the day *is* difficult!

They must face so many hard-to-read social cues. They are baffled by all the abstract thinking. Their sensitivities to light, noise, heat, cold, tastes, and smells make them feel bombarded. Day-to-day life is truly a challenge for reasons far different than it is for the rest of us.

Consequently, any little success they achieve is much bigger than you think because their scale of achievement is not the same as the one for neurotypicals. With all the criticism they hear for being disorganized, quirky, blunt, anxious, uncooperative, etc., they need to hear something other than what they're doing wrong . . . a little praise goes a long way for the little things they do right.

So if you know your child has kept going to finish a hard assignment, remembered to brush his teeth on his own, or climbed higher on the jungle gym than ever before, please praise him. He probably won't recognize his victory, so you need to point it out for him.

Let your child know how proud you are whenever he does the right thing and does it well (or well enough). This will make him feel better about himself and feel more hopeful about his future.

Again, our Asperger's Friends hear all day long about how slow they are or messy or off topic or annoying or rude. So whenever you can offer them a kind word about what they're doing right, it's a great idea to do so. That's the kind of praise that will build their self-esteem.

See also Conversation, Curiosity About People,
Empathy, Listening to Others, and Perspectives
and Point of View

SELFISHNESS

Let's face it, it's easy for Asperger's individuals to appear quite selfish to neurotypicals.

First, they don't pay attention to or show any curiosity about other people, usually preferring to be alone, on their own.

Second, they prefer to talk only about their ideas without asking other people what they think. There are no niceties. They don't ask others how their day went or what they would like to do.

Third, Aspies prefer to do things their way, convinced that it is the "right" and only way. They will reject others' notions and suggestions outright.

And finally, being bombarded by sensory stimuli and blindsided by the unexpected, an Aspie spends his time fending off anxiety and trying to keep calm and get through the day.

Is it any wonder that they seem quite selfish?

What other people don't know is that Asperger's folks are wired to only see things from their unique perspective, which means they can't read the social cues or signals sent by other people. Research indicates that their mirror neurons are deficient, preventing them from intuitively knowing what someone else is thinking or feeling. This makes them appear all the more self-centered, since they are trapped in their own perspective with everything coming from only their viewpoint.

Our goal at the Friends' Club is to help our kids make friends by becoming more socially aware. If they can learn some basic skills to help them read social cues, then they will be able to make friends.

The most fundamental skill is active listening. Learning to listen to others is critical to friendships. It is not just talking and expecting them to always listen to you, which is what Aspies do, but you pausing to listen to them and following up with questions. This is one of our kids' toughest challenges to master.

We work on teaching them the reciprocal nature of conversation: someone talks and you listen, then you talk and they listen. It takes a lot of practice and reinforcement for our Friends to realize that conversation is not about spouting off your views, expecting everyone to be quiet and then agree with you. Conversation is about an exchange of ideas and opinions. Everyone should get a turn.

Of course, just teaching this in a straightforward way would be boring, especially to the younger kids. So we've found a few games that help teach giving up your point of view and adopting someone else's viewpoint, all while you converse with others. The games are Apples to Apples, Whoonu, and Cranium. (See the Perspectives and Point of View section for instructions on Apples to Apples.)

Cranium involves more than reading and words. It has a drawing component, a drama bit, and other activities. But it still requires group effort and perceptions. It takes into account how another player will perceive your hints, clues, or pantomime to get to the right answer. You can't just think from your own point of view. You must think of your teammate and how he will interpret your gestures and squiggles.

With the card game Whoonu, each player gets five cards showing things that people like or dislike. One player is It, and the other players have to think about what that person would like the most. When the cards are played, the chooser ranks them on a scale from one to six with six being his most liked thing. The winner is the player who put down the highest-ranking card and he gets to be It next.

The bottom line is that any game, activity, or interaction that encourages our Friends to think about someone else's point of view, requires them to listen to someone else's opinion, and makes them practice the give-and-take of conversation is moving them in the right direction.

The less selfish and self-centered our Asperger's kids seem to others, the more likely they are to make friends. And even gaining one friend makes them feel so much less alone, and more part of this world.

them more socially appropriate ways to stim. The goal is to be less obvious. If their behavior is less distracting to others, then it makes them less of a target for teasing. Our kids stand out enough without drawing attention to themselves through repetitive behaviors.

One of our boys would flap his hands whenever he was anxious. We taught him to wring his hands, which is a more subtle gesture, or better still, put his hands in his pockets so they would be less noticeable. It worked! Once he was aware that he had an alternative, and with some practice, he switched from flapping to tucking his hands in his pockets.

Remember, whenever your child gets anxious or stressed, the less emotion you show, the less upset your child will get. Then the faster they can recover and calm down. Use a quiet voice, show no emotion, and offer a logical explanation whenever possible.

The key is to look at their surroundings and at the adult supervision available. Often, stimming increases when Aspie kids are on their own in difficult situations where other kids are running around and playing and supervision is minimal. At parks, playgrounds, and birthday parties, be sure to keep an eye on your child and never leave them unattended or assume someone else will keep an eye on him for you.

Structured settings are less stressful for Asperger's children. Unstructured settings and activities mean **supervision is necessary** by you or another understanding adult.

See also Admitting When You're Scared,
Anxiety, Appearance, Calming Down and
Focusing, Change and "Change-ups," Fear,
Grooming and Personal Hygiene, Holiday
Gatherings, Leaving the House, Meltdowns,
Physical Inactivity, Self-regulation or
"Stimming," Staying Calm, *and* Travel

SENSORY SENSITIVITIES

Yes, your child really is bothered by that little tag in his T-shirt or the seam in his sock.

Yes, a vacuum cleaner, a trash truck, and any kind of music really can be way too loud for your Asperger's child to tolerate.

And yes, certain foods (perhaps many foods) may not appeal to your child. The flavor is too strong. The texture is too strange. The smell or look of the food is somewhat suspicious. The temperature is too hot or too cold, or perhaps only room temperature is the tolerable choice whether it's soup or ice cream.

It's kind of like living with Goldilocks, where it can't be too this or too that and it has to be just right or your Aspie child won't accept it.

Welcome to the world of heightened sensory sensitivities experienced by our Friends on the autism spectrum.

Sounds, sights, smells, tastes, and textures that would never give the rest of us another thought truly bother many Asperger's children. As Tony Attwood relays in his book *The Complete Guide to Asperger's Syndrome*, 70 to 85 percent of Asperger's kids are extremely sensitive to certain sounds. More than 50 percent are extremely sensitive to the feel or touch of certain tactile experiences. And more than 50 percent of our Friends have smell and taste sensitivities that can be remarkably acute, but which also can make them incredibly fussy when it comes to food.

Of course, with this group, one size never fits all. What bothers one Asperger's child may not bother another. And even the same child may be hypersensitive to one sound, then not even hear another! Commonly, there is a mix of oversensitivity and undersensitivity in individuals, which may fluctuate randomly.

It is safe to say, though, that they are all prone to being assaulted by sensory stimuli far more than any of us realize. Both Tony Attwood and Temple Grandin, a well-known author, professor, and business consultant who has high-functioning autism, have confirmed that when Aspies are asked what is the one thing that they wish they could change about their condition, all say that they would want to reduce their sensory sensitivities.

Such sensitivities are the hardest thing for them to live with—even harder than all the social miscommunications and their difficulty in getting organized, being on time, etc. Their sensory issues make it difficult for them to understand and tolerate a normal environment. Places like stores, swimming pools, parties, and classrooms can overwhelm their senses.

And those who are undersensitive to sensory input may self-stimulate (called "stimming") or even self-injure in order to get the input their nervous system needs. This is the kind of behavior that impacts our Friends in social settings.

So what can we do to help?

As always, being understanding instead of condemning is the best first step. They really can't help being so sensitive.

No matter how hard you try, you won't convince them that a certain sound, smell, or taste is no big deal. It is a big deal to them. Arguing is futile, so it's better to console them and listen. Why make the situation more antagonistic and difficult than it has to be?

What helps is to realize that sensory avoidance or overload is behind much of their quirky behavior and seeming misbehavior. The more you accept this, the less frustrated and emotional you'll be. Then the more they'll feel understood and the faster they'll calm down.

The obvious next step is to ask what's bothering them. If they can't tell you, look around and guess what is upsetting them so that you can remove the offending item or lower the volume.

Always let them leave the space where they are feeling assaulted. Allowing them to go elsewhere to find peace is important to their ability to regain their self-control.

But sometimes, they can't leave. One of our young Friends was having problems staying at the lunch table where the teachers wanted him to sit. Even when they realized that it was being so close to the lunch cart with its strong smells that was bothering the boy, the staff said it was the only place he could sit. No one knew what to do.

Then one of my staff members asked the boy what he thought might work to help him stay at the table. The boy suggested packing something that smelled good in his lunch, and he could hold that up to his nose whenever he needed it. Guess what? It worked.

Speaking of food, many children on the autism spectrum are very picky eaters. This is often because the taste, smell, or texture of a food bothers them. Research has shown that some Aspies suffer gastrointestinal problems, which may be relieved by a casein-free and gluten-free diet. This diet does not cure autism, but it can reduce their discomfort, which helps them deal with their quirky behavior.

The good news is that, as they grow older, many of our Friends' sensitivities diminish or they find better ways to cope so that they are less bothered than when they were younger. By late adolescence or early adulthood, such offending conditions as bright sunlight, loud stereos, and scratchy cloth may become more tolerable. They may not even mind if their food servings are touching each other or that things are cut a certain way.

At the Friends' Club, we keep in mind their sensitivities and respect their wishes, to a degree. We also know that the real world will not always be peaceful or quiet, so we don't shelter them either. **It's called pushing with understanding.**

Being trained in sensory integration strategies, as are most of my staff, I make sure that we incorporate activities from Brain Gym and other sensory strategies into our group settings. The video *Brainercize* from Brain Gym is a good way to get our kids energized, which we like to do at the beginning of a session. Then it's followed by a calming activity like a hum-along or breathing exercise, before we begin the discussion on the carpet.

This progression of fast to medium to quiet activities has worked quite well. By incorporating more sensory activities in a natural way with a stimulating activity up front followed by a "cooldown," we've found that our Friends are better able to focus and will fidget less.

Even then, though, some of our kids need help to sit and listen to one another. That's why we offer weighted stuffed animals like snakes and geckos that are filled with dry beans or rice kernels. Our Friends like to drape these objects over their shoulders or rest them on their laps. There is an obvious calming effect for those children who have a sensitivity to touch and pressure. It definitely helps them pay attention better to the group discussion.

With our younger Friends, we play games like How Does Your Engine Run? and musical chairs and musical pillows. All of these teach sensory regulation.

How Does Your Engine Run? teaches the kids to think of their bodies as engines. Then they are to figure out what speed they're going at—whether it's "slow," "medium slow," "fast," or "very fast." What we're aiming for is not too slow, not too fast, but the "just right" setting.

The more aware they are of their speed, the better they can self-regulate and the less they will need to move and physically shift their bodies in order to calm themselves or to feel their space.

At the beginning of every group meeting, we gauge our Friends' sensory systems and we willingly alter our group lesson, if necessary, to match their current state. Such customization is critical to the success of our whole program. Our kids' and teens' sensory sensitivities will interfere with any learning that goes on, their own and that of the others in the group, if someone is being disruptive.

So we must be attuned to our Friends' level of sensory stress. And we have no qualms about changing our written schedule to accommodate the group members' needs. Flexibility is the name of the game.

Plus such changes to the written schedule show our boys and girls how "change-ups" happen. It reinforces that change must be taken in stride as a part of life. Just because you have planned something doesn't mean that everything must or will go according to plan.

Life throws *all* of us curveballs. We want to teach our Friends how to catch curveballs rather than be knocked out by them. We want them to know that the goal is to stay in the game, not to be rigid or "right" or sidelined by sensory sensitivities.

This is also why our curriculum is never set in stone, because what is planned is not necessarily what happens. These are Asperger's kids—we learned in the very first sessions that we have to expect the unexpected. Staying flexible allows us to tap into our Asperger's kids' current state of mind and body for the maximum teaching and learning effect, so the trade-off is worth it.

During our group sessions, we've also learned to read the children to know when they need a quick break. Then we bring out things like *SongGames*, which is a music CD produced by an occupational therapist to incorporate sensory integration into music. Or we'll take the whole group out into the parking lot to play a game of football. Sometimes we have them run around the block or play tag.

When some of our Friends' sensory sensitivities are being triggered, we like to have the children tell one another when they're being too loud or if something is annoying them. The ability to communicate that someone is bothering them is an important friendship skill. Since our kids are apt to put their hands over their ears if someone is being too loud—and such a gesture is not appropriate for older children—we teach them to ask that person to be quiet. We want them to be assertive while still appropriate.

In one group, a girl was whining because she hadn't won a game. Another girl said, "Stop crying. It's too loud." This was great! First, we want our Friends to hear such a comment from one another and not always from an adult. And second, she used a simple and direct approach without being too blunt.

As much as we try to take into account our group's sensory sensitivities, we also believe in working on the issue and pushing with understanding.

So when those things occur that are out of our control, like when one of the kids becomes very excited or agitated and whoops and hollers and makes loud noises, we don't get upset or try to force them to do what we intended. We turn such outbursts into teachable moments and learning opportunities. Calmly, unemotionally, we address the behavior and once it's resolved, we go back to the group's activity.

One parent told us how her son spent most of first grade under the table. His teacher told her, "This is the weirdest kid I've ever had."

Fortunately, the boy's mother had figured out that the noise and liveliness of a first-grade class were overwhelming her son's ultrasensitive senses. So she asked the teacher to let her son continue to sit under the table and to *not* worry about teaching her son. The mom even drew up a contract to make it clear that it was okay for her son to observe and not participate in class for the first month of school.

What the mother and father knew was that their first-grade son was perfectly bright. He could already read at a fifth-grade level and do algebra. What he couldn't do was handle the noise and confusion of a primary school classroom. What he needed, the mother realized, was to be comfortable and get used to being in class before he could learn.

And sure enough, her son did come out from under the table eventually and settled into the classroom routine. He went on to take many Advanced Placement classes in high school and continued on to college.

Albert Einstein had sensory issues, particularly with touch. He wore slippers and other comfortable clothes to the Swiss patent office where he worked. And later, when teaching at Princeton University, he wore sweatshirts to class instead of a suit and tie like other professors.

Einstein's hair was long and wild, rather than fashionably cut, which probably meant that he was avoiding scissors and trimming shears, commonly loathed by Asperger's folks.

Where you can take heart is that Einstein's sensory issues didn't stop him from tapping his potential and changing the way we all look at our world. These sensory issues are one more challenge for your child, but not an insurmountable one.

See also Bullying and Bullies, Conversation, Literal Language, Talking with Peers, *and* Teasing

SLANG AND IDIOMS

All of us grow up hearing idioms, slang, and colorful expressions. They are part of the liveliness and nature of contemporary language.

Kids, and teens in particular, adopt new expressions all the time. They take a typical word and change its meaning into something quite different; for example, *sick* means "terrific" and *wicked* means "cool." Or they make up new words altogether, as in *bodilicious* for being "very attractive."

Since we hear slang expressions and idioms every day, we learn to understand their meaning through the context of how they're used. We listen for and learn to find the hidden meaning. We become so good at it that we don't give it a second thought. It's so automatic, we don't stop and think when or why we use them, we just do.

This is not the case for Asperger's kids. Born to be *very* literal with language, they take words strictly at face value. One of our girls thought that being called a "fruitcake" meant that the person was sweet. Our Friends are unable to detect and understand the underlying message of idioms and slang.

And some are bothered that words are not being used the "right" way. This happened in one group when a boy refused to participate in an idiom lesson that we had planned. Instead of getting angry or forcing him to participate, I pulled him aside and asked what he was afraid of. "I don't want to say those things because they don't sound right," he said.

I explained that the purpose of the activity was for him to understand what idioms meant when he heard them said by others. "I don't have to say them?" he asked. When I said, "No," then he went right back in to join the group in the activity.

Our intent is not to make these kids become someone they're not. We don't want them to become fakes or to parrot every slang expression spoken by other kids. Our Asperger's children are original thinkers and independently minded. They should be valued for that. But they will get along better and blend in to a degree if they understand what slang and idiomatic expressions mean, so they can respond appropriately.

Not being able to detect the underlying meaning of idioms or slang makes it all the more difficult for our Friends to communicate with their peers and gain a measure of acceptance. Without coaching, they just don't get it when it comes to spoken slang.

That's why we work on this social skill all the time at the Friends' Club. For them to be even minimally accepted by their peers, and more important, to become less of a target for bullies and others who would use our Friends' vulnerabilities against them, our Friends must learn to understand the hidden meaning of the language of their age group. Again, they don't have to use the idiom, just understand it.

Of course, slang and idioms baffle nonnative English-speaking kids as well. They struggle with American slang and idioms, which are foreign to them. They have to learn the hidden meanings. But they're quicker to figure them out and remember them because, first, they have similar phrases in their native language and can make the association, and, second, they know not to take the words so literally.

One night, one of our Friends told me, "This is so confusing when normal people say these expressions! Why do they do it?" Whenever we get that question, we bring out books on the history of idioms and slang expressions to help make sense of it all. Look in the Children's Books section of Further Reading in Part Three: Resources for our favorites.

We developed a very simple activity called the Ultimate Friends' Club Idiom Game that we play with our kids. It uses a deck of cards with idiomatic expressions and a two-sheet "board" with seven spaces on each sheet. The whole idea is to engage the children in play while practicing idioms and talking about these expressions. This increases their familiarity and comfort level with this baffling part of our language.

As with humor, once some Asperger's kids unlock the secret code of how slang works, they tend to overuse it. They're so excited by the new possibilities opened up by idioms and slang, they become obsessed with this new language option. They try so hard to impress other kids, but instead annoy them. So we also cover *when* and *how much* slang to use.

Just as important is teaching them when *not* to use slang! For example, if talking slang will be misconstrued as a challenge to someone else or as making one seem a smart aleck, then it can be dangerous. If our Friends use slang around teachers and other adults, it could be seen as disrespectful or worse.

So we let them know that, to paraphrase Spider-Man's Uncle Ben, "With this new knowledge and power comes great responsibility." They must be discerning as to when and how they use the slang they've learned, and consider whom they're talking to.

Applies to all areas but see also
Change and "Change-ups," Cooperation,
Discipline, Letting Go and Refocusing,
Perfectionism and Unrealistic Expectations,
Perspectives and Point of View, *and* Writing
Things Down

SOCIAL STORIES

As we keep mentioning, Asperger's folks do not intend to say or do the wrong thing socially. It's their obliviousness, their inability to pick up social cues from the setting, and their lack of intuition about other people's feelings and thoughts that get them into trouble.

Telling Asperger's kids what they've done wrong usually just upsets and baffles them. What they need is to understand your expectations of them and the logic behind it. Then they need to be told *exactly* what you want them to do.

But so often, they don't hear the spoken words if they're engaged in an activity of interest. They have a "deaf" ear when they're absorbed in doing something they like.

Or if there is a lot of emotion in the delivery, like an angry tone or a loud voice, then Asperger's kids do hear that their parents or teachers are upset with them, but they don't know why. Such emotions throw them, so they may become argumentative and refuse to cooperate.

Again, this is not out of defiance or willfulness, but out of confusion and not wanting to change. They become stuck in the moment.

What can you do? How can you help them get unstuck?

Well, as Hans Asperger himself noted in 1944, since these kids do not have an instinctive ability to acquire social habits, then "Social adaptation has to proceed via the intellect."

The best way you can help is to use reason and facts to reach the child. Take the emotion out of any interaction with your Asperger's child and appeal to his rational side. If it's a rule or law, be sure to mention it.

Keeping a calm, level voice that is not loud and not emotional works most of the time. Go ahead and count to ten first, if that will help you regain your composure. Then talk as calmly as possible about what your child needs to do next. Usually they'll comply.

If that doesn't work, you can also take the emotion out of your message by writing it down. A piece of paper or a whiteboard work well. With short, simple sentences, your black-and-white words can be the best way for your child to "hear" you communicate what needs doing.

But what kinds of sentences?

Descriptive sentences set the stage for when they will use the skill: "When I ride in a car, I will try to stay in my seat and stay buckled."

And then **perspective sentences** teach them how others will think about them, because how others perceive their behavior never occurs to Asperger's folks: "My friends will think I'm being rude if I don't behave in their car and don't say 'thank you' when I get out."

These kinds of sentences are called Social Stories, a very visual tool pioneered by Carol Gray. Social Stories have proven to be highly successful and effective.

A Social Story is simply a few written sentences, or a long paragraph, told in the first person. Each is addressed to the individual child to highlight certain social skills that the child is struggling with. The story reads like a cue card and reminds them how they need to behave and explains how others will think of them, because they really don't know.

Remember, no matter how obvious their social mistake or misbehavior is to you, Asperger's kids don't see what they've done wrong nor do they know how to fix it.

Social Stories provide the stage for using the people skills that our Friends need to learn. These stories help put things in perspective and reduce the confusion Asperger's folks so often feel. It's best if they're kept positive with the expectation made very clear.

What Carol taught me is that it's not that they don't know the skill, but they don't know *when* to use it. A Social Story is like a script for them to read and absorb. It has the right action and characters spelled out. It tells the child what to do next in that specific situation.

Ever since my training with Carol in how to write Social Stories, I've made sure that all of us use them. These stories help our kids grasp what it is that they're doing wrong, but more important, what they *should* do in that particular situation to get along and why.

What I've also done is try to take the basic Social Story to the next level by individualizing it so that the child or teen says to himself, "This is me." I will start their story with statements about their special inter-ests, for example, "My name is Cody and I really like *Star Wars*."

One of our very smart eight-year-old Friends was unintentionally hurting other children's feelings. Since he loved *Star Wars*, I built the Jedi Code into his Social Story:

> Lately, some things have been occurring where I get upset and I cause others to get hurt. Hurt can be hurt feelings or actual physical hurt. When I say something in a rude tone of voice, I also can hurt others. This means that when I talk rudely, I'm not showing respect. I need to practice my tone of voice so that I can tell the difference between a rude voice and a friendly voice. Something that may help me is to remember the Jedi Code. It goes like this:
>
> > *There is no emotion,*
> > *there is peace.*
> > *There is no ignorance,*
> > *there is knowledge.*
> > *There is no passion,*
> > *there is serenity.*
> > *There is no death,*
> > *there is the Force.*
>
> I will try to remember that my rude tone of voice hurts others and I will try to use a gentler tone. This will mean that I am giving others respect, and being a good Jedi. My mom will like this because she will be able to say that in addition to being smart, I am also respectful.

As you can see, I mention to him how smart he is. I always try to include something about intelligence because it is a very important trait to highlight when working with our Friends. The intellect is something they understand and value, while emotions perplex and elude them. I encourage them to make a "smart" choice, which is more precise and appealing to them than if I said a "good" choice, which is vague.

This boy's mother said that this Social Story worked so well that when his tone was getting disrespectful or hurtful, all she had to do was lean over and say, "The Jedi Code," and her son immediately un-derstood how to change his tone.

That's the beauty of a Social Story tailored to the individual. It pro-vides parents and teachers with phrases or code words to be able to whisper to the Asperger's child, and that will help trigger their memory of how not to behave and how to act more appropriately.

Another type of Social Story that I write rather often for our Asperger's Friends, young and old, is about private versus public behavior. These kids are truly unaware of what you should do *only* when no one else is around and when you are in private. This includes such minor gross-outs as picking your nose or burping out loud as well as major offensive behavior like undressing in public or masturbating.

Here is a social story about private versus public behavior that I recently wrote for a twelve-year-old boy (all names have been changed):

> My name is Alan. I like a lot of things but I especially like going to school at Thornfield Middle School. I like my teachers, Renaldo, Mrs. Gordon, Devon, and of course Miss Caroline.
>
> Sometimes, at home and at school, I like to do things that should be kept private. Sometimes I do things with other people that are okay. I can eat my lunch with a friend or even play a game.
>
> Rubbing myself so that it feels good should be kept private. This is something that boys who are my age like to do but they don't do it when others can see them. It's something natural because it is something that happens to my body. Sometimes I think of something, like girls. However, it is also something very private. Private means something that I do alone. Usually I ask to use the bathroom to do this, but only at break or recess.
>
> Sometimes I want to do it in front of others. That's not a good idea. It offends other people to watch me do this. Offending others means that they don't want to watch me do this. It's a private thing.
>
> Devon and Miss Caroline tell me, "Put your hands on the table." This means that they see me doing the rubbing. They don't like it because they are offended by it. That means that they are uncomfortable. It doesn't make them feel good. It's okay to make myself feel good, but I need to do it in private.
>
> When I rub myself in public, my teachers really don't like it. Renaldo and Mrs. Gordon really don't like it. My friends don't like it. They think that I am being rude. They will talk about me and say, "Alan is being rude." My parents won't like it because Devon will need to call my mom to tell her what I am doing at school. I want De-

von and Miss Caroline to tell my mom the good things that I do at school, not the things that should be private. I need to remember this when I rub myself.

I have learned that when my Asperger's Friends argue with a Social Story that I have written for them, or correct the grammar, that's actually a good sign, behaviorally. That means that they have bought into it and it's working.

Very often, parents say to me, "But don't you think they *know* this? Isn't it obvious?" Well, to you, yes. But to someone with Asperger's, definitely not. We can't assume that anything is obvious to them.

So keep those whiteboards and sheets of paper handy, along with felt pens or pencils. Social Stories are powerful visual tools to use with Asperger's kids who need to see what you're saying in black-and-white and to gain a new perspective to function in a neurotypical world.

See also Compromise, Losing Gracefully,
Perfectionism and Unrealistic Expectations,
Perspectives and Point of View, Physical
Inactivity, Rules, Selfishness, *and* Teamwork

SPORTSMANSHIP

First, let's make it clear that Asperger's children are not typically competitive. They hate to lose, but it's not from a competitive streak. It stems from their perfectionism and their need to be right.

To them, losing at anything means that they did something wrong. Their need to win is not fired up by the quest for victory, like for most kids, but to keep from being wrong. And when they lose, they can be very bad sports.

It should be no surprise, then, that most of our Friends are rarely interested in team sports, as they are not team players by nature. Being on a team means that you share the ball or puck or whatever. Our kids hate to share because then they would have to give up control.

Also, Asperger's kids crave predictability. Sharing means that others have control and you don't know what will happen next.

And finally, the concept of sharing and team play truly eludes them. It's not selfishness, although it can look that way. They see things only from their perspective, so they cannot understand why it's important to share and include someone else.

When playing sports, you have to trust other people to do what they're supposed to do, or what you think they should do. All players have different skill levels, abilities, and maturity levels. This means that team play is full of surprises and mistakes made by teammates, our Friends included. But Asperger's kids are less able to see their own failings. They focus on everyone else's, which is hardly team friendly or sportsmanlike.

Our Friends' lack of coordination and gross motor challenges make it harder for them to pick up the skills of whatever sport they're playing. This means coaches and other players need more patience.

What's best is to find the position on the field that will play to their strengths.

One of our Friends played soccer throughout his elementary school years because even though he wasn't very good at scoring or passing the ball, he was terrific at defense and blocking the ball. Finding an Asperger's child's strengths and playing to those is always the best approach to anything.

Being a good sport in whatever you do is important in making and keeping friends. So we work on our kids' struggle with taking turns. Whether for sports, board games, or video games, all they know is that they want to play the activity and have the controls. It really doesn't occur to them that anyone else wants a turn.

And they don't realize that someone else might want to go first. While neurotypical kids at a very early age understand taking turns and alternating who goes first, our Friends don't realize that this is an important part of playing with others. It's good sportsmanship.

So that's why we play games every week with our Friends, especially the younger ones. They get continual practice at letting others go first, taking turns, maybe winning or maybe losing, and being good sports when they do lose. Practice is the best solution for this blind spot that comes from their neurological wiring. Practice, that is, in a safe place where they aren't ostracized.

Most of these stumbling blocks to sportsmanship for our Friends comes from their lack of a "theory of mind." This is the ability to think like another person would think. It's the mental version of empathy, which is being able to feel what someone else might feel. To be successful in sports, you need to guess what someone else might be thinking and anticipate their next move to stay ahead of them, whether they're the opponent or your own teammate.

Suffice it to say, becoming team-minded is highly unlikely for our Asperger's kids. Individual sports like swimming, fencing, rock climbing, karate, and running are better avenues for their physical pursuits. Because of their sensory sensitivities, it's better to avoid contact sports and big audience sports where there will be loud cheering and noise, which could upset our Friends.

Still, they need to learn the basic elements of sportsmanship because that comes out in everyday life, both at home and at school. Whether they're playing a board game with their siblings or working with a group on a school project, the concepts of being fair, taking turns and sharing information, and giving up control are embedded in *everything*.

A favorite game that we play at the Friends' Club is called SPLAT! If your Play-Doh "bug" is in the wrong space at the wrong time, it gets flattened and you are out of the game. And being out is a big deal to our Friends! Being a good loser is difficult for them.

One night, when one boy got out, he became so upset that he threw the dice and his bug across the room. We didn't get mad. We didn't punish him. All we said was, "You need to repair this."

At first, the boy resisted. Then he came up with an offer to help clean up, which worked.

One thing that neurotypical kids do more than Asperger's kids is to make up games where someone is "out." Chasing games such as tag and Capture the Flag involve escaping from someone who is It in order to keep playing and not get tagged out.

As you've undoubtedly noticed, it's more devastating for Asperger's kids to be "out" than other kids because it is seen as failure and losing. Unfortunately, they also make the easiest targets because they aren't as agile and quick at dodging out of the way. We've found that if they are told the "why" or logic behind the rules, then they resent it less.

And what we've also noticed is that many of our Friends will come up with new games or they will modify existing games. Their originality may or may not cater to their own limited sports ability, but it shows signs of creativity and can intrigue other players, if they listen and give it a chance.

See also Anxiety, Bluntness and Unintentional Insults, Calming Down and Focusing, Fear, Holiday Gatherings, Meltdowns, Self-regulation or "Stimming," *and* Sensory Sensitivities

STAYING CALM

Social interactions tend to make Asperger's kids anxious. Lacking the skills to interpret the myriad messages involved in even the simplest exchanges, our Friends get stressed. The unexpected can happen, and often does.

Our Friends have a chronic tendency to interrupt and to talk out of turn. They become too excitable around strangers, and even around people they know. Some kids are completely unable to keep their hands to themselves or their bodies in check during a group activity or conversation. They may invade someone's personal space. All of this becomes disruptive in any gathering.

Being unable to behave calmly in a group setting does not endear our Friends to others. Neurotypicals, young and old, wonder why these kids can't show more self-control. Why are they so quirky and annoying and disrespectful in what they say and do?

What's important to remember is that an Asperger's child's odd behavior is never intentional. They are not acting out or being disruptive for attention. They struggle to exercise self-control, and they even know when they're not succeeding. "Most people distract me twenty-three times a day," said one of our boys, "but I distract people only twelve and a half times a day." Staying calm and not being distracting is something they have to practice and work on so that it will become more automatic.

To make and keep friends, our Asperger's kids need to be able to remain calm enough not to scare off others. So we have the kids practice staying calm even if they're getting anxious or excitable.

One such concept we've introduced is, "Stop, think, what would happen?" This is to help our boys and girls remember to think about

their actions and the possible consequences, which may affect friendships. When the leaders demonstrated this catchphrase to a group, one
boy said, "I have to think a lot. My head is getting too big!"

This shows how unused he is to stopping and thinking about what
he says or does, and what a *chore* it feels like to these kids to slow down
and be more reflective before acting. But their social lives will improve
if they are able to stay calmer, so it's an essential lesson to learn.

We also teach basic calming techniques that our Friends can use
anytime. Deep breathing in a slow, measured way has been proven to
reduce anxiety and calm the body as it gains more oxygen.

Since our kids' inability to stay calm is often because they feel threatened by too many people or too much stimulation, we encourage them
to talk about it. Talking about a fear with safe people often makes the
problem grow smaller. Drawing a picture about what is bothering them
channels their energy into an activity, and makes the worry in their
mind more tangible.

Humming also has a calming effect, whether it's humming a song
or just doing a group hum-along. The younger kids especially respond
to a few rounds of "shhhhh—hmmmmm" to gain focus and to regain
their sense of calm.

One of our newer activities is teaching the kids a few yoga poses.
Yoga is about listening to your body, which is great for Aspies who
need to be more aware of their bodies and how they feel. Our leader
demonstrates a couple of poses or shows a video, along with showing
the kids cards with the positions.

The kids have been very willing and interested in trying it themselves. And leaders have noticed results. The kids have been calmer and
better at paying attention after a brief yoga activity.

As you can see in this and all of the lessons at the Friends' Club, our
formula is to offer a balance of empathy, support, mediation, education,
boundaries, practice, and the opportunity for kids to be with, as one
girl said, "my species." This formula has worked in reducing meltdowns,
raising participation, and instilling skills to help our kids do better in
social settings.

See also Obsessions and Obsessive Behavior
and Thinking in Pictures and Patterns

STRENGTHS AND HOW TO
CULTIVATE THEM

Many Asperger's folks are overly fond of certain things—trains, planes, computers, video games, etc.—to the point of obsession. Our Friends *love* their obsessions and special interests, which often remain lifelong passions.

Because Aspies have the social disability of not being able to read facial expressions or social signals, they cannot see how annoying and alienating their obsessions can be. On the one hand, their social blindness makes them free to love and pursue their special interests, while on the other hand, it keeps them from making friends.

Is there a way to turn our Asperger's Friends' obsessions into strengths? Can they help them function in school, in the workplace, in the real world?

Very often, yes! Their special interests do become lifelong hobbies, if not careers. And those interests can be used as teaching tools as well.

At Friends' Club, we use such interests as a context to convey information. By using a boy's fascination with trains, we get his attention by reading a book like *Tobin Learns to Make a Friend* by Diane Murrell. Since Tobin is a train, the abstract friendship skills in the book become concrete and meaningful for the boy who loves trains.

Talk to any expert in the field and you'll hear the same advice over and over: "Play to their strengths" and "Cultivate their strengths" and "Choose their activities or jobs based on strengths, not deficits."

What are Asperger's children's strengths?

Although everyone on the spectrum is different, as a whole, Asperger's kids have definite assets.

For one, they are knowledge driven. They love information. They love to learn new facts. They also have terrific concentration when asked to do something that interests them.

Aspies have a unique perspective. Born out-of-the-box thinkers, they don't have to work at being unconventional or original. Their unusual, fresh take on things is like no one else's and often bucks the status quo, but they don't care. Think Charles Darwin, Gregor Mendel, and Hans Christian Andersen.

Their unconventionality and unique point of view can sometimes lead to revolutionary thinking, which they embrace instead of ignore. By not caring if they fit in, they are free to go against conventional wisdom.

These are all strengths. What helps is if our Friends are in the type of school or work environment where such nonconformity is allowed, or better still appreciated and encouraged.

The reason school is so difficult from elementary grades to high school is that socializing is such an integral part of each school day. Conformity in and out of the classroom is expected. While most kids go to school to see their friends and to mix and talk with others, Asperger's kids go to school to learn.

Fortunately, once they get to college, specialization kicks in. Professors appreciate the serious student who wants to learn and think original thoughts, instead of the student who's a passive learner or is more interested in socializing.

Unfortunately, many of our Asperger's Friends struggle in school because of written expression and other motor or processing challenges. Yet there are usually certain subjects in which they excel.

Some are whizzes in math. Some are stellar in science. History can be enticing because it's a fact-filled subject. The Aspie artistic geniuses-in-the-making may struggle in math or history, but dazzle people with their animation, fine art, or sculpture.

Having peaks and valleys of skills and abilities is typical for Asperger's kids. It is wisest to keep an eye on those peaks and help your child make the most of them, while getting extra help for their valleys through tutoring or summer school or whatever will get them a passing grade.

It's not fair to expect them to excel in everything. But it is also not fair to let them get discouraged and feel like failures because they do poorly in certain subjects. Help your child develop good study habits and follow through on her homework. Then she'll do better on quizzes and tests in the classroom. Keep in touch with teachers so you can work together to help your child succeed.

As for jobs or extracurricular activities, the less socially demanding, the better. Lots of people means lots of noise, confusion, and stress. Aspies usually prefer quieter pursuits.

Typically, our Friends have trouble with their peers, who give them the hardest time and the least amount of understanding. Yet they get along well with younger kids, who are happy to have an older child or teen pay attention to them. Asperger's kids also get along with adults who appreciate their intellect.

A paid or volunteer job with plenty of structure and routine is best. The more predictable their duties, the less anxious and more secure our Friends will be. They like to know what to expect and what is expected of them.

And if you can find a mentor who appreciates your child's unique-ness and, yes, obsessions, you should cultivate that relationship! This mentor could help build up your child's self-esteem, which will make him more motivated. If the mentor is in the field of your child's special interest or skills, this could pave the way to discovering your child's life's work. Seeing the real-world application of a special interest would make it less abstract and seem more possible, which would be a boon to your child.

A great resource for using a special interest as a strength is *Power Cards: Using Special Interests to Motivate Children and Youth with Asperger's Syndrome and Autism* by Elisa Gagnon. It's best to consider an individual's strengths on a case-by-case basis. There are no general Social Stories or stories in books that will work for every individual.

There are two books by Michael Fitzgerald, an Irish autism and Asperger's expert and professor, that will give all parents and teachers hope for their Asperger's kids. They are *The Genesis of Artistic Creativity: Asperger's Syndrome and the Arts* and *Genius Genes: How Asperger Talents Changed the World*.

Each volume has short biographies on almost two dozen famous statesmen, scientists, philosophers, artists, musicians, writers, and other luminaries who exhibited all the signs of having had Asperger's. Fitzger-ald reveals how this condition enabled them to do the extraordinary work that they did, even if they were quite quirky and so different from their contemporaries.

Many experts agree that success is the best remedy for these socially disabled and communicationally challenged kids. So whatever you can do to help them use their talents, insights, and love of facts, and steer them in the right direction, the better it will be for them and the better for you, your whole family, and probably society at large.

See also Compliments, Conversation, Eye
Contact, Greetings, Holiday Gatherings,
Manners, *and* Responding to Others

TAKING ONE'S LEAVE

Although most of us don't realize it, there are many steps involved in leaving any social gathering.

Unlike at school, where a teacher prepares a class for dismissal by reminding them to write down their homework and collect all their things before the bell rings, at a party or event there is no bell or teacher to say that you can leave. Social gatherings are very open-ended, which makes them very difficult for Asperger's folks to figure out.

Timing can be tricky. Unless specific hours are designated, how do you know when an event is over?

Most of us look for clues.

Are people still engaged in lively conversation or is the energy winding down? Do the host and hostess look ready for people to go or do they give signs of wanting to continue?

The social dynamic to a gathering is what we sense intuitively, but not our Friends. Asperger's folks can't read any of the social signals, so it is tough for them to gauge when it's time to go.

And then there's the tricky bit of making sure that you collect whatever you brought so you don't leave anything behind. Our Friends have a hard time remembering such details. How can you look for your things if you don't remember what things you brought in the first place?

And finally, before leaving, it's essential to find the host or hostess to say "thank you." Saying good-bye means making eye contact again and possibly shaking hands or giving hugs, just as our Friends needed to do when they arrived. You ought to say something flattering about the event so the hosts know you had a good time, but that's just the kind of small talk that Asperger's people struggle with, so none of this is easy.

Try to imagine a social event from our Friends' point of view. Any gathering is like a fast-moving river, sweeping everyone along. The arrival and departure from the party are stage-five rapids. Greeting and leaving are the biggest trouble zones. They require many small but important steps, and there are no firm rules to hang on to, other than to be polite.

What makes leaving even more difficult than arriving is that you're not usually the only one going. The chaos and confusion at the door make it harder and more uncertain for our Friends to know what to say and do.

At Friends' Club, we always try to see from our Asperger's kids' perspective first. And we know that they have a tendency to think that everyone can see them leave, so why should they have to say "good-bye"? It seems unnecessary to them.

So we explain that it's good manners. We point out that they must say "good-bye," just as they're expected to say "hello" whenever they enter a room. Other people appreciate it and will like them for it.

Then we break down the leave-taking into smaller pieces. Just as we practice greetings at the beginning of every session, we practice good-byes at the end. For all ages, we start with making eye contact when they are telling us "good-bye." The more practice our Friends have making eye contact, the better. Then we adapt the rest according to the group's age.

For the younger kids, we have them sit in a circle and pass a "good-bye ball" around. Whoever is holding it looks at the rest of the group and the leaders and says, "Good-bye," before passing the ball to the next member.

Other times, we'll use a colorful parachute with the young kids. They lie on the floor as the parachute is waved over them. Then a leader will say, "Good-bye, Travis" or "Good-bye, Kate," and that child gets up and says "good-bye" when leaving.

For those groups where we ask the kids to take their shoes off as they come into the room each time we meet, there is a good-bye ritual that we go through as they put their shoes back on.

And for our older Friends, especially the teen groups where it can't be too formal, we forego the handshakes but leaders do say "good-bye" to each member and wait to hear a "good-bye" back. If not, the leader will move closer and repeat the farewell, to prompt the boy or girl to respond.

As with any behavior, if it's done frequently enough, it should become automatic. We strive to have our Friends adopt the "good-bye" habit and they do quite well, once it's part of their routine.

See also Asking for Help, Bullying and Bullies, Conversation, Dating and Gender Talk, Further Information About Bullying, Intentions, Literal Language, Peer Pressure and Avoiding Dares, Phone Skills, Slang and Idioms, *and* Teasing

TALKING WITH PEERS

An interesting thing about Asperger's children is that they are not drawn to their peers like other kids. In fact, they have the most trouble getting along with kids their own age.

Why?

The short answer is, intellectually they're often ahead of their age, but socially they're behind.

Driven more by facts and ideas, these kids gravitate to older kids and adults who would understand and appreciate what they want to talk about. In his 1944 paper that first identified these special children, Hans Asperger called them "little professors" because they talked about higher-level subjects in a straightforward, almost academic way.

Asperger's children also get along well with younger kids who are thrilled to have an older kid play with them. Plus our Friends often still like the same things the younger kids like, such as Pokémon, Legos, anime, cartoons, etc.

With our kids, especially our middle-schoolers and teens, we try to help them understand which topics are "cool" to talk about with their peers. We teach them how to show an interest in what others say, and to not just talk about their own special interests.

Most of our Friends are profoundly fascinated with anything electronic, especially video and computer games. This is fortunate in that many other kids their age are interested, too. However, our Friends often go overboard when it comes to talking about such games.

In our weekly groups, we help them see that it's okay to talk about video games a little, but if others try to change the subject, it's important to let them. The give-and-take of conversation is always a challenge for Asperger's kids, and giving up a favorite topic is even harder, but they need to listen and switch topics to make and keep friends.

One of our girls once told us, quite adamantly, that it was okay to talk about Pokémon in the Friends' Club group because she's understood there, but it was not something that the kids at her middle school would want to hear. We agreed with her, and applauded her perceptiveness.

Our Big Picture goal is not to take away the topics that interest our Friends. It's more a goal of teaching them that others may want to talk about something else. In teen groups, we offer an environment to practice talking about "in" topics like music, movies, and even makeup and boys for the girls, or for our boy teens, girls and dating. This way, our teens will be more aware and accepting of typical interests.

One of our leaders came up with a list of discussion topics for her teen groups, to help them understand what is on other teens' minds. The ideas range from graduation night and school dances, gossip in the locker room, and using slang, to yearbooks and what to write in them. For instance, if they don't like the person handing them a yearbook to sign, we recommend that our Friends just sign their name. However, if they like someone, then it's a good idea to personalize the message—yes, these things need to be spelled out for Asperger's teens and younger kids.

The trickiest part, of course, is all the unspoken but very pervasive boy-girl social stuff that goes on all day long at school, which is lost on anyone with Asperger's. In our teen groups, we demonstrate the difference between staring versus looking at girls and boys. We discuss other subtle spoken and unspoken messages sent by the opposite sex.

While these signals are tough enough for neurotypical teens to pick up properly, for someone with a social disability that blinds them to such cues, it's truly baffling and nearly impossible. They need coaching from parents, siblings, and social skills groups. We've even developed a special lesson called "Gender Talk" to help our Aspie teens understand adolescent physical and emotional changes, as well as dating dynamics, with everything broken down into small pieces.

It's amazing that our Friends manage to navigate through their middle school and high school campuses as well as they do on any given day. Unable to see the hidden meaning of things, they don't detect suspiciously friendly or insidious behavior. This makes them such easy targets and victims.

For instance, one of our teen boys was tricked into making a bet at his high school, and he lost. He was told to deliver the forty dollars or he'd get beat up! Yes, this kind of behavior is bullying, as well as being illegal since it's gambling on a high school campus.

What did he do? He stole the money from his mother's purse. He was so focused on stopping anyone from hurting him that he did the first thing that came to mind. He didn't ask for help because Asperger's kids don't think to do that naturally. He just focused on paying a debt that he never should have had to pay in the first place.

This is why we address such possibilities in our groups. Almost weekly, we cover some aspect of language, especially slang, which confounds our Friends. It's important to make them aware and open their eyes to what someone is *really* saying, to listen to the true intentions and to keep someone from taking advantage of them.

As we've mentioned in our Literal Language section earlier in this book, slang also throws our kids because the meaning can be so opposite from what it seems to be. For example, "What up, fool?" can be a very friendly greeting and a joke among teens who are goofing around. But to a literal-minded person, it sounds offensive, like the person is calling you a name.

It can also be said in a menacing way, which our Friends wouldn't detect. Rather than hear it as a warning, our kids might think it's a hip greeting. The variations are endless, which is why it's so confusing— there are no hard-and-fast rules on slang for our kids to learn.

Something you could do when you're with your Asperger's teen is to listen for slang on the radio, TV, or in movies. By explaining these expressions to your child, you will help make them more aware of the true meanings of phrases and become less vulnerable to their peers.

And keep reminding your child that it is okay and good to talk with a trusted adult about any problems that may come up. Encourage them to tell you or a grandparent, teacher, therapist, librarian, counselor, *someone* who can help gauge what is really happening and put it in perspective for them.

Another thing that peers do to bug an Asperger's child is to call them by another name. With our Friends' rigidity and strong sense of what's right, they think they should only be called by their own name. Any other name is wrong. So this makes for easy teasing by their peers.

As a counterstrike, we've incorporated some flexibility training within the group by playing one of our standard games, What's *Up?* a different way. We've now called it What's Up, Dude? to get all the children used to being called something other than their own name. They also will get used to being called "dude," a term that their peers might use.

A recent example of how out of step our kids are with their peers occurred when I went to observe one of our Friends at his middle school. During his math class, I noticed how all of the students were standing near the teacher's desk to see the grades posted on the wall. Our Friend was sitting, as he always does, at his desk waiting for instructions on what to do next.

Yes, he was following the teacher's instructions, but he was not following the "hidden curriculum" of what his peers were doing. They were checking out grades but also chitchatting with one another and doing what we call the "social glue" of life. By not joining his peers or talking with them in this casual way, our Friend missed out on relating with his classmates and making friends.

See also Cooperation, Letting Go and
Refocusing, Listening to Others, Perfectionism
and Unrealistic Expectations, Perspectives and
Point of View, Problem Solving, Sportsmanship,
and Thinking in Pictures and Patterns

TEAMWORK

The need to be a team player is everywhere. In families. At school. On
the playing field. On the job. In the community. All require being able
to join others in working together at some point, in some way.

But teamwork requires sharing control. Teamwork requires taking
turns listening to one another and giving someone else's idea a chance
to be heard and considered.

Teamwork means that things may not go as you had envisioned.
The group effort may be nothing like what you would have done, if left
to your own devices. But you must let go enough to incorporate others'
input because, when working as a team, everyone must be allowed to
contribute and work together to get it done.

What a challenge this is for our Friends!

The very essence of teamwork is so difficult for Asperger's kids to
grasp. Yet becoming a team player is the key to friendship because only
then do all parties feel heard, which leads to bonding.

Asperger's children would much rather work on any project, game,
or activity by themselves and pursue their own "picture" of how it
should be done. Because they think in pictures, it's very hard for them
to adjust their vision to incorporate someone else's ideas. Their conviction that their view is the "right" view doesn't help. And their inability
to empathize, their inability to put themselves in the other person's
shoes, or see things from anyone else's perspective, only adds to the
problem.

It's hard for our Friends to believe that the whole, with input from
individuals, could possibly be better than their own singular approach.
Our Friends value their own ideas and the way they see things much
more than what anyone else thinks. Again, it's not arrogance or selfish-

ness. It's neurological. Their mirror neurons seem to be impaired, which prevents them from taking into account other people's feelings and ideas. They do not naturally know how to work with others, who seem truly alien to them.

That's why, at Friends' Club, a huge part of our activities is playing cooperative games. These kids need to learn how to take turns, how to listen to others, and how to work together toward a mutual goal.

They also need as much practice at these skills as possible so that such team behavior becomes more automatic.

If you watch any Asperger's children at work on a project, there is no conversation. They work quietly and determinedly, doing their own thing. They prefer to work alone, quite convinced that they "do it better alone," as they constantly assure us.

That's exactly why we ask them to build something *together* with others in the group. Whether it's with Legos, K'NEX, ZOOB Tubes, or some other kind of building blocks, they are asked to work together to create a single structure. This forces them to interact *and* to take into account someone else's viewpoint or ideas. They have to share materials, build onto each other's parts, and accept the uncertainty of how the whole thing will turn out.

Of course, before they start, we tell them that we know they are fantastic builders on their own, because they are. Then we tell them that now they're ready for a new challenge—to build something with others, as a team.

There are minor tiffs, some differences of opinion, sometimes even an outburst or two. Some want to say, "But you're not doing it right," which we forbid because there is no right or wrong in creating something new. These are the growing pains of learning to share and give up control. These kids are learning to accept not having everything their way, perhaps not having the project turn out as they see it.

But they do succeed! They do learn, through practice and weekly exposure, that teamwork also produces creative, interesting, fun results.

In these building projects, we often ask only one Friend to add a piece at a time. Then the kids say what we made when it's all done. With imaginations fired up, the same project has been called a windmill and an observatory. Embedded in this discussion is the realization that there is no "right" or "wrong" answer.

Sometimes we play Silent Builder. This is when our Friends pretend to put their voices "in a box" and we use a real box as a tangible prop to remind them that they cannot talk during the game. This concrete reminder is a fun way to help them follow the rules.

Building in silence forces the kids to use nonverbal cues and gestures to tell their teammates how to build the structure. More than once, we've been so caught up in the game that the kids have had to remind us to give them back their voices as they left the session.

Another teamwork project the kids enjoy is when we put out a giant sheet of paper. Then we ask each Friend to draw one part of a whole picture. This is an ideal team activity as they see an ever-evolving picture with each person's addition.

In the end, while it's not the exact image that any of our Friends had in their mind, it does become an image that sparks conversation, laughs, and camaraderie.

See also Asking for Help, Bullying and Bullies, Further Information About Bullying, Humor, Intentions, Literal Language, Sarcasm, Slang and Idioms, *and* Talking with Peers

TEASING

One of our boys once said, "The worst thing is teasing. I can take punches. But I can't take teasing."

This admission confirms what recent research has revealed: psychological abuse is *worse* than physical abuse, and it can leave lifelong, invisible scars. The expression "Sticks and stones may break my bones, but words can never hurt me" is both a ridiculous lie and no line of defense for a child being picked on verbally.

What teasers claim to be doing, once they've pushed their target to the point of anger or tears, is just kidding around. They skillfully twist the whole episode so that it's the victim's fault for not having a sense of humor.

It's the victim's fault for being too sensitive, or not "playing" along and getting the joke in their taunts or insults.

That's why we spend a lot of time talking about teasing at Friends' Club—so-called friendly and unfriendly teasing. We want our kids to learn to recognize the difference because teasing is a form of bullying. Asperger's kids make perfect targets for any kind of bullying for many reasons.

First, they never see it coming. Aspies are a guileless group and don't recognize other people's true intentions, nor do they expect others to be tricky or mean.

Second, our Friends take all words literally, even sarcastic ones. In spoken language, the words are only 7 percent of the meaning. Body language conveys a whopping 55 percent of the message and tone of voice, speed, and style account for 38 percent of the meaning. Since our Friends take the literal meaning of what is said, they are trying to discern the teasing from just 7 percent of the message. Of course it's going to be difficult for them to realize what is friendly teasing and what is mean teasing.

And third, they take the teasing to heart. They get upset easily, giving the kind of reaction the teaser is after.

On the plus side, our Friends' cluelessness about people and social cues works for them when it comes to teasing. If it's very subtle, it may go right over their head. They don't even hear it, so there is no immediate hurt and perhaps no effect.

On the negative side, if they don't react because they don't get it, that may push the teaser to try harder or louder to get a rise out of our Friend.

What's unfortunate is that *if* they do recognize the teasing and are hurt by it, they usually don't know how to react. They don't have quick comebacks. They don't know how to ignore it and walk away. Aspies often do or say something that makes them even more vulnerable and bigger targets.

What we teach our Friends is that they must say *something* to the person teasing them, otherwise the teasing tends to escalate. A short, standard comeback is the best, before turning and walking away. We have them practice saying, as matter-of-factly as possible, things like "That's not funny" or "That's mean" or "Be nice." As long as teasers get some kind of reaction, then usually they will stop.

If the teasing persists, we teach the kids to find an adult and tell them what is going on. Our Friends are not tattletales. But they do need a cavalry. They need an adult who is on their side and better able to assess the situation and stop the teasing or bullying when it surfaces.

If your child's school is not striving to have a zero-tolerance policy toward bullying—and teasing is a form of bullying—then take action! You would help not only your child but every child who is being picked on, by campaigning for such a policy.

There should be zero tolerance in the classroom, and especially out on the playground and playing fields. The play areas are where there are the most children roaming around with the fewest adults watching, an ideal venue for teasing.

Not surprisingly, it's during recess and lunch hour when our Friends are teased and bullied the most. If your school allows parents to volunteer for yard duty, then consider helping out.

Or if your child reports any teasing or bullying in the classroom, be sure to tell the teacher. Perhaps you can volunteer and help out in the classroom. This would allow you to see for yourself what the dynamics are with your child's peers.

Sometimes you may discover that your child thinks kids are teasing or trying to annoy him, when they're not. They're just being themselves! It's really your child who finds the other child's behavior annoying or doesn't understand her sense of humor.

This has happened to a few of our Friends, so it's good to get a clear picture before making final judgments. Go to your child's classroom or talk with the teacher about the student annoying your child, to find out if it's unintentional or intentional.

The good news is that our Friends can build up a resistance to teasing. One of our middle school Friends said that, looking back, he was glad that he got teased in elementary school because it made him tougher. "I've got a thick armor now," he said confidently. "Nothing can bother me anymore." This armor is serving him well through middle school, some of the toughest terrain for any preteen, let alone for our Asperger's Friends.

Interestingly, this same boy has no desire to go back to his elementary school to visit. Why? Because it holds too many bad memories of very painful social episodes.

Teasing takes its toll. Please keep talking to your child or teen and let them know that you want to hear if they're being teased. They need to know that you care and will take it seriously. Assure them that you will do everything you can to stop it.

You are their cavalry . . . in this and all things.

See also Depression, Diagnosis, *and* Parental Sainthood and Your Need for Support

TELLING YOUR CHILD THAT HE OR SHE HAS ASPERGER'S SYNDROME

Experts agree that your child is better off knowing that he or she has Asperger's syndrome.

Why? Because first off, these kids usually know they're different by the time they enter school. By the age of nine or ten, they can see that their classmates all seem to know what to do next without being told, while the Asperger's child is at a loss. Without the ability to predict what comes next, they don't pick up the clues and unspoken messages sent by the teacher. Aspies tend to feel out of step and in the dark most of the time.

Second, on the playground as well as in the classroom, they can tell that the other kids are making friends and managing social interactions better than they are. Our Friends are truly baffled by what people really mean when they say or do something. Socializing is very, very abstract for them, and they struggle to decode the signals.

As one of our boys said, "I didn't have any friends, and I wanted some, but I didn't know what to do about it." Once he was told that he had Asperger's, it was more reassuring for him than not knowing. Now he had a reason to explain why he wasn't like the other kids. This knowledge, he said, made him "no longer feel like a freak."

Finally, perhaps the best reason to tell your child is because it's not something he's going to outgrow. There is no "snapping out of it." There is no cure for Asperger's. The sooner your son or daughter comes to terms with it, and the sooner you do as parents, then the sooner their awareness can be used to help them modify their behavior to be more successful in social encounters at school and, later, in the workplace.

When do you tell your child?

As soon as you know, because the sooner children know, the better. Becoming aware of their Asperger's helps them feel less like failures. It takes the mystery out of why they think so differently from other people. It demystifies their struggles with social interactions.

You should definitely tell your child if they ask about, or demonstrate an awareness of, being different. Usually that's around the age of eight or so, but it may be younger or older than that.

What do you tell your child?

That depends on their age. But in this case, not so much their calendar age as their intellectual age. Some of our Asperger's Friends are quite precocious. They read and reason beyond their years. So it's best to tailor what you say to how old they seem intellectually.

The best approach is pretty much the way that you would handle other sensitive subjects that parents need to talk with their kids about (sex education comes to mind). You choose carefully what you say based on what they can understand.

If I'm talking with eight- or nine-year-olds, I've found it best to say something very simple and direct like, "There are people thinkers and there are thing thinkers, and you are a thing thinker." Believe it or not, they get it. They know that they get how things work, yet they do not realize how people work or what other people are thinking about.

If I'm talking with a ten-year-old, then I'll go into a little more detail. I've said, "Different kinds of brains have different wiring. It's like computers. Some people are Macs and some people are PCs."

If they're twelve or so, and seem to want to know more, I'll say, "You're very smart. You have an original view on things because your brain is wired a bit differently. So was Albert Einstein's brain and Mozart's. They both had Asperger's and so do you."

And if a child is in his or her teens, then I usually go ahead and tell them, "You have the Einstein syndrome, which is Asperger's. It's named after Hans Asperger, a doctor who first noticed some very smart kids who also struggled with socializing. They were not great at reading people, but they were great at coming up with cool ideas and original thinking."

What do you risk by *not* telling your child he or she has Asperger's?

A lot, according to Tony Attwood. When individuals are told, he says that they may react in any of four ways, two good and two bad.

The two good reactions are imitation, when they copy or rehearse how other people behave so they know how to behave, or imagination, when they create imaginary friends or imaginary worlds that are always there and always nice for them to think about.

The bad reactions are arrogance, when they see themselves as superior and think they're always right and everyone else is an "idiot" or "stupid" and they deny they have any problems, or depression, when they know they're different and feel out of step. This last group might intensely overreact to minor social errors to the point of considering suicide. The last two reactions are definitely not friend makers and are the most difficult to treat.

It is especially important to tell teens because they may be at risk for suicide if they see the differences between themselves and their peers as insurmountable. While the statistics appear to be very low for suicide among depressed Asperger's teens, averaging two or three a year in Attwood's experience, the risk is there. Telling your child or teen about their condition should help fend off despair because it gives a reason for their differences. It can set a course for developing more awareness and a better outcome.

And please don't stop at just telling your child that he or she has Asperger's syndrome. Be sure to tell anyone else who will be working with your child.

At the start of each school year, talk to elementary school teachers and hand them a one-page guide, filling them in about your child. For middle school and high school teachers, send them a group e-mail letting them know that your child has Asperger's syndrome and describe what kind of student she is. The sooner they know, the more understanding they can be.

Besides, they're going to notice the quirky behavior, the lack of eye contact, and the undeniable fact that your child is a bit different, so it's better to tell them than to leave them guessing. It will probably make your child's transition into the class smoother, too.

Even if your child has an IEP (Individualized Education Program), a copy of it rarely reaches teachers until well after school has begun. So in the first week of school, it's better to inform them right away before any frustrations or misunderstandings arise. It also opens the lines of communication between you and the teachers from the beginning.

Some parents prefer to ask counselors for their child's schedule the week before school starts, so they can familiarize their child before the first day. Others wait until a few days have passed to contact teachers, so the teachers have a better idea of who their child is.

One of our teens' parents sends an e-mail on the first Friday of the new school year. She thanks all of the teachers for a good start (not much usually goes wrong for her son that first week, so it's easy to be positive). Then she goes into how her son loves to learn, that he is very bright but he has Asperger's syndrome, which is high-functioning autism. This means that he will be eager to participate in class and will have no qualms about raising his hand to share information, but he will be slower in writing and usually need extra time on quizzes, tests, and projects.

She lets them know that she works with him every afternoon after school, to keep him on track while he does his homework (and she helps modify it, if it's taking too long). Then she asks them to contact her if they notice her son falling behind or if he's not handing in homework, or if they have any questions (see the sample parent-teacher e-mail in Part Three: Resources).

Most teachers are quick to answer back. They appreciate the heads-up. They are glad to know that her son has support and homework help at home. It makes for a positive team effort.

Because, yes, it takes a group effort to get an Asperger's child successfully through school. You don't have to feel alone. The sooner you engage and inform teachers and other school personnel, the greater the likelihood of getting the help that you and your child will need in order to finish their formal education in a timely manner.

And just because children know they have Asperger's does not mean that they can use it as an excuse to not do any homework or to ditch anything else. If they want to go on to college, reminding them of that bigger goal often helps motivate them.

I have told parents that their child shouldn't adopt the attitude that would lead him to say something like "I have Asperger's, so I don't have to tie my shoes." Being on the spectrum should not be an excuse to not do something. It only means that your child may do it differently, and take longer doing it, but he should always try.

See also Disorganization, Obsessions and Obsessive Behavior, *and* Strengths and How to Cultivate Them

THINKING IN PICTURES AND PATTERNS

Most people with Asperger's syndrome think in pictures rather than words. Because Albert Einstein possessed this unique ability, he was able to develop the theory of relativity. It is based on the visual imagery of moving boxcars, mirrors, and bursts of light.

While Einstein's calculation skills were slow, his genius lay in his ability to connect visual and mathematical thinking. He was able to turn pictures in his head into mathematical equations. Einstein once told a friend that his thoughts did not come in verbal formulation. When a thought came, it took a while before he could express it in words.

According to *Genius Genes: How Asperger Talents Changed the World* by Michael Fitzgerald and Brendan O'Brien, Einstein's extraordinary scientific achievements would not have been possible if he had not had Asperger's syndrome. His theory was so radical that it was criticized and rejected at first. But like other Aspies, Einstein did not care if he pleased other people, nor did he care what they thought about him.

With physics as his prime obsession, Einstein spent long periods working on problems, whether they would gain acceptance or not. His Asperger's ability to think in pictures enabled him to create some of the most important scientific theories ever. *Genius Genes* goes into greater detail of how this revolutionary thinker exhibited many traits of someone on the spectrum.

In *Elijah's Cup: A Family's Journey into the Community and Culture of High-Functioning Autism and Asperger's Syndrome* by Valerie Paradiz, she suggests that pop art icon Andy Warhol displayed many traits that would put him on the autism spectrum.

Warhol's obsession with Campbell's soup cans reflected the kind of sameness and repetitiveness that so often appeals to people with Asperger's. She writes, "Andy moved in the realm of the literal, a common autistic trait. Abstractions, theories and concepts are not as graspable as objects and images, which Andy rolled out in different colors. He lined up in assorted rows and sizes: 210 *Coca-Cola Bottles*, 80 *Two-Dollar Bills*, 16 *Jackies*, 20 *Jackies*, and 168 *repetitions of the lips of Marilyn Monroe*."

While Paradiz goes into Warhol's childhood when he was described as "shy, serious and withdrawn," she notes that when he retreated from others, he drew. Paradiz interprets his famous blank stare and emotionless demeanor not as an affectation, which many have thought, but as a true sign of his Asperger's. Warhol himself often said that he didn't have a clue how to relate to people, yet another classic trait.

In another book about cultural trailblazers on the spectrum, *The Genesis of Artistic Creativity: Asperger's Syndrome and the Arts* by Michael Fitzgerald (which is a companion book to his earlier title, *Austism and Creativity: Is There a Link Between Autism in Men and Exceptional Ability?*), Fitzgerald adds Vincent van Gogh to the Asperger's pantheon of masterful artists. The artist's well-known difficulty in getting along with people, his serial paintings of starry nights and other subjects, and his obsessive desire to paint and only paint, regardless of his health or the fact that his paintings didn't sell, make for a very strong case.

Many of the Asperger's children with whom I've worked have told me themselves how they see their world in pictures and patterns. One boy was brought to me for a diagnosis. I pulled out a game called Mastermind as a way to assess him. In the game, one player makes a pattern with colored pieces while the other guesses what the pattern is.

As I was making my erroneous guesses on the game board, the boy looked up at me and said, "You don't think in the optical color spectrum, do you?"

Rather than be taken aback, I asked him, "What information tells you that?"

"Your guesses don't follow the pattern of the optical color spectrum," he said.

I asked him if that was the way that he thought of things.

"My thoughts are in patterns," he said. "The color spectrum is one such pattern."

Believe it or not, he was seven years old.

In working with other such children, I've learned that they have to process the information into a pattern—consciously thinking about what they are seeing—before it makes sense to them. Yet they can process concrete details, some extraordinarily small, almost automatically.

Take, for instance, another boy who came into my office and started talking about a video game. I thought that his remarks were just random until I looked up to see where his eyes were looking. In an obscure corner of my desk was the very video game that he was talking about. Few would have spotted it in the jumble in my office, but his keen eye for the obscure detail picked it up. This is typical of these kids' tendency to focus in on a detail, while often missing the Big Picture.

What is interesting is that children on the spectrum have often been thought to not be involved in imaginative play. This is not true. It is just that the kind of imaginative play is qualitatively different in Asperger's and autism than it is with neurotypical children.

Asperger's children and adults spend a lot of time thinking of ideas. They are literally lost in thought, in seeing visions and patterns invisible to the rest of us. Often, they are thinking of ideas to change things, to make something better for others.

Thomas Edison, who displayed a considerable number of Asperger's traits, was a classic example of a child on the spectrum. He spent almost all of his time in thinking up ideas to better our world—electricity, phonographs, movie cameras, etc.—and obsessively throwing himself into his scientific pursuits. But he did "play" with those ideas before turning them into drawings, calculations, experiments, and patents.

One thing that should be noted is that these Asperger's thinkers and geniuses need a helpmate—parent, sibling, spouse, fellow worker—to assist them in turning their radical, out-of-the-box ideas into reality. Einstein's first wife, Mileva Maric, excelled in physics and mathematics. She is now acknowledged to have helped considerably in working out the details of her husband's theories.

While not all our Friends will achieve the pinnacles of scientific or artistic achievements reached by the standouts mentioned here, these kids and teens do have the power of vision and unconventional thinking.

They have the ability to persevere in the face of criticism and naysaying because having Asperger's frees them from caring about what others think.

And they tend to be single-minded to the point of obsession in pursuing their visions, creating things no one has thought of before.

Temple Grandin has stated that if we were all neurotypical in our development, then humans would still be living in caves just talking to one another.

History has shown that the world is much better off from the revolutionary thinking and fresh approaches taken by our Asperger's Friends.

So if they need a lot of understanding and a little help, let's give it!

See also Disorganization *and* Writing Things Down

TIME BLINDNESS

Individuals with Asperger's have frontal lobe deficits, which make it hard for them (and anyone with attention-deficit/hyperactivity disorder and Tourette's) to be organized. It also sabotages their sense of time. They have no idea how much time has passed or how much time it will take to do something. They may not know what day or month it is either.

"My homework will take a half hour," says your Asperger's child, when it's obvious to you that it will take at least an hour, if not longer.

Their time blindness comes from their inability to quantify time. It's too abstract. They can't figure out in their head how much time something will take because they have no grasp of the passage of time in the first place. In fact, it takes them much longer to learn how to tell time on an analog clock.

Digital clocks are straightforward. The hour and minute numbers are shown, even separated by a colon. No confusion. But a clock with a face and hands is much more difficult. Even neurotypical kids in first grade struggle while they're learning to tell the time, but for our Friends, it's totally baffling long past first grade.

Michelle Garcia Winner insists that we must teach these kids to read an analog clock because these clocks teach us the movement of time. A digital clock just jumps to the next number. An analog clock has minute and hour hands that sweep around and around. These tangibly show time moving. What our Friends have trouble discerning is which hand is which and what hour it is when that hand is between numerals.

The more you have your child practice reading a clock with a face and hands at home, the better he'll get at it. It will take a long time and many trials and errors, but practice is what he needs. As usual, there is no quick fix or secret shortcut for these kids. Practice and repetition is the key.

Michelle has been successful using different-colored Lego blocks to show her clients how much time is being talked about. As concrete objects, the Legos represent invisible, slippery chunks of time.

For example, Michelle will stack three blue blocks to represent the number of half hours that a homework assignment will take. Then she'll top it with a single yellow brick to represent a half hour of free time that the child can have when the work is done. This seems to help some Asperger's kids see the proportion of work time to play time.

There are two-colored timers available in the Free Spirit catalog (at www.freespiritcatalog.com) of special education items, which offer a visual approach. The clock face is one color. When you spin the dial to the number of minutes that you want to allot to a certain task, the underlying color is different up to that number. As the minutes tick down, the second color's area shrinks. It's an excellent visual way of showing our Friends how the minutes are passing. They can see how little time they have left by the lessening of that second color.

Another factor contributing to their inability to sense time, according to Ami Klin, Ph.D., director of the Autism Program at Yale Child Study Center, is that they cannot anchor time in a social context. He says that what gives other children a sense of time is the social cues all around them. Our Friends are unaware of those cues, which makes them unaware of time.

There is no amount of training that will help overcome this general inability to sense time. Asperger's kids will be time blind their whole lives. Still, they can benefit from all the new tools that are being offered to keep all of us on schedule and aware of time: digital clocks, timers, PDAs, devices that beep when time is up, etc.

But Aspies need extra help—a caring adult to act as their executive assistant to help them with managing their time and coping with confusing details. No matter what you think they should be able to do, they really can't handle it alone.

At Friends' Club, we found that writing things down is the most effective way to help our kids plan ahead. When we announce what is planned for the hour, we also write it all out on a whiteboard. This way our Friends can see and anticipate what activities are coming up. As we move from conversation to activity to discussion, we try to reinforce a sense of time.

Writing things down will also give your Asperger's child a more concrete clue about how their time needs to be spent and what they need to work on next. Just be sure to also give them their favorite kind of time—quiet time. Time to play alone. Time to think their own thoughts. It's not a waste of time. It's free time that is vital to their well-being.

See also Anxiety, Calming Down and Focusing, Change and "Change-ups," Cooperation, Leaving the House, Letting Go and Refocusing, Meltdowns, Sensory Sensitivities, Social Stories, Thinking in Pictures and Patterns, Time Blindness, *and* Vacations and School Breaks

TRAVEL

As we've mentioned before, and as you know all too well, change can be very difficult for any Asperger's child. Change means unpredictability, uncertainty, and the unknown.

What is the epitome of those three elements? Travel, of course.

While those of us who like to travel seek it out because of the new sights, sounds, and tastes that we'll experience, and while we crave the surprises and delightful discoveries found in new places, our Asperger's Friends do not share our enthusiasm.

Unfamiliar places, unfamiliar faces, and unfamiliar foods alarm them. Throw in a foreign language and strange smells, sounds, and sights, and travel can be very upsetting to your Asperger's child in ways that you will never be able to fathom and they can rarely express.

Does that mean that you should never travel with your child?

No, not at all.

What it means is that if you want a trip to be a pleasant experience for your child, and thus, a more pleasant experience for you and the rest of the family, then you need to prepare your Asperger's child for what the trip will entail.

Besides announcing the destination, you need to break into small steps how the trip will unfold from beginning to end. Of course there will be unexpected changes that happen along the way—that's what traveling is all about—but at least if your child has the comfort of knowing what is supposed to happen, then when the unexpected happens, it won't be as disturbing.

Preparation and priming go a long way in alleviating our Friends' anxieties aroused by new places and new faces.

Since Asperger's kids don't have a sense of time, and very much live in the present, you'll need to mention the upcoming trip a few times before it sinks in. The bigger the trip, the earlier you should start talking about it. By the time you start packing, you should have mentioned the trip several times and pointed out the fun things you'll all be doing.

Showing your child pictures of the place will give him a more concrete idea of it. Images give Asperger's kids visuals to hang on to, which is good because they tend to think in pictures themselves. Help your child fill a backpack with books, toys, travel games, a stuffed animal, an iPod, or whatever he enjoys most. It is important for him to have some objects from home. Their familiarity will be comforting, and help ground your child.

Before heading to the airport or train station, or loading up the car for a road trip, be sure your child has enough warm clothes. Our Friends' heightened sensitivities can make them miserable in the air-conditioning in planes, trains, and cars. Don't forget hats to block the too-bright sun or waterproof pants and extra-long underwear to shield him from the freezing snow.

In the airport or train terminal, in a subway or bus station, make sure you hang on to your Aspie child extra tightly, far more than you would your other children. All too often, these kids stray if they see something none of the rest of you have noticed. They'll just wander off to examine it, unaware that they've left the group. We've had some parents resort to a child leash (or use a cat leash) to hang on to our Friends during a trip, so they can't get lost.

A more high-tech option is one of the electronic locating devices now available. Check your local gadget store. Many parents give their older Asperger's children cell phones. This works both ways—the parents can call their children if they haven't shown up and the children can call for help or to be located if they get lost. Cell phones also have built-in clocks, so it's easy for your child to know what time it is.

An identification bracelet is an excellent precaution. In case your child gets separated from the family, an ID bracelet with their name and your names, cell phone numbers, and/or the address where you're staying is important. Asperger's kids, even the older ones, don't know or remember these kinds of details.

Be prepared to find a quiet place for them en route, to decompress and calm themselves, before you move on. It would also be wise to set aside a block of time every day for your child to simply hang out at the hotel or cabin or to play in the tent if you're camping. They still need downtime, usually inside, to keep up their spirits and stay calm.

The biggest challenge can be to get them to go sightseeing. This means leaving wherever you're staying and going outside. Just because you left home doesn't mean that your Asperger's child left behind their desire to stay indoors. They can quickly become attached to their new "home," wherever you're staying, and prefer to stay inside rather than be bombarded by strange sights, loud sounds, and unpleasant weather.

The good news is that you can coax them out. You can use meals, playing in parks, or visiting animals in a zoo or pet store as lures to get them to agree to an outing. Natural history, science, and technology museums are usually a bigger draw than art museums or palaces.

If you do what interests them first, then you can tack on what you'd like to do afterward.

At the Friends' Club, we encourage our kids to talk about any trips that they've taken or are going to take. We love to hear them share their stories and to find out what they enjoyed (or didn't) about traveling.

I have also written many Social Stories to help parents prepare their child for a trip or vacation. Here's an example of one that I wrote for a Canadian Friend going with his family to the Dominican Republic. This one is quite explicit, which some kids need and is good if you know enough details in advance. I also found color photos from the Internet to accompany each scene. Such pictures really help our boys and girls, who are so visual, to understand more fully the place that they are visiting.

> My name is Jason and I am really smart. I really like playing Bionicles. I am going to be traveling on vacation to the Dominican Republic [map]. This is going to be so much fun because I am going to be flying in an airplane.
>
> When I am on the airplane [photo], I need to respect the other people on the plane by using kind words and not talking too loudly. The inside of the airplane might look like this: [photo]. I will have my own seat. When I am on the plane, I have a seat that is assigned to me and I cannot get another seat because this is the one the people at the airline have saved for me [photo of people in seats].

There might be some lines at the airport and this is okay. I need to stay with my mom and dad because the airport will be big and there will be a lot of people there and I do not want to get lost. There will be lines that I have to wait in. There are lines because a lot of people will be traveling at the same time and this is okay. I need to find things that I can do like listen to my dad's iPod [photo], bring some toys I can play with like Bionicles or read a book.

When I get to the airport, we have to wait to check in. This means I will be waiting at an airline ticket counter where I will have to give my luggage to a person who will be putting it on the plane [photo].

After checking in, I will have to wait in a line that is for security. This means I will be walking through a machine that looks like this: [photo].

It is okay that I have to walk through this machine because it will make sure that I am safe. This is a good thing.

When I land in the Dominican Republic, I will have to wait my turn to get off the plane. I will then have to go through what is called customs. This is an area where police from the Dominican Republic keep track of who is coming into the country [customs photo].

Then I get to go pick up my luggage. This area is called baggage claim and might look like this: [photo].

It can be tiring but fun to travel. I will try to remain calm and use nice words to tell people what I don't like. I will try to wait my turn and will try to wait to ask questions until it is my turn. This will make my family happy. Going on vacation is so much fun.

If you need any added incentive to take your child to far-off places, you might like to know that many Asperger's adults have told Tony Attwood they can live quite happily and more socially successfully in a foreign country than in their own. Their social awkwardness is attributed to their being a foreigner and not knowing the culture. Social blunders are more easily forgiven because they are strangers in a strange land, and therefore deserve understanding and not chastisement. And if they are willing to learn the language, then the locals appreciate them all the more.

See also Anxiety, Calming Down and Focusing,
Change and "Change-ups," Cooperation,
Leaving the House, Sensory Sensitivities, Social
Stories, Time Blindness, *and* Travel

VACATIONS AND SCHOOL BREAKS

Most of us look forward to a day off or a vacation. We appreciate the break from our routine. We enjoy the freedom to travel and the chance to indulge in a change of scenery. We plan ahead and look forward to spicing up our lives with the discovery of new places or a return to favorite destinations, often with family or friends. Or, if we choose to stay home, we have a chance to pursue our own interests.

Not surprisingly, our Asperger's Friends are quite different. Many don't really welcome vacations and school breaks. They can even become grouchy, upset, and outright angry at the disruption to their routine.

Sure, most are glad to be out of the classroom and not have any homework. But school itself provides a steady, reliable structure to their days. Our young Friends appreciate that school offers predictable places and familiar faces, which gives them a sense of comfort and security.

Since our Friends know what to expect at school for the most part, this daily pattern appeals to them. If taken away, they often miss it. They may be a bit sad or even seem lost without the predictability and pattern that school days offer.

If you don't leave home during a holiday or school vacation, we recommend that you suggest specific things that your child can do during the day. Set up certain times for them like "Lego hour" or "computer hour" or a specific time to walk the dog. This will help them feel more assured. Many of our Friends are unable to choose what to do because of their innate indecisiveness. Structuring their day is comforting and gives them that sense of time that they lack and the predictability that they crave.

For teens, volunteering at the local library or elsewhere during a school break will earn them community service hours. It will also give them a good reason to leave the house. If there is a summer job that is less customer-oriented and more computer- or animal-oriented, then that can make a perfect first step into the work world.

Volunteering and summer jobs give our Asperger's teens two benefits: a schedule, providing structure; and a sense of purpose and independence, boosting their self-esteem. That's a winning combination.

If your family decides to travel during vacation, that means leaving comfort and familiarity to go someplace new and strange. Vacations, even to other relatives' houses, are fraught with uncertainty. The more the surroundings are unlike home, the more unsettling and upsetting it can be for our Asperger Friends.

So, does that mean that you avoid travel vacations?

Do you not leave town to avoid possible meltdowns and public scenes?

Or do you find someone to stay at home with your Asperger's child while you and your spouse, maybe with the other kids, go on vacation?

Just as with any individual on the autism spectrum, every family's case is different. You have to do what's best for you and your family. However, with proper preparation and encouragement, your Asperger's child can rally for an out-of-town vacation. It's not impossible to go to new places.

In fact, it's necessary. If they are never exposed to new places and new experiences, how will they get over their aversion to them? How will they learn that they will be fine away from home and the familiar?

When you do leave town with your Asperger's child, keep in mind what we've learned at the Friends' Club: expect the unexpected.

One of our four-year-old Friends went on a summer vacation with his parents. He was a very bright boy who could already read. The first night of their trip, he refused to take his shoes off when he went to bed. Frustrated and worried, his parents called our office the next day from out of town to ask what they should do.

One of our staff members who knew this boy suggested showing him a calendar. She said to point to all the days that they would be on vacation and then to the last day, when they would return. As soon as they did that, voilà! The shoes came off at bedtime.

Why? Because by knowing how long the vacation would last and when it was going to end, he knew he didn't need to have his shoes on to be ready to leave the next day. Keeping his shoes on, in his mind, made him ready to go back home at any time. Now he could relax and enjoy the vacation along with his parents.

To travel with Asperger's kids is a lot like traveling with younger children, who need playtime, quiet time for naps, and to be taken to places and do activities that will interest them. Because our Friends have heightened sensitivities to taste, smell, and sights, and an aversion to the unknown, they need quiet time, indoor playtimes that will give their senses a break, and to be taken to sights that entice them.

I encourage all parents to prepare their Aspie child. First, talk up the things they will like, and engage their interest by looking at books and brochures to see what there is to do on your vacation.

Then it helps to ask them to choose three places or activities that sound the most interesting to them, so they have a vested interest in going. This gives them specific things to look forward to, which gives the vacation more meaning and gives them a sense of purpose.

I have written Social Stories for children going off on vacation. Again, the more specific and customized, the better it seems to work. Here is one for a Friend going on a vacation with her family, with sentences accompanied by color photos off the Internet:

> My name is Lindsey and I am going to have fun traveling to Cancún [photo] because it is fun to explore new places. When I am there, the weather is going to be different than it is in Minnesota. The weather will be warm or hot. They speak Spanish there. My mom and dad will be able to help if I don't understand something.
>
> I will be seeing the ocean [photo]. I might even try snorkeling, which looks like this: [photo]. I will see lots of beaches and colorful sunsets here [photos of beach and sunset].
>
> If I get upset, I need to try to use my kind words and explain to people what is wrong so they can help me. I am going to be spending nights here with my family. The hotel that I am staying in may not have a TV, and that's okay. We will have lots of fun things to do. This will be fun to sleep in a different bed and a new place. We will eat at restaurants and that can be fun, too. I will be okay because Mom and

> Dad will be there to help me if I need it. I can also remember those things that make me feel better when I am upset, like music, making things with my hands, or reading a book.
>
> Cancún is going to be a lot of fun. I can be a neat big sister and help Andrew so that he has fun, too.

Reading this kind of descriptive and predictive script to your child, or having them read it themselves, helps lower their worry of the unknown on a vacation and warm up to the possibilities.

To make it a more enjoyable experience for all, be sensitive to your Asperger's child's limits. If they are overloaded by sensory stimulation, then they will become anxious, perhaps uncooperative and difficult to manage. By structuring the vacation so that they have pockets of peace, small doses of sightseeing, and are offered familiar foods along with the new, then things should go more smoothly.

One of our teen Friends had the good fortune to go to France for a couple of weeks with his family during summer vacation. They even had French friends to stay with, so they had a home base instead of bouncing about from hotel to hotel.

While the mother and older brother saw this as a golden opportunity to revel in the beauty and deliciousness of France, the fifteen-year-old with Asperger's was not thrilled. "But they don't speak English," he said. He also worried about the strange food and what they would be doing.

How did the family help him out?

First, his mother asked him to look through a photo-filled guidebook on Paris and to choose three things that he wanted to do.

Then, as soon as they arrived, the whole family went to the Eiffel Tower, which was number one on his list.

That first night for dinner, they ate at a simple bistro in Paris, which offered pasta, chicken, and familiar fare that he liked. This won him over to dining out when he could see that things he liked eating at home were also available on menus in France.

He had brought his Game Boy in his backpack, and was allowed some downtime at the apartment each day. And since dinners in France can take two hours or more, he was allowed to leave the table after the main course and retreat to his bedroom, skipping the other courses and lengthy conversation.

The best things you can bring on vacation are your child's favorite books, Legos, handheld electronic games (conditional to a time limit), and other toys. These will give your Aspie child a mental escape from his surroundings, and a healthy diversion. Tossing in a new book or toy for a surprise is also effective. But be forewarned about an electronic game—if you don't set a time limit, Aspie kids tend to want to spend all of their time on it. It's important to make a rule about how long they can play.

But above all, prepare your child for where your family is going and what he is likely to see, so that the challenge of being away on vacation is less challenging for him . . . and for you.

See also Conversation, Empathy, Eye Contact, Listening to Others, Selfishness, *and* Time Blindness

WAITING

None of us like to wait—wait for our turn to talk, wait for a cab or bus, wait for a friend to show at a restaurant, wait for our meal to be served, and so on.

It's even harder to wait when you have no sense of time.

Asperger's kids and teens have no sense of time.

This seems to be caused by a frontal lobe deficiency, the same thing that ADHD and Tourette's folks have. It short-circuits their ability to sense the passage of time (it also sabotages their ability to be organized). The brain's frontal lobe is where executive functions take place.

Neurotypical people are wired to be able to keep track of how much time has passed, to gauge how long something will take, to estimate how long they've been kept waiting, etc.

Asperger's people are not.

Our Friends are pretty oblivious about time in all its forms. While this gives them that Zenlike ability to live truly in the moment, it also makes it harder for them to wait. To Asperger's boys and girls, everything can and should happen as soon as they think of it. To wait for anyone or anything does not compute. They don't understand that waiting is just a part of life.

Couple this inability to wait with the fact that they can't see things from anyone else's perspective, and they can seem downright selfish. Their deficient mirror neurons keep them from thinking of someone else's needs or desires. It simply doesn't occur to our Friends that someone else would like a turn, or wants to finish speaking, or isn't ready to go yet—they don't understand why waiting is required.

As selfish as they can seem, it's just the same lack of awareness that pervades so much of our Asperger Friends' being. They don't dwell only on themselves because of their ego or vanity. They are just locked into their own point of view, incapable of putting themselves in someone else's shoes or head.

That's why at the Friends' Club, we play lots of board games and other games that require turn taking. The more they play, the more they learn that they have to wait. They wait for the game to begin. They wait for their turn. They wait for everyone else to take a turn. They *wait!*

By the end of all that waiting, our Friends become more accepting. The need to wait eventually sinks in.

We also play other games like Zoom! This activity works on many skills at once: eye contact, conversation speed, sudden topic switching, and waiting your turn. (See the section on eye contact for instructions on how to play this game.)

What we explain to the kids is that a conversation is like driving a car. You can be going too fast and the person can't stay with you. Or you can be going too slow and you lose the other person's interest. And there are always times in talking with someone when they will put on the "brakes" and switch topics, taking the conversation in a completely new direction.

In our meeting rooms, we also post a colorful, illustrated handout as a reminder about waiting during conversations. It says:

WHEN TALKING TO OTHER PEOPLE, REMEMBER . . .	ILLUSTRATION
When to accelerate	A man waving from a car
When to brake	A car at a stop sign
When to slow down	A race car with a parachute open

As always, our Friends benefit from illustrations and specific instructions of what to do. Being concrete thinkers, they also think in pictures, so it's good to have written words accompanied by visuals.

Our Friends will need your help in learning to wait. These kids need help gaining perspective on delays, or perceived delays. Otherwise, they may start to fret, get frustrated, or even get angry.

And you, as parents, grandparents, or teachers, will need to learn to wait as well whenever you ask them to do something. Aspies tend not to have quick reaction times because it takes them a long time to process what you've said and to turn your words into actions.

Sometimes there is *no* reaction at first, which seems like they are ignoring you or not listening. This is really frustrating, but it's actually a signal for you to wait.

Wait after each request, to allow them to absorb the message.

Wait for them to give up what they've been doing and were engrossed in, and then switch gears to act on what you want them to do.

Wait for them to finally get up and follow through on your request.

While "Please brush your teeth" seems like a simple enough thing to do, it has many more steps than you realize: hearing the direction, stopping what you're doing (which is harder still if it's something you love doing like playing with Legos or studying schedules or playing on the computer), understanding what you're supposed to do next, getting up, and, finally, doing what you've been asked to do.

Beware of throwing too many requests too fast at your Asperger's child. You'll lose him with "Please brush your teeth, wash your face, get into your pajamas, and put your dirty clothes in the hamper."

These kids do so much better with just one change of activity at a time. Yes, it's slower. Yes, it takes longer. And, yes, you'll have to repeat yourself if they don't hear you the first or second time—which means you should write it down and hold it for them to read to get results.

The bright side of this "one step at a time" approach is that you'll be less frustrated, they'll be less confused, and there will be a lot less stress all the way around. It's the end result that counts, right? So if you have to slow down a little to give them time to react, as long as they do what you ask, then all is good.

Remember, the more logical and unemotional your explanation, the better it is. If they experience emotional distress, it can prevent them from hearing what you're saying. If calmly delivered, the message will be heard, which will lower their anxiety over having to wait.

See also Bluntness and Unintentional Insults,
Conversation, Empathy, Manners, *and* Rudeness

"WHITE LIES" AND SPARING OTHERS' FEELINGS

You've heard it before and I'll say it again—people with Asperger's syndrome are purveyors of truth. Telling the truth is paramount to them, and they will not deviate. To their credit, Asperger's boys and girls are generally honest, loyal, and trustworthy.

Asperger's folks say things as they see them or think them, period, end of story. It never occurs to them to act like they are interested in something that they're not, or to pretend that they like something they don't. In their minds, this would be deceitful, and they do not deceive.

The good news for parents of Asperger's children is that they don't have to worry about their kids lying. Of course, there are some exceptions, which doesn't mean that your child doesn't have Asperger's. It means that they're among the few Aspies to figure out that someone wants to hear a different story than what actually happened. But when they try to lie, they're usually pretty bad at it.

That's because to figure out the intent behind a lie requires "theory of mind," which is a psychological term for being able to infer another person's thoughts. Although anyone with Asperger's doesn't have this ability naturally, due to a mirror neurons deficiency, it can be developed to some degree. But even then, Aspie kids usually confess to lying eventually because they are hardwired to tell the truth and to never deceive.

Not being able to lie makes it difficult when an Aspie needs to act friendly. I've had several clients who have told me that it would never occur to them to "act" friendly. That would be deceptive, and from their perspective, it would be dishonest.

For example, this became a problem with one of my adult clients who refused to "appear" interested in what his roommate had to say because he felt that would be a lie. He didn't realize that faking just a minimal interest in what someone was saying would create a friendlier environment. Later, he overcame his fear of being dishonest and worked on appearing more interested, which improved his roommate situation.

While being truthful is admirable, it does not help one become socially successful if adhered to too tightly. Truthfulness can sound brutal and rude all too easily. People with Asperger's are totally unaware of this. The concept, let alone the importance, of "little white lies" in sparing someone's feelings and in friendships is foreign to them.

Since our goal is to improve our kids' social success and their ability to connect with other kids, we introduce the concept that not all lies are bad. We teach them that a "little white lie" is actually a good thing because it spares people's feelings. In fact, people will be quite hurt without the occasional white lie.

Here is an example of an acceptable white lie. Let's say you are visiting friends and they offer you a meal. Even if the food served is not something you like, when your hosts ask, "How is it?" you reply, "It's good." This white lie is to avoid hurting their feelings, but praising food they did not enjoy would not occur to our too-truthful Friends. They do not try to hide their dislike of something to spare someone's feelings, so we need to teach them to do it.

The first step is to make our Friends aware of feelings in general, then to make them realize that one can hurt another's feelings without physically hurting the person. These are the kind of abstract notions that are hard for our kids to grasp, so we show photos and video clips as visual, concrete examples. The irony is that even though our Friends have had their feelings hurt many times, it doesn't make them conscious of the feelings of others.

Then we teach them the difference between when a lie is truly dishonest and when a lie is okay because it is protecting someone's feelings by not being the whole truth. We've had the most success by turning to literature to get this point across.

A wonderful book, *The Honest-to-Goodness Truth* by Patricia C. McKissack, has a main character who learns exactly what it means to hurt another person's feelings by being too honest.

To make this concept more concrete for our Friends, we've compared being punched in the arm to being verbally insulted. When you get punched in the arm, it hurts on the outside. When you are told something that is too truthful, it's like getting punched on the inside and you hurt and ache inside.

We've found that our Friends need lots of practice to really understand the concept of sparing others' feelings. For them, the need for white lies and how to deliver them is very murky. It takes a lot of trial and error. That's why it's best for our kids to practice toning down their truthfulness in a safe haven like at the Friends' Club or at home. This way they won't have to suffer the social consequences of their inappropriateness.

Softening the truth and practicing white lies in the company of understanding people is the best way for our Friends to learn this tricky social skill. The more encouraging you can be, the better. It's important to make your child feel that it's safe for them to make mistakes and you won't get mad. That's when the true learning will occur.

See also Awareness, Change and "Change-ups," Letting Go and Refocusing, Moving On to New Things, *and* Social Stories

WRITING THINGS DOWN

Parents often ask me how they should deal with their child's oppositional behavior, that is, when the child won't listen to them or argues a point with them. Usually, this occurs when the parent is asking the child to change, or transition, to a new activity or place.

Asperger's children have a hard time coping with change, no matter how small. And if they're enjoying what they're doing, it's even more difficult to coax them away. But it's not a control issue and they're not intentionally misbehaving.

What I tell parents is that their child is "stuck" in the current activity, or in thinking about the activity. How stuck? So stuck that it can make them literally deaf to what anyone is saying to them.

Again, they are not ignoring you on purpose. They really don't hear you! Talk about being in the zone—these kids are so wrapped up in what they're doing (especially if it's one of their special interests) that they literally don't hear you. It's true.

Problems arise when you repeat your request, they continue not to respond, and the situation becomes emotional. And often, once the child finally reacts, he'll argue and it becomes an emotional tug-of-war over whatever it is he's being asked to do. This verbal tussle leaves everyone frustrated, parents angry, and kids entrenched in their position.

What we've found is that if we stop talking and **write down, in a few words, what it is they should be doing,** it's much easier to get through to these kids.

Writing down what you want them to "hear" is the best way to reach them peacefully. Writing it down takes all emotion out of the exchange. They can't argue with the whiteboard. They can't argue with the written words. Seeing the words written on a whiteboard or piece of paper makes it real and concrete. And they usually cooperate.

For example, a six-year-old boy was intensely playing with a toy in my waiting room when his mother said, "It's time to go." He kept on playing, without even looking up. His mother said to me, "See? This is what I mean. He won't listen to me."

I pulled out a whiteboard, and with a felt marker, wrote, "It's time to go. It's best to say 'good-bye' and go with Mom out the door."

He read it, got up, said, "Good-bye," and went happily out the door with his mom. Visuals are that powerful. I can't emphasize enough how important written words or images are in communicating with our Friends, especially the younger ones. Your life will be easier and your child will make changes more easily if you use visual aids to "talk" to him or her.

One day, at the end of a group session, one of our younger Friends was having a hard time leaving the room. We have all the kids take their shoes off before coming in (both to practice transitions as well as to protect our rug) and he was at a loss as to what to do next. The leader pulled out a picture of shoes from our "Super Symbol" book made especially for transitions in the groups, and showed it to the boy.

The results were immediate. He got up, grabbed his shoes, and headed out the door! The next week, when it was time for everyone to leave, he actually asked to see the picture of the shoes again.

We keep small whiteboards in every room where our groups meet. I encourage parents to buy lots of them and keep them everywhere—in the house, in the car, etc. All you have to do is pull it out and write what you want them to "hear." Most of our Friends read early and this is the most powerful tool for reaching them, especially when they're absorbed in something else.

One mother told us about the dramatic results she achieved when her boy was four years old. He was having screaming episodes throughout the day and she was at her wit's end. So one morning she told him, "Let's see how many times you scream today." She put a blank sheet on the refrigerator and marked down each time he had a screaming outburst.

At the end of the day, she showed him the chart and said, "You screamed eleven times today. Let's see if you can do less tomorrow."

The next day, he did scream less—only eight times. The next day, it dropped again, and the day after that, too. Within one week, her son had stopped screaming altogether.

The chart made him aware of what he was doing, and by being aware, he could change his behavior. He wasn't screaming for attention or to annoy her or to manipulate her. Being only four, he couldn't express why he was screaming, but it could have easily been a sensory issue or an unconscious reflex.

The key is that if you write things down for these kids, they can see what you're talking about and take action.

Think of these words on the whiteboard like the white lines painted on a blacktop road. If the road has been freshly paved, there would be no lines. Nothing to follow. Only an endless stretch of black road. How would you know where to drive on the road?

Writing things down for Asperger's kids helps guide them down the baffling road of life. The words give them directions as to what to do next. It may seem like an unusual and unnecessary extra step to you, but it works.

PART THREE | RESOURCES

DSM-IV-TR DIAGNOSTIC CRITERIA FOR ASPERGER'S DISORDER

A. Qualitative impairment in social interaction, as manifested by at least two of the following:

   1. marked impairment in the use of multiple nonverbal behaviors such as eye-to-eye gaze, facial expression, body postures, and gestures to regulate social interaction

   2. failure to develop peer relationships appropriate to developmental level

   3. a lack of spontaneous seeking to share enjoyment, interests, or achievements with other people (e.g., by a lack of showing, bringing, or pointing out objects of interest to other people)

   4. lack of social or emotional reciprocity

B. Restricted repetitive and stereotyped patterns of behavior, interests, and activities, as manifested by at least one of the following:

   1. encompassing preoccupation with one or more stereotyped and restricted patterns of interest that is abnormal either in intensity or focus

   2. apparently inflexible adherence to specific, nonfunctional routines or rituals

   3. stereotyped and repetitive motor mannerisms (e.g., hand or finger flapping or twisting, or complex whole-body movements)

   4. persistent preoccupation with parts of objects

C. The disturbance causes clinically significant impairment in so-cial, occupational, or other important areas of functioning.

D. There is no clinically significant general delay in language (e.g., single word used by age 2 years, communicative phrases used by age 3 years).

E. There is no clinically significant delay in cognitive development or in the development of age-appropriate self-help skills, adaptive behavior (other than in social interaction), and curiosity about the environment in childhood.

F. Criteria are not met for another specific Pervasive Developmental Disorder or Schizophrenia.

Note: There is an ongoing debate among clinicians about these guidelines. Although this is currently the official diagnostic tool for now, some consider the DSM-IV criteria incomplete. Modifications are being suggested and the use of other assessment tools (especially the Gillberg criteria) is often encouraged.

GLOSSARY OF TERMS

amygdala The emotional part of the brain where fight, flight, or freeze reactions are triggered.

Asperger's syndrome A neurological condition that affects an individual's ability to "read" other people or make intuitive predictions, hampering their social skills. Named after Hans Asperger, an Austrian pediatrician who first recognized and described the traits in 1944, calling the condition "autistic personality disorder."

attention-deficit/hyperactivity disorder (ADHD) A condition that makes it difficult for an individual to pay attention and increases the tendency to daydream and/or to act impulsively and to be overactive.

autism A developmental disorder discovered in 1943 by Leo Kanner, an Austrian psychiatrist living in the United States. He observed certain behaviors and termed the individuals "autistic," from the Greek word *autos*, meaning "self."

autism spectrum The broad range of symptoms seen in individuals with autism, with many shared but rarely identical traits.

casein A protein in cow's and goat's milk with a molecular structure that is extremely similar to that of gluten (a wheat protein substance).

casein-free diet An elimination diet that removes all dairy products and all foods containing casein from all meals, which may help alleviate gastrointestinal discomfort for some children with Asperger's or autism.

cognitive behavior therapy (CBT) Therapeutic techniques to improve individuals' reactions to their emotions through conscious thought and behavior modification.

corpus callosum   The part of the brain that connects the left and right hemispheres.

DSM-IV-TR   Abbreviation for the official publication, *Diagnostic and Statistical Manual of Mental Disorders*, *Text Revision*, *Fourth Edition*, used in diagnosing children and adults with neurological conditions—the first edition identifying the diagnostic characteristics of Asperger's syndrome as suggested by Christopher Gillberg, a Swedish physician who specialized in the study of Asperger's children.

empathy   The ability to guess another person's feelings and thoughts, to put oneself "in another's shoes" and imagine what another is experiencing without ever having experienced it oneself.

executive function   The ability to plan, organize, and sense time and place. This function takes place in the frontal lobe of the brain.

frontal lobe deficits   When the part of the brain called the frontal lobe lacks the wiring to function typically. Such deficits hinder organizational, directional, time-measuring, and planning abilities.

gluten   A protein found in the grass family of wheat, oats, barley, rye, and their derivatives.

gluten-free diet   An elimination diet that removes all gluten, a wheat protein substance, from one's meals. It is thought to help reduce gastrointestinal discomfort for some children with Asperger's or autism, but research is still being conducted and results are not yet definitive.

hidden curriculum   A term coined by Richard Lavoie concerning the subtle social signals and unspoken intentions of individuals, which are intuitively picked up by most people but are missed by those with Asperger's.

high-functioning autism   A condition where autistic issues are more pronounced in the first three years of life, then developmental abilities improve until they are on par with Asperger's syndrome individuals.

Individualized Education Program (IEP)   A meeting with your child's teacher, a school administrator, and other specialists working with your child to discuss goals and objectives, proper placement, accommodations, and what is going well and what is not.

mindblindness   The inability to predict or intuit what someone else is feeling or thinking; a term coined by Simon Baron-Cohen in 1990 for the deficit in theory of mind.

mirror neuron deficiency   When mirror neurons are not performing as they normally would.

mirror neurons   Neurons that command motor functions and enable one to imitate the motions of another individual. They are thought to play a role in empathetic responses.

mirror neuron system   Special nerve cells in the brain that may be part of the basis of learning, empathy, and compassion and enable an individual to determine the intentions of other individuals.

neocortex   The rational brain; the reasoning part of the brain.

neurotypical   A term for those who do not have Asperger's syndrome. Also called "Tippies" by Asperger's people who call themselves "Aspies."

nonverbal communication   Body language, intonation, eye contact—any communication that is not verbal.

perseverating   Repeated behavior or conversation usually caused by stress.

self-regulation   The ability to manage sensory input and emotions in appropriate ways so as to not stand out socially.

sensory sensitivities   Being very sensitive to elements in one's surroundings that affect the senses (sound, sight, smell, taste, etc.).

sensory stimuli   Any sights, sounds, smells, tastes, or textures that stimulate the senses.

social skills   Also known as "people" skills, including greetings, conversation, good manners, good personal hygiene, respecting personal space, intuiting someone's feelings and thoughts, etc.

Social Story   A written tool, conceived and trademarked by Carol Gray, that uses a personalized story to address a specific situation, concept, or skill, laying out what it is, what may happen, and typical responses.

stimulatory behavior or "stimming"   Repeated gestures like flapping arms, rocking, pacing, hand waving, etc., to release anxiety and stress or to become more aware of one's body.

theory of mind   A novel idea introduced by Simon Baron-Cohen in 1985 about the ability to be aware that other people have thoughts, feelings, and intentions that are not the same as yours.

Tourette's syndrome   A neurological disorder causing random physical and verbal tics.

visual cortex   The part of the brain that is highly specialized for processing information about stationary and moving objects, and that excels in pattern recognition.

Hello—

I'm Ben Brust's mom and I want to thank you for a successful first week of school for Ben. He likes school and it's always nice to have a smooth start to the new school year.

As you may have noticed, Ben is eager to learn, a good student and unself-conscious about speaking up. He's also a bit quirky because he has Asperger's syndrome, which means he may not catch unspoken signals very well and he may take things too literally. It's best to tell him exactly what you want him to do, instead of what you don't want him to do, and he'll usually comply.

Ben also has ADHD, the inattentive type. He takes Adderall every morning, which helps him focus in class, but it does wear off by the time he comes home, so homework takes a lot longer to do than for other students. I work alongside him on my things and keep him on track, but we do have to modify the amount of homework sometimes if it's getting too late.

Ben has an IEP, which allows for some modifications and accommodations in class:

1. Please encourage him to sit up front, if he's not already doing it. That helps Ben focus and keeps distractions to a minimum.

2. You may see my handwriting sometimes because if it's a long writing assignment (or too late at night), Ben dictates the answers or essay to me to move things along.

3. The good news is Ben retains information very well, and usually does well on tests—but if there are essays on the test, he will need extra time because it takes him so long to get his thoughts out of his head and onto paper.

4. If Ben ever gets very agitated about something, it's best for him to leave the classroom and go outside to compose himself or to be given a pass to see Ms. Jones, the school psychologist. Or he could go see John McCann, his resource person (whom he rarely sees, so Ben will need to be told John's room number).

Thank you again for this good launch into Ben's junior year. If you have any questions or would like to tell me something, please feel free to call me at (xxx) xxx-xxxx or e-mail me. I work out of the house, so I'm usually around during the day.

Happy Friday and have a great Labor Day weekend!
Beth Brust

Bullying occurs when someone uses power to hurt or reject someone else. Physical bullying is more than pushing or hitting. It's also tripping, throwing food, taking or damaging someone's belongings, and being physically intimidating.

Verbal bullying is more than name-calling and teasing. It can include spreading false rumors, writing nasty comments, making a person the butt of a joke, making threats, and saying things that make others uncomfortable.

Bullying *is not* and *should not* be an inevitable part of childhood. Bullying is not a life lesson that anyone needs to learn. This is not a mandatory step toward adulthood.

There is *no* value in experiencing being bullied—it causes only hurt and frustration and potential lifelong damage.

Just as important, bullying is *not* something that kids can or should be expected to work out for themselves. Parents, teachers, coaches, neighbors, and any adults who witness bullying going on, or are told about it, should intervene immediately to stop the incident from escalating or recurring.

It has been proven that if one person—just one—steps in and says, "Enough" or "Stop" or "That's not funny, quit it," it tilts the balance enough that the bullying will usually stop.

Our Asperger's children and teens are so unsuspecting and literal-minded, they make very easy targets for bullies. Being unable to discern the true intentions of others, Aspies are especially vulnerable to a third type of bullying—the false friend bullies.

These bullies smile as they coerce their target into doing something he doesn't want to do and are nice when they want something. The bully's smile and friendly actions fool our Friends into thinking that all is well. Aspies don't see that the bully is only friendly when no one else is around, and is using them.

Plenty of bullies have low self-esteem and are friendless, fringe kids, but some can be quite popular. They seem to enjoy the power and attention they attract when they pick on someone. These bullies are dominant types, maybe even emotionally troubled, who realize that they can use aggression to become a group leader. Humiliation is another weapon of choice.

While more than 50 percent of elementary school students report that they've been bullied at some time or another, research shows that children fall into three main groups when it comes to bullying:

1. About 8 to 15 percent of kids are bullies

2. About 8 to 10 percent of children are repeated targets of bullying and a higher proportion of these victims tend to be children with Asperger's or those with other conditions

3. About 70 to 80 percent of students—the social majority—are neither bullies nor targets, and they react in a variety of ways from simply ignoring what's going on and waiting for it to end to being drawn into the drama and even egging on the bully

A Canadian study by two university researchers, Debra Pepler and Wendy Craig, revealed that bullying episodes occurred once every seven and a half minutes on the playground. Other kids were watching 85 percent of the time and often encouraged the bully. Only 10 percent of the time did kids intervene, and adults got involved only 20 percent of the time.

The bottom line is that bullying incidents affect all involved and are toxic to the class climate and school environment. Bullying spreads a poison that erodes students' sense of safety and interferes with their ability to concentrate on what matters—academics.

What's the best way to address bullying?

All the experts agree: nip it in the bud.

Stop the incident as soon as it starts. Break up the negative dynamic as soon as possible.

While many in the social majority say they want to help stop bullying, two things hold them back: they don't know exactly what steps to take, and they worry that if they get involved, they may be the next victim. So they stay silent, waiting and hoping for the bully to finish or for the whole thing to go away.

What has been proven to help students is training. Various antibullying, human relations classes or programs have been created to give students—targets, bystanders, *and* bullies—the skills training they need to avoid such incidents and to minimize bullying on a campus.

The reason it's so important to stop bullying is that it can be very damaging to individuals in the long run, affecting the bullies and especially the targets, who are so often our Asperger's Friends.

There is clear evidence that young students who have been bullied feel the effects well into their adulthood. The damage includes lower self-esteem or sense of self-worth, anxiety, insecurity, depression, and a feeling of helplessness and powerlessness that can stir up latent anger, loneliness, and lower performance in school or on the job.

The bullies are not unscathed by their actions either. If their behavior is left uncurbed, young bullies tend to become adults who engage in criminal behavior, substance abuse, and rocky relationships.

It takes a tremendous amount of courage and confidence for a child or peer to speak up and tell a bully, "Enough!" It is much easier for an adult, who is perceived to have more authority, to put an end to any bully's attempts at intimidation. So adults do need to step in and speak up, if they see any form of bullying going on or if children report such behavior.

If you are told by your Asperger's child that a bullying episode has happened, believe him or her. These kids do not typically make up such stories for attention or to get someone in trouble for fun. Aspies are wired to be truthful and they call it as they see it or as it happened, so such a report is always worth investigating.

Granted, not all teasing is bad. Friendly teasing is used by kids of all ages to bond with their peers through verbal dueling and ribbing. Friendships evolve from jokes between friends, sarcasm, poking fun, and "razzing" friends to get a rise out of them and to make sure they're not taking themselves too seriously.

Unfortunately, our Aspie Friends cannot detect the underlying tone and meaning of sarcasm, so they fail to hear the embedded humor. In Friends' Club, we'll show a movie clip of friendly teasing and our kids think that it is mean teasing because they just can't hear the joking tone of voice or see the subtleties of inside humor.

Because there can be such a fine line between friendly teasing and mean teasing, it's best to check out any reports by your child of mean teasing or bullying. It will make him or her feel better and less alone, plus it will give you a chance to see what is really going on.

It's also important that children or teens who have been targets of bullying are not made to feel helpless to defend themselves and turn into victims. They need to be instructed, as we do at the Friends' Club, in various ways to respond to bullying attempts and practice those techniques over and over, so they will be more comfortable in standing up for themselves.

The following tips and techniques provide a valuable supplement to those found in the Bullying and Bullies section in Part Two. These come from a variety of sources, including our Friends' Club activities, to give your child more tools to use.

STRATEGIES AND CONCEPTS TO CONVEY TO KIDS

- Many of our Friends are afraid they will be considered tattle-tales, so they don't tell anyone about being bullied. They need to understand that **telling an adult is essential**, so that something can be done. Learning the difference between "tattling" and "telling" is very important. *Tattling* is intended to get someone into trouble and is usually done in front of others. *Telling* is intended to get help and should be done privately. Telling is like reporting—just the facts: "Tim called me a purple pig for three days in a row at recess. I ignore him but he keeps following me."

- The best way to find shelter from bullies is by being with other kids at lunch or at recess. To be alone with no allies makes any child more vulnerable to a bullying incident. Encourage your child to hang out near others, even if he's not playing with them.

- Talk with your child about a plan for him to follow if he is bullied at school. Who can he talk with? Make a list together of the people at school who can help and be trusted. For instance, if the teacher is busy, your child should go to the school psychologist or perhaps the school nurse. If they're not available, then perhaps the librarian or school secretary. It's important to identify, discuss, and list these trusted adults so your child has a plan to follow of whom to go to and what to say. And then contact these adults so they know that your child considers them trusted people who would help if your child is being bullied.

- Even your teen would benefit from making a list of all the places where he goes—school, clubs, after-school care, sports teams, etc.—and talking about who would be the best person at each place to speak to about a bullying incident. Many teens have told me that adults do *not* help them when they've asked for assistance. Even when the teen goes back again, the adult does nothing. That's why it's important for your teen to know who else they should approach to get help. They need to be told the next step because they will not think of it on their own. And then it's up to you to contact those adults to let them know that your son or daughter may come to them, expecting and trusting them to do something to help if your teen is being bullied.

- Humor is a great way to defuse a bullying situation. Since a bully is expecting the target to be fearful, if the victim uses humor to respond to the bully's actions, it can tip the balance and get our Aspie Friends off the hook and out of the situation. For example, if the bully said, "What ugly shoes," the child who is being targeted could answer, "I agree. They're like clown shoes. My mom made me buy them," and then just walk away.

- Marilyn Langevin, a speech-language pathologist and clinical director of the Institute for Stuttering Treatment and Research in Canada, offers "Speak Up—Five Finger Strategy" to give children who are being bullied a handy strategy to fend off mean teasing, direct insults, or anything making them uncomfortable:
  1. Use the person's name: "Jason"
  2. Say how you feel: "I don't like it"
  3. Cite behavior: "When you call me names"
  4. Be respectful: "Please"
  5. Say what you want: "Stop"
     Breaking it into these five elements—one for each finger on a hand—may make it easier for Asperger's kids to remember what to say to a bully.

- At Friends' Club, we teach the concept "Stick Up for Yourself." We read stories where a character is not being treated well and we discuss solutions. While our kids have suggested retaliation, we point out that to stick up for yourself doesn't mean that you have to get back at the person. It means remembering who you are and what you believe is right and standing up for that. We've found that the book *Pinky, Rex and the Bully* by James Howe is an effective story to use since the boy's name is Pinky and his best friend, Rex, is a girl—such unexpected twists grab our kids' attention.

- We practice the tried-and-true method of facing a bully: Stand up straight, look them in the eye, and say something simple like "Leave me alone" or "That's not funny." Then walk away toward other people and join a group, because bullies don't usually pick on people in groups.

- Our kids need to know that if they're being singled out and bullied, it doesn't help to cry, make threats, or fight back. Bullies want an emotional response. They want to see that they've had an effect. The best defense is to be as stoic and unemotional as possible. Unfortunately, our Aspie Friends can be very sensitive and socially immature, so again, they need to practice the kinds of firm and unemotional responses that work best to deflect a bully.

- Bullies usually have an unfair edge over their victim. Maybe it's physical strength, but it could be social status or emotional resilience. Just by recruiting some help, a bully can easily outnumber his target, gaining the edge by being more than one against one. Make sure that your child isn't walking home alone or left alone before or after school in a place where other kids could zero in on him. And let him know that to keep himself safe, he sometimes has to give in to the bully. If a bully is trying to take something from him, tell your child to let him take it and get away as fast as possible.

- Build up your child's self-confidence and hope for the future by enrolling her in something she's good at. Play to her strengths and let her be with others who share her interests and skills. Being with like-minded kids may produce a new friend or two, too, which could help buffer your child from bullies.

- Teach your child how to play board games and playground games. These are good skills for your child to have, so he can interact with other children. Knowing and practicing games will give them something to do at recess with the other kids, so that they're not alone.

- Practicing eye contact is helpful because if your child can look the bully in the eye briefly while he talks, that will make your child appear less intimidated. This is not to encourage staring down the bully. Just look at him long enough to say, "Leave me alone," and then walk away.

- Talk about your own experiences with bullies to help your child know that she's not alone. By hearing that it happened to you when you were younger, and that you made it through, your child will be more reassured that she, too, will live through this tough time. Be sure to talk about how you felt—that it's normal to feel scared and alone and to want to cry but you didn't want the bully to see that.

- Help your child make a list of his positive traits. Keep this list in his room, so he can reread it and remind himself of his strengths, talents, and interests.

- If our Aspie Friends can keep calm when approached by a bully, it will make them look more confident, even if they're not. Having them practice keeping calm, focusing on breathing slowly, and speaking with a confident voice will better equip them to handle future bullying incidents. It's also good for them to practice keeping a safe distance between themselves and the bully. Moving too close could trigger a physical confrontation. But Aspies tend not to be aware of personal boundaries, so learning to step back to make space is important and something our Friends need to work on.

What we want to avoid at all costs is a silent buildup of anger that may plague those being bullied. The stress, a lowered sense of self-worth, and an increased feeling of helplessness may give kids suicidal thoughts. Or, as the spate of school shootings has shown, an irrational need to "get back at" other students or a sudden need to protect themselves can drive some teens who were targets of bullying to bring weapons to school and use them.

While Asperger's children and teens are not naturally prone to violence, anyone who is in enough pain and despair and has access to weapons may see that as their only recourse. We want to avoid this kind of tragedy by having a clear course of action for our Aspie Friends, so if they are being harassed and bullied, they can go to trusted adults and find help before things get out of control.

As Marilyn Langevin has stated so well:

I believe that it is our responsibility to ask ourselves each day, "Is there anything I do or say that supports or reinforces bullying?" and "What behaviors am I modeling for the children?" Equally important, we—parents, teachers, speech language pathologists and all members of the community—must not simply rescue children and enable the development of a "victim" role. It is important that we help children learn conflict resolution strategies; help them acquire resiliency to prevent internalizing teasing, taunting, and other types of bullying; and help them maintain their power or regain it when it has been lost to a child or a group of children who bully. And finally, we must make it safe for children to report bullying and to ask for help.

INTERNET RESOURCES

www.addwarehouse.com   Resource for the understanding and treatment of all developmental disorders, including ADHD and related issues.

www.advocatesforspecialkids.org   A nonprofit organization promoting "parents helping parents to understand special education."

www.aspergersyndrome.org   Online information and support for parents and professionals about Asperger's syndrome.

www.autism.fm   Yale Child Study Center and Laboratory for Social Neuroscience.

www.autismpartnership.com   International organization that provides services and therapy for autistic and Asperger's children.

www.autismservicesfdn.org   A nonprofit organization focused on education and public awareness.

www.autismshopper.com   Visual aids for visual kids!

www.autism-society.org   Autism Society of America is the nation's leading grassroots organization that promotes autism awareness and provides the latest information to improve the lives of those with autism.

www.autismspeaks.com   America's largest autism advocacy organization, sponsoring public service campaigns to increase awareness of autism, funding research, and offering an online family resource guide.

www.autismtoday.com   An all-inclusive Web site of autism resources.

www.barbaradoyle.com   Helpful handouts and other information for children with developmental disabilities, particularly those on the autism spectrum.

www.brainhighways.com   Special physical activities to increase the basic brain-processing skills needed to learn more easily.

www.bullying.org   Addresses new findings on bullying and ways to avoid being a target.

www.cesa7.k12.wi.us/sped/autism/structure/str11.htm   The site of the Cooperative Educational Service Agency Number 7 of Green Bay,

Wisconsin, showing tools for teachers to use with students, created by autism consultant Susan Stokes.

www.chantalsicile-kira.com   An advocate and author of reference books on autism, incorporating her experiences with her autistic son.

www.childswork.com   Activities, books, and games for children.

www.cyberbullying.org   Focuses on Internet and high-tech bullying dangers and strategies for avoiding it.

www.cynthianorall.com   Dr. Norall's Web site and home of the Friends' Club and Comprehensive Autism Services and Education (C.A.S.E.), which helps children with autism spectrum disorders (ASD).

www.dotolearn.com   Do2Learn offers special education teaching materials.

www.freespirit.com   Books, games, etc., for special education needs offered by the Free Spirit publishing company.

www.grasp.org   Stands for the Global and Regional Asperger Syndrome Partnership, an advocacy and educational organization serving individuals on the autism spectrum.

www.icdl.com   The Interdisciplinary Council on Developmental and Learning Disorders offers extensive information about learning and developmental challenges, including autism spectrum disorders.

www.igive.com   Supports organizations doing autism research by allowing customers to shop online at many stores through the iGive Web site. IGive will donate a percentage to the charity of your choice.

www.k9webprotection.com   Free Internet filtering and control service for home computers to protect children.

www.nccasa.com   Organization aimed at preventing sexual assault through education, advocacy, and legislation.

www.nfar.org   National Foundation for Autism Research offers educational grants and funds research in the Southern California area, to date.

For the Web site for O.A.S.I.S. or Online Asperger Syndrome Information and Support, go to www.udel.edu cited on p. 325.

www.ricklavoie.com   Great information for educators and parents to help motivate and support students with special needs.

www.safefamilies.org   Offers free Internet filtering software to protect kids and issues a newsletter.

www.socialthinking.com   Web site for the Center for Social Thinking, headed by Michelle Garcia Winner, offering advice and strategies for families and teachers for students with speech and social cognition disabilities.

www.specialed.us/autism/assist/assist10.htm   Offers a detailed article about using various tech strategies to help children on the autism spectrum, written by Susan Stokes of Wisconsin.

www.superduperinc.com   Fun learning materials for kids with special needs.

www.taskca.org   Team of Advocates for Special Kids is a parent training and information center offering help in early intervention, educational, medical, or therapeutic support services for children.

www.thegraycenter.org   Web site for the Gray Center for Social Learning and Understanding, directed by Carol Gray, creator of Social Stories, Comic Strip Conversations, and bullying information.

www.tonyattwood.com   Offers guidance to parents, professionals, and spouses for children and adults with Asperger's syndrome.

www.udel.edu/bkirby.asperger   The Online Asperger Syndrome Information and Support (O.A.S.I.S.) Web site for parents and professionals.

www.valerieslist.com   An e-newsletter offering the latest news in the world of autism, listing resources useful to parents and others.

www.wiredsafety.org   World's largest Internet information and education source concerning cyberabuse, cyberbullying, and cyberstalking.

www.wrongplanet.net   Designed to allow Asperger's teens to connect with one another online. Lots of blogs.

FURTHER READING

ASPERGER'S SYNDROME, HIGH-FUNCTIONING AUTISM, AND AUTISM

Adolescents on the Autism Spectrum: A Parent's Guide to the Cognitive, Social, Physical, and Transition Needs of Teenagers with Autism Spectrum Disorders by Chantal Sicile-Kira. New York: Perigee, 2006.

American Normal: The Hidden World of Asperger Syndrome by Lawrence Osborne. New York: Copernicus Books, 2002.

An Asperger Dictionary of Everyday Expressions by Ian Stuart-Hamilton. Philadelphia: Jessica Kingsley Publishers, 2007.
A humorous explanation of idioms incorporating a literal take typical of the Asperger mind.

The Asperger's Answer Book: Top 300 Questions Parents Ask by Susan Ashley, Ph.D. Naperville, IL: Sourcebook, 2007.

Asperger Syndrome by Ami Klin, Fred R. Volkmar, and Sara S. Sparrow, eds. New York: Guilford Press, 2000.

Textbook on the subject.

Asperger's Syndrome: A Guide for Parents and Professionals by Tony Attwood, Ph.D. London and Philadelphia: Jessica Kingsley Publishers, 1998.

Autism: The Facts by Simon Baron-Cohen, Ph.D., and Patrick Bolton. Oxford: Oxford University Press, 1993.

Autism and Asperger Syndrome: The Facts by Simon Baron-Cohen, Ph.D. Oxford: Oxford University Press, 2008.

Autism and Creativity: Is There a Link Between Autism in Men and Exceptional Ability? by Michael Fitzgerald, Ph.D. East Sussex and New York: Brunner-Routledge, 2004.

Autism Aspergers: Solving the Relationship Puzzle—A New Developmental Program That Opens the Door to Lifelong Social and Emotional Growth by Steven E. Gutstein. Arlington, TX: Future Horizons, 2000.

Autism Life Skills: From Communication and Safety to Self-Esteem and More—10 Essential Abilities Every Child Needs and Deserves to Learn by Chantal Sicile-Kira. New York: Perigee, 2008.
From the viewpoint of teens and adults on the spectrum, the importance of communication, safety, self esteem, and more.

The Autism Sourcebook: Everything You Need to Know About Diagnosis, Treatment, Coping, and Healing by Karen Siff Exkorn. New York: HarperCollins, 2005.

Autism Spectrum Disorders: The Complete Guide to Understanding Autism, Asperger's Syndrome, Pervasive Developmental Disorder, and Other ASDs by Chantal Sicile-Kira. New York: Perigee, 2004.

Autism Spectrum Disorders from A to Z: Assessment . . . Diagnosis & More by Barbara Doyle and Emily Doyle Iland. Arlington, TX: Future Horizons, 2004.

A Brief Tour of Human Consciousness by V. S. Ramachandran, M.D. New York: P. I. Press, 2004.

The Complete Guide to Asperger's Syndrome by Tony Attwood, Ph.D. London and Philadelphia: Jessica Kingsley Publishers, 2007.

The Curious Incident of the Dog in the Night-Time by Mark Haddon. New York: Doubleday, 2003.

Diagnosing Jefferson: Evidence of a Condition that Guided His Beliefs, Behavior, and Personal Associations by Norm Ledgin. Arlington, TX: Future Horizons, 1998.

Elijah's Cup: A Family's Journey into the Community and Culture of High-Functioning Autism and Asperger's Syndrome by Valerie Paradiz. New York: The Free Press, 2002.

The Essential Difference: Male and Female Brains and the Truth About Autism by Simon Baron-Cohen, Ph.D. New York: Basic Books, 2004.

The Genesis of Artistic Creativity: Asperger's Syndrome and the Arts by Michael Fitzgerald, Ph.D. London and Philadelphia: Jessica Kingsley Publishers, 2005.

Genius Genes: How Asperger Talents Changed the World by Michael Fitzgerald and Brendan O'Brien. Shawnee Mission, KS: Autism Asperger Publishing Company, 2007.

Mindblindness: An Essay on Autism and Theory of Mind by Simon Baron-Cohen. Cambridge, MA: MIT Press, 1997.

The Official Autism 101 Manual compiled by Karen L. Simmons, featuring forty-four experts. Alberta, CN: Autism Today, 2006.

Phantoms in the Brain: Probing the Mysteries of the Human Mind by V. S. Ramachandran, M.D., Ph.D., and Sandra Blakelee. New York: Harper Perennial, 1998.

Ten Things Every Child With Autism Wishes You Knew by Ellen Notbohm. Arlington, TX: Future Horizons, 2005.
Defines the top-ten characteristics that reveal the hearts and minds of children with autism and how others can better understand them.

PARENTING, FAMILY ISSUES, AND PARENTS' PERSPECTIVES

Alone Together: Making an Asperger Marriage Work by Katrin Bentley. London and Philadelphia: Jessica Kingsley Publishers, 2007.

An Asperger Marriage by Gisela and Christopher Slater-Walker. London: Jessica Kingsley Publishers, 2002.

Aspergers in Love: Couple Relationships and Family Affairs by Maxine C. Aston. London and New York: Jessica Kingsley Publishers, 2003.

Asperger Syndrome and Your Child: A Parent's Guide by Michael D. Powers with Janet Poland. New York: HarperCollins, 2002.

Bully-Proofing Your Child: A Parent's Guide by Carla B. Garrity, Mitchell Baris, and William Porter. Longmont, CO: Sopris West, 2000.

Communicating Partners: 30 Years of Building Responsive Relationships with Late-Talking Children Including Autism, Asperger's Syndrome (ASD), Down Syndrome, and Typical Development—Developmental Guides for Professionals and Parents by James D. MacDonald. London and Philadelphia: Jessica Kingsley Publishers, 2004.

Employment for Individuals with Asperger Syndrome or Non-Verbal Learning Disability: Stories and Strategies by Yvona Fast, et al. London and New York: Jessica Kingsley Publishers, 2004.

The Explosive Child: A New Approach for Understanding and Parenting Easily Frustrated, Chronically Inflexible Children by Ross W. Greene, Ph.D. New York: HarperCollins, 1998.

Great Kids: Helping Your Baby and Child Develop the 10 Essential Qualities for a Healthy, Happy Life by Stanley I. Greenspan, M.D. Cambridge, MA: Da Capo Press, 2007.

How Rude!: The Teenagers' Guide to Good Manners, Proper Behavior, and Not Grossing People Out by Alex J. Packer, Ph.D. Minneapolis, MN: Free Spirit Publishing, 1997.

Just This Side of Normal: Glimpses into Life with Autism by Elizabeth King Gerlach. Arlington, TX: Future Horizons, 2004.
A powerful depiction of one mother's journey toward understanding and accepting her son's autism.

Louder Than Words: A Mother's Journey in Healing Autism by Jenny McCarthy. New York: Dutton, 2007.

The Out-of-Sync Child: Recognizing and Coping with Sensory Integration Dysfunction by Carol Stock Kranowitz. New York: Perigee, 1998.

A Parent's Guide to Asperger Syndrome and High-Functioning Autism: How to Meet the Challenges and Help Your Child Thrive by Sally Ozonoff, Ph.D., Geraldine Dawson, Ph.D., and James McPartland, Ph.D. New York: Guilford Press, 2002.

Play and Imagination in Children with Autism Spectrum Disorders by Pamela J. Wolfberg. New York: Teachers College Press, 1999.

Raising a Sensory Smart Child: The Definitive Handbook for Helping Your Child with Sensory Integration Issues by Lindsey Biel, M.A., OTR, and Nancy Peske. New York: Penguin, 2005.

Unlocking the Mysteries of Sensory Dysfunction: A Resource for Anyone Who Works With or Lives With a Child with Sensory Issues by Elizabeth Anderson and Pauline Emmons. Arlington, TX: Future Horizons, 1996.

Your Life Is Not a Label: A Guide to Living Fully with Autism and Asperger's Syndrome for Parents, Professionals and You! by Jerry Newport. Arlington, TX: Future Horizons, 2001.

EDUCATIONAL ISSUES

Asperger Syndrome: A Guide for Educators and Parents by Brenda Smith Myles and Richard Simpson. Austin, TX: Pro-Ed, 1997.

Creating a Win-Win IEP for Students with Autism: A How-To Manual for Parents and Educators by Beth Fouse. Arlington, TX: Future Horizons, 1999.

Incorporating Social Goals in the Classroom: A Guide for Teachers and Parents of Children with High-Functioning Autism and Asperger's Syndrome by Rebecca Moyes and Susan Moreno. London and Philadelphia: Jessica Kingsley Publishers, 2001.

Navigating the Social World: A Curriculum for Individuals with Asperger's Syndrome, High Functioning Autism and Related Disorders by Jeanette McAfee, M.D. Arlington, TX: Future Horizons, 2001.

Playground Politics: The Emotional Development of Your School-Aged Child by Stanley I. Greenspan, M.D., with Jacqueline Salmon. New York: Perseus Books, 1993.

Power Cards: Using Special Interests to Motivate Children and Youth with Asperger's Syndrome and Autism by Elisa Gagnon. Shawnee Mission, KS: Autism Asperger Publishing Co., 2001.
This book shows parents and educators how to change unwanted behavior by appealing to Aspies' special interests and visual nature.

School Success for Kids with Asperger's Syndrome by Stephan Silverman, Ph.D., and Rich Weinfeld. Waco, TX: Profrock Press, 2007.

Teaching Children with Autism: Strategies to Enhance Communication and Socialization by Kathleen Ann Quill. Albany, NY: Del Mar Publishers/International Thomson Publishing Company, 1995.

Ten Things Your Student with Autism Wishes You Knew by Ellen Notbohm. Arlington, TX: Future Horizons, 2006.
A straight-talking guide for educators to better understand the unique thinking patterns of children on the spectrum and how to better approach them.

A Treasure Chest of Behavioral Strategies for Individuals with Autism Spectrum Disorders by Beth Fouse, Ph.D., and Maria Wheeler, M.Ed. Arlington, TX: Future Horizons, 1997.

A Work in Progress: Behavior Management Strategies and a Curriculum for Intensive Behavioral Treatment of Autism by Ron Leaf, Ph.D., and John McEachin, Ph.D., editors. New York: DRL Books, 1999.

"You're Going to Love This Kid!" Teaching Students with Autism in the Inclusive Classroom by Paula Kluth. Baltimore, MD: Paul H. Brookes, 2003.

SOCIAL SKILLS TRAINING AND OTHER SOCIAL INTERVENTIONS

Building Social Relationships: A Systematic Approach to Teaching Social Interaction Skills to Children and Adolescents with Autism Spectrum Disorders and Other Social Difficulties by Scott Bellini, Ph.D. Shawnee Mission, KS: Autism Asperger's Publishing Co., 2006.

Comic Strip Conversations by Carol Gray. Arlington, TX: Future Horizons, 1994.

Gray's Guide to Bullying (includes *Bully Workbook*) by Carol Gray. (Go to www.thegraycenter.org for more information.)

Do-Watch-Listen-Say: Social and Communication Intervention for Children with Autism by Kathleen Ann Quill. Baltimore, MD: Brookes, 2000.

Inside Out: What Makes a Person with Social Cognitive Deficits Tick? by Michelle Garcia Winner. San Jose, CA: Winner Publications, 2000.

It's So Much Work to Be Your Friend: Helping the Child with Learning Disabilities Find Social Success by Richard Lavoie. New York: Touchstone, 2005.

The Motivation Breakthrough: 6 Secrets for Turning On the Tuned-out Child by Richard Lavoie. New York: Simon & Schuster, 2008.

The New Social Story Book by Carol Gray. Arlington, TX: Future Horizons, 2000.

Taming the Recess Jungle by Carol Gray. Arlington, TX: Future Horizons, 1993.

Teaching Children with Autism to Mind-Read: A Practical Guide for Teachers and Parents by Patricia Howlin, Simon Baron-Cohen, and Julie Hadwin. New York: John Wiley & Sons, 1998.

Teaching Your Child the Language of Social Success by Marshall Duke, Stephen Nowicki, and Elisabeth Martin. Atlanta, GA: Peachtree, 1996.

Teach Me Language: A Social Language Manual for Children with Autism, Asperger's Syndrome and Related Developmental Disorders by Sabrina Freeman and Lorelei Dake. Langley, BC: SKF Books, 1997.

Thinking About YOU, Thinking About ME, second edition, by Michelle Garcia Winner. San Jose, CA: Winner Publications, 2007.

PERSONAL ACCOUNTS

Beyond the Wall: Personal Experiences with Autism and Asperger's Syndrome by Stephen Shore. Shawnee Mission, KS: Autism Asperger Publishing Co., 2003.

The Boy Who Loved Windows: Opening the Heart and Mind of a Child Threatened with Autism by Patricia Stacey. Cambridge, MA: Da Capo Press, 2004.

Emergence: Labeled Autistic by Temple Grandin and Margaret M. Scariano. New York: Warner Books, 1986.

Freaks, Geeks and Asperger Syndrome: A User Guide to Adolescence by Luke Jackson. London: Jessica Kingsley Publishers, 2002.

Look Me in the Eye: My Life with Asperger's by John Elder Robison. New York: Three Rivers Press, 2007.

Mozart and the Whale: An Asperger's Love Story by Jerry Newport, Mary Newport, and Johnny Dodd. New York: Touchstone Books, 2007.

Pretending to Be Normal: Living with Asperger's Syndrome by Liane Holliday Willey. London and Philadelphia: Jessica Kingsley Publishers, 1999.

Thinking in Pictures: And Other Reports from My Life with Autism by Temple Grandin. New York: Vintage Books, 1996.

The Way I See It: A Personal Look at Autism and Asperger's by Temple Grandin, Ph.D. Arlington, TX: Future Horizons, 2008.

CHILDREN'S BOOKS

At the Friends' Club, we have more than two hundred children's books that we use with our groups, and our library is growing. We've discovered that many books illustrate the social skills or issues that we're addressing, ranging from feelings, manners, and friendship to bullying, perspectives, literal language, and making sense of idioms and slang.

The following titles are those mentioned in this book. To see the complete list of books that we have found useful when teaching social skills to our Friends, please go to our Web site, at www.cynthianorall.com.

Amelia Bedelia and the Baby (and other books in the series) by Peggy Parish. New York: Prentice-Hall Books for Young Readers, 1970.
A family's housekeeper takes everything very, very literally, which causes havoc and good humor.

The Berenstain Bears and the In-Crowd (and other books in the series) written and illustrated by Stan and Jan Berenstain. New York: Random House, 1989.
Sister Bear decides not to go along with a bossy new cub's tactics of putting down other cubs, and resists peer pressure.

Enemy Pie by Derek Munson, illustrated by Tara Calahan King. San
    Francisco, CA: Chronicle Books, 2000.
A boy decides the new boy who moves in across the street is an enemy, so his
    father offers to make an "enemy pie" to get rid of him.

Excuse Me!: A Little Book of Manners by Karen Katz. New York: Grosset &
    Dunlap, 2002.
A lift-the-flap book for preschoolers about basic manners.

Flotsam by David Wiesner. New York: Clarion Books, 2006.
A stunning, wordless picture book about a boy who finds an unusual camera
    washed up on the beach.

Franklin Is Bossy (and other books in the series) by Paulette Bourgeois,
    illustrated by Brenda Clark. Toronto: Scholastic, 1994.
Franklin is a young turtle who learns many character-building lessons,
    including that no one likes a bossy friend.

The Gas We Pass: The Story of Farts (part of the My Body Science series) by
    Shinta Cho. La Jolla, CA: Kane/Miller Book Publisher, 2001.
Provides facts about all types of human and animal flatulence.

The Honest-to-Goodness Truth by Patricia C. McKissack, illustrated by Giselle
    Potter. New York: Atheneum Books for Young Readers, 2000.
Libby gets in trouble for lying to her mother and vows to only tell the truth,
    only to discover there is a right and wrong way to tell the truth.

Hooway for Wodney Wat by Helen Lester, illustrated by Lynn Munsinger.
    Boston: Houghton Mifflin, 1999.
Rodney Rat is teased mercilessly for not being able to pronounce his *R*s, yet
    he manages to deal with the class bully to everyone's surprise.

How Humans Make Friends by Loreen Leedy. New York: Holiday House,
    1996.
A space alien returns from Earth offering his interpretations of human
    interactions.

*How Rude!: The Teenagers' Guide to Good Manners, Proper Behavior, and Not
    Grossing People Out* by Alex J. Packer, Ph.D. Minneapolis, MN.:
    Free Spirit Publishing, 1997.
Funny, casual, teen-friendly approach to getting along with others by being
    considerate, well-mannered, and more.

How to Be a Friend: A Guide to Making Friends and Keeping Them by Laurie
    Krasny Brown and illustrated by Marc Brown. Boston: Little
    Brown Young Readers, 2001.
Practical suggestions for resolving arguments, coping with bullies, handling
    shyness, and more.

If You Give a Mouse a Cookie by Laura Numeroff, illustrated by Felicia Bond.
    New York: HarperCollins, 1985.
Circular tale of a little mouse that keeps a boy very busy fetching things
    from around the house.

It's Not Easy Being a Bunny by Marilyn Sadler, illustrated by Roger Bollen.
    New York: Random House Books for Young Readers, 1983.
P. J. Funnybunny tries out being other animals, thinking their lives are more
    interesting than his.

King of the Playground by Phyllis Reynolds Naylor, illustrated by Nola
    Langner Malone. New York: Aladdin Books, 1994.
Sammy the bully tries to keep Kevin out of the sandbox, but through
    problem solving and persistence, Kevin turns things around.

The King Who Rained by Fred Gwynne. New York: Prentice-Hall Books for
    Young Readers, 1970.
The literal interpretations of idioms make a hilarious picture book full of
    crazy images.

The Meanest Thing to Say (and other books in the Little Bill series) by Bill
    Cosby. New York: Scholastic Cartwheel Books, 1997.
Gives good suggestions for how to deal with a school-yard bully.

Milo and the Magical Stones written and illustrated by Marcus Pfister. New
    York: North-South Books, 1997.
A mouse discovers an unusual stone that can bring good or bad to the world,
    and midway through the story splits, offering two different endings.

Milo and the Mysterious Island written and illustrated by Marcus Pfister. New
    York: North-South Books, 2000.
Sequel picks up after the happy ending of the first book, when Milo goes on
    a voyage and comes to a tropical island where the story splits for two
    possible endings, leaving it for kids to decide.

Mr. Men and Little Miss (book series) by Roger Hargreaves. New York:
    Price Stern Sloan, 1998.
Simple characters represent a wide array of emotions, including Mr.
    Grumpy, Little Miss Shy, Mr. Daydream, and Mr. Forgetful.

Odd Velvet by Mary Whitcomb, illustrated by Tara Calahan King. San
    Francisco, CA: Chronicle Books, 1998.
Dressing and acting differently than the other kids, quiet Velvet is teased
    and unappreciated by her classmates until her special talent is revealed.

Oops!: The Manners Guide for Girls (American Girl Library) by Nancy
    Holyoke, illustrated by Debbie Tilley. Middleton, WI: American
    Girl Publishing, 1997.
Covers appropriate manners in a light, entertaining way.

The Paperbag Princess by Robert Munsch, illustrated by Michael Martch-
    enko. Buffalo, NY: Annick Press, 1980.
When a dragon kidnaps her prince, a princess uses her wits and courage to
    rescue him only to find the prince less than grateful.

Pinky, Rex and the Bully by James Howe, illustrated by Melissa Sweet. New
    York: Aladdin Books, 1996.
A boy named Pinky and a girl named Rex take on the local bully.

The Recess Queen by Alexis O'Neill, illustrated by Laura Huliska-Beith. New
    York: Scholastic Press, 2002.
Mean Jean, the reigning recess queen, threatens and pushes others around
    until a new girl surprises them by making the playground safe again.

Sector 7 by David Wiesner. New York: Clarion Books, 1999.
A boy takes to the clouds and discovers a fantastic new world in this word-
    less picture book.

*The Slangman Guide to Street Speak 1: The Complete Course in American Slang
    and Idioms* by David Burke. Studio City, CA: Slangman Publish-
    ing, 2000.
Self-teaching guide to American slang and idioms offering word games,
    crossword puzzles, and exercises.

Stand Tall, Molly Lou Melon by Patty Lovell, illustrated by David Catrow.
    New York: G. P. Putnam's Sons, 2001.

Small, buck-toothed Molly Lou faces a determined bully at her new school armed only with the strength of believing in herself.

Tacky the Penguin by Helen Lester, illustrated by Lynn Munsinger. Boston: Houghton Mifflin, 1988.
Naturally different, Tacky seems odd to his look-and-act-the-same penguin buddies until his different ways help repel hunters to save the day.

365 Manners Kids Should Know: Games, Activities, and Other Fun Ways to Help Children Learn Etiquette by Sheryl Eberly. New York: Three Rivers Press, 2001.
One-manner-a-day format offers role-playing games, exercises, and activities to teach and reinforce good manners.

Tobin Learns to Make a Friend written and illustrated by Diane Murrell. Arlington, TX: Future Horizons, 2001.
Tobin is a lonely train who wants to make friends and connect with others.

The True Story of the Three Little Pigs by Jon Scieszka, illustrated by Lane Smith. New York: Viking Penguin, 1989.
Familiar tale retold from the "innocent" wolf's perspective.

GAMES

American Girl 300 Wishes Game: Wish Big, Share Dreams, Friends Forever (Mattel)

Apples to Apples Junior!: The Game of Funny Comparisons! (Out of the Box)

Ask and Answer Social Skills Game (Super Duper Publications)

Balloon Lagoon: The Four-in-One Carnival Game for Kids (Cranium)

Battleship (Milton Bradley)

Bingo Bunch: The Mix-and-Match Bunch that is Bonkers for Bingo (Cranium)

Blurt! The Webster's Game of Word Racing—Junior Edition (Keys Publishing and Patch)

Bop It! (Hasbro)

Cadoo: The Outrageous Game That's All Kinds of Fun (Cranium)

Cariboo: A Magical Treasure Hunt Game (Cranium)

Catch Phrase!: Fast-passing, Fast-talking Game (Parker Brothers)

The Charade Game: It's Charades Like It's Never Been Played Before (Pressman)

Chicken Limbo: Listen to the Chicken Cluck a Limbo Song (Milton Bradley)

Conga: The Hilarious "Guess What I'm Thinking" Game (Cranium)

Constructionary: The Lego Game of Charades (Lego)

Cover to Cover: The Fast-Flippin' Magazine Game (Milton Bradley)

Creator: The Race to Build-It Board Game (Lego)

Crocodile Dentist (Milton Bradley)

Disney's Princess Spinning Wishes Game: Find the Prince's Hidden Gift (Milton Bradley)

Doodletales: The Game of Silly Sketches and Crazy Captions (Cranium)

Guesstures: The Game of Split-Second Charades (Hasbro)

Guess Who?: The Mystery Face Game (Milton Bradley)

Hangman: The Original "Risk Your Neck" Word Guessing Game (Milton Bradley)

Hear Me Out!: The Game That's More Than a Game (Toresite)

Hoopla: Outrageously Fun Game Where Every Second Counts (Cranium)

Hullaballoo: An Amazing Animal Adventure (Cranium)

I Can Do That! (I Can Do That Games)

Jenga: Girl Talk Edition (Parker Brothers)

Jeopardy Game (Milton Bradley)

Lego Racers Super Speedway Game (Lego)

Mad Libs (Penguin)

Mastermind: The Challenging Game of Logic and Deduction (Pressman)

Mighty Beanz (Moose)

Monster Stomp: The Game that Puts Monsters in Their Place (Aristoplay)

Moods: It's All In the Way You Say It Game (Hasbro)

Operation: A Skills Game (Hasbro)

Puzzles Plus: Where the Puzzle Is Only Half the Fun (Cranium)

Scattergories (Hasbro)

Scene It?: The DVD Movie Trivia Game (Screenlife)

Scrabble Junior: Your Child's First Crossword Puzzle Game (Milton Bradley)

Screwball Scramble: Set the Screwball Scrambling on Its Zany Race Against the Clock (Tomy)

Sounds of the Seashore: The Magical Matching and Memory Game (Cranium)

Splash: The Game of Fast Action and Fast Fun (Great American Puzzle Factory)

SPLAT! The Bug Squishin' Race Game (Milton Bradley)

Squint: The Game Where Pictures Take Shape (Out of the Box)

Stare! Juniors Edition (Game Development Group)

Super Showdown: The Game of Crazy Characters and Dynamic Debates (Cranium)

Taboo: The Game of Unspeakable Fun (Milton Bradley)

Think Blot Game: What Can You Spot in a Blot? (Mattel)

Tickle Toes (Milton Bradley)

Topple: Winning or Losing Hangs in the Balance of Every Move! (Pressman)

Trivial Pursuit: What Mighty Contests Rise from Trivial Things (Horn Abbot)

What's in Ned's Head?: The Wacky, Silly, Icky, Sticky and Fun Gross-Out Game (Fundex)

What Would Lizzie Do? Can You Get Inside Lizzie McGuire's Head? (Milton Bradley)

Whoonu: The Fun-filled "What's Your Favorite Thing?" Game (Cranium)

Wonder Works Super Story Recorder (Cranium)

Zingers: The Game of Wacky Situations and Off-the-Wall Responses (Play All Day Games)

INDEX

abstraction/abstract thinking
  difficulty in, 6, 11, 13, 14, 33, 53, 91, 106–7, 297–98, 300
  emotions as, 183–88, 214–15
  humor/underlying meaning as, 150–51
  money as, 133–34
academic support, 22
  extra time for tests, 149
  homework, 109–11, 260
  IEP, 17, 21, 147–48, 278, 310–11
  parent-teacher communication, 244, 261, 279, 313–14
acquaintances
  forming interpersonal bridges, 40, 72, 97, 103, 158
  friends v., 29–31
ACT college entrance exam, 149
Addison, Joseph, xv
ADHD. *See* attention-deficit/ hyperactivity disorder
advocating, self-, 41–42, 204–5, 244
age-appropriate explanation, 277
agenda, school, 110
airplane emergency rule, 22
alone time, 14, 34–35, 42, 108
Amelia Bedelia, 171
amygdala, 37, 122–23, 309
Andersen, Hans Christian, 8, 163, 200, 228, 260
anger/frustration, 4, 7, 59, 103, 161, 176–77, 182–88, 303–4. *See also* anxiety; calming techniques
  daily talking to prevent, 161
  expression of, 36, 117
  from fear, 32–33, 127–28, 129
  Friends' Club approach to, xvii
  losing gracefully v., 176–77
  parental, 18

tantrums and meltdowns from, 7, 59, 182–88, 303–4
  techniques for defusing, 36–38, 105
animals
  bean bag (calming technique), 8, 242–43
  fear of, 128–29
annoying behavior
  avoiding eye contact, xv, 3, 31, 88, 95, 115, 122–26, 137–38, 297
  blunt speech, 14, 39, 63–65, 84, 105, 112–13
  purveyors of truth, 3, 40, 43, 63, 81, 112, 116, 178, 299–301
  "stimming," 16–17, 237–39, 241, 312
anxiety, 32–33, 41–42, 92, 104. *See also* anger/frustration; calming techniques
  defusing, 36–38, 105
  parental, 18
  "stimming" due to, 16–17, 237–39, 241, 312
apologizing, 43–45, 64–65, 112–13, 178
Apples to Apples game, 169, 204, 236
  Aspie modifying, 230
Aristotle, 69
arrogant attitude, 102–5, 277
  self-esteem v., 233–34
Asperger, Hans, 86, 249, 266
Asperger Syndrome (Klin), xxii
Asperger's syndrome
  criteria for, 307–8
  defined, 309
  entering world of, xvii–xviii
  Golden Rule for, 161
  telling your child, 276–79
Asperger's Syndrome: A Guide for Parents and Professionals (Attwood), xxi

Cynthia La Brie Norall, Ph.D., is a licensed educational psychologist who has specialized in the diagnosis and treatment of children and teens with Asperger's syndrome for more than twenty years. As founder and clinical director of Comprehensive Autism Services and Education (C.A.S.E.), Inc., Dr. Norall is an educational and behavioral consultant who oversees a team of therapists, social coaches, and group leaders. As founder of the Friends' Club, launched in 2000, she has created a safe, special place where children and teens with Asperger's can come together in small groups on a weekly basis to learn social awareness and "people" skills. Based in Carlsbad, California, satellite Friends' Clubs are now in northern California, western Canada, and Hawaii. Dr. Norall lives in San Diego with her husband and two children. For more information, go to www.cynthianorall.com.

Beth Wagner Brust is an award-winning author of thirteen children's books as well as articles published in the *Los Angeles Times*, *San Diego Union*, and *The Horn Book*. A graduate of Stanford University, she has a son who was diagnosed with Asperger's syndrome in third grade. Now a teenager, his social skills have noticeably improved by attending the Friends' Club. This is the book that she wishes she'd had when her son was first diagnosed. She lives in San Diego, California, with her two sons and their noble but unpredictable dog. Visit her Web site, at www .bethbrust.com.